THE BUSINESS OF EMPIRE

A volume in the series

The United States in the World

edited by Mark Philip Bradley and Paul A. Kramer

A list of titles in this series is available at www.cornellpress.cornell.edu.

THE BUSINESS OF EMPIRE

United Fruit, Race, and U.S.
Expansion in Central America

Jason M. Colby

Cornell University Press
Ithaca and London

First published 2011 by Cornell University Press
First printing, Cornell Paperbacks, 2013

Printed in the United States of America

Library of Congress Cataloging-in-Publication Data

Colby, Jason M. (Jason Michael), 1974–
    The business of empire : United Fruit, race, and U.S. expansion in
Central America / Jason M. Colby.
        p. cm. — (The United States in the world)
    Includes bibliographical references and index.
    ISBN 978-0-8014-4915-4 (cloth : alk. paper)
    ISBN 978-0-8014-7899-4 (paper : alk. paper)
    1. Central America—Foreign relations—United States. 2. United
States—Foreign relations—Central America. 3. Central America—
Commerce—United States—History. 4. United States—
Commerce—Central America—History. 5. Central America—Race
relations—History. 6. Industrial relations—Central America—History.
7. United Fruit Company—History. I. Title. II. Series: United States in
the world.
    F1436.8.U6C65   2011
    327.730728—dc23   2011020198

Cornell University Press strives to use environmentally responsible
suppliers and materials to the fullest extent possible in the publishing
of its books. Such materials include vegetable-based, low-VOC inks
and acid-free papers that are recycled, totally chlorine-free, or partly
composed of nonwood fibers. For further information, visit our website
at www.cornellpress.cornell.edu.

Cloth printing   10 9 8 7 6 5 4 3 2 1
Paperback printing   10 9 8 7 6 5 4 3 2 1

for Kelly

Contents

Acknowledgments

The seeds of this book were planted fifteen years ago, when I attended the University of Costa Rica as an exchange student. I went there to polish my Spanish and to have a good time. Instead, the people I met in and beyond San José opened a new world for me. It was there that I first heard of United Fruit and Minor Keith, first felt the staggering heat of a banana plantation, and first thought seriously about the U.S. role in the world. My time in Central America raised questions and instilled intellectual passions that remain with me to this day.

In the ensuing years, I had the good fortune to learn from extraordinary scholars and teachers. During my final year at Whitman College, I took three courses with David Schmitz, who inspired me to choose the field of U.S. international history and helped me navigate the passage to graduate school. At Cornell University, I encountered a group of remarkable historians, among them Walt LaFeber, Tom Holloway, Mary Roldán, Mary Beth Norton, and Raymond Craib. But I must extend special thanks to Tim Borstelmann and Nick Salvatore. Tim is a superb mentor and dear friend who has guided me through the vagaries of academia and parenthood alike. For his part, Nick not only trained me in the craft of history but also (along with his wife, Ann) treated me and my wife, Kelly, as family. I would be a different man, and this would be a different book, had I never met him.

This project also benefited from significant financial support. The research that took me to Central America, Great Britain, and throughout the United States was made possible by a number of grants and fellowships. At Cornell, the generous gifts of Martha and David Maisel funded several research trips to Washington, D.C. I also received a Gilder Lehrman Institute of American History Fellowship, a W. M. Keck Foundation Fellowship from the Huntington Library, a W. Stull Holt Memorial Fellowship from the Society for Historians of American Foreign Relations, and an Andrew W. Mellon Fellowship at the Massachusetts Historical Society. In the later stages, research grants from the University of Texas at El Paso and the University of Victoria enabled me to chase down crucial leads.

It is far more difficult to list those with whom I have incurred non-monetary debts. First and foremost are the many librarians and archivists who guided me along my way and without whom this study would not have been possible. I also benefited from the encouragement and advice of other scholars. When I was just beginning my research, two fine historians of black migration to Guatemala, Fred Opie and Doug Kraft, generously shared their time and research with me. Although some of my findings may differ from theirs, I am grateful to both of them. I was also lucky enough to hold a fellowship at the Huntington Library at the same time as Aims McGuinness, who listened patiently to my ramblings on United Fruit and shared his own research on the Panama Railroad Company. As I moved to turn dissertation into manuscript, Kyle Longley provided friendship, guidance, and cajoling, as well as astute criticism of an early draft. For his part, Ole Heggen, the University of Victoria's resident cartographer (and B.C.'s finest political cartoonist), dove into this project on short notice and drew maps that greatly improved the book. Finally, I would like to acknowledge the editors of *Diplomatic History* for graciously allowing me to reproduce some material that originally appeared in my article "'Banana Growing and Negro Management': Race, Labor, and Jim Crow Colonialism in Guatemala, 1884–1930," *Diplomatic History* 30, no. 4 (September 2006): 595–621.

Publishing my first book with Cornell University Press has been a true pleasure. The academic editors of the United States in the World series, Paul Kramer and Mark Bradley, believed in this project from the start and gave the many versions of the manuscript careful attention. Likewise, the press's three anonymous readers raised questions and offered suggestions that improved the book immeasurably, and Candace Akins and Kay Scheuer provided superb copyediting. Above all, it was wonderful to work with Cornell acquisitions editor Michael McGandy, who walked me through each step of the process with patience and grace.

In my short career as a gainfully employed academic, I have been a member of two splendid history departments. I could not have asked for friendlier or more supportive colleagues than those I met at the University of Texas at El Paso. Department Chair Michael Topp, in particular, made me feel involved and appreciated from the start. Despite my ties to the Pacific Northwest, it was hard to leave. My colleagues at the University of Victoria have been equally welcoming. Chairs Tom Saunders and Lynne Marks have proven unfailingly supportive and tolerant of their transplanted Yank, and my fellow Americanist, Rachel Cleves, fills our tiny U.S. section with intellectual dynamism. And then there is Jordan Stanger-Ross, a fine scholar and a good friend. As I agreed to take the blame for his book's errors and shortcomings, I assume he will do the same for me. Let us hope, for his sake, that there aren't any.

Finally, *mi familia.* I had an unconventional childhood, to say the least, involving orcas, abalone diving, salmon fishing, mussel farming, and visiting zoos and aquariums up and down the Pacific Coast. Through it all, my parents, John and Jan Colby, cultivated a deep sense of curiosity and adventure in me. They also taught me the importance of hard and honest work. In all ways but material, it was a privileged upbringing, one that I hope to pass on to my two sons. My first, Ben, was born on the U.S.–Mexican border and came into my life when I needed him most. Two years later, after we had moved to the blue-water border that is Victoria, Canada, came Nate, whose grins and giggles have brightened all of our lives. I hope someday to convey to them the place they have in their father's heart. For her part, Kelly has accompanied me on many journeys and lived the ups and downs of an academic spouse, including a distinctly unromantic "honeymoon" to Central America's Caribbean coast. She can never know how much she has meant to me, and I will never know how much she has sacrificed for me. *Por eso, Kelita,* this book is dedicated to you. Someday, I hope, all three will forgive me the time and love this book diverted from them. For now, it gives me great pleasure to answer a question put often to me by my boys: Yes, now daddy can come out to play.

THE BUSINESS OF EMPIRE

Introduction

In December 1909, black workers in the United Fruit Company's Guatemala Division rose up against their American supervisors. The trouble began on 7 December with a surprise pay cut on the Cayuga plantation. In response to protests from laborers, nearly all of whom were British West Indians, the farm's white timekeeper declared, "You damned niggers! Mr. Smith says you are all getting too much pay. He says $30 a month is enough for any nigger." News of the racial slur and pay reduction spread quickly among the laborers, who were already simmering over their poor treatment in the enclave. When the same timekeeper shot a Jamaican worker nine days later, their anger boiled over: laborers declared a strike, chased their white supervisors off the farm, and began marching along the company railway toward the division headquarters of "Virginia." As they passed the nearby Dartmouth plantation, workers there joined the strike and raided the company commissary. Fearing for American lives and property, U.S. government and United Fruit officials demanded that the Guatemalan government crush the uprising. British diplomats quickly intervened, however, persuading Guatemalan authorities to refrain from violent repression. Over the following days, the British vice consul convinced the laborers to return to work, in part by promising to investigate their grievances against United Fruit. The strike ended peacefully, but it left company officials badly shaken.[1]

This West Indian uprising points to the complex relationship between race, work, and U.S. expansion in Central America in the late nineteenth and early twentieth centuries. At first glance, the nature of the relationship may seem obvious. White supervisors' racial attitudes, seemingly drawn from the U.S. South, had offended black West Indians unaccustomed to such treatment. Many British observers certainly perceived a difference in racial cultures. In 1911, for example, white Anglican Bishop Herbert Bury claimed that in the British West Indies, "we all worship together, receive Communion together, and meet together socially without restraint, black and white and coloured." In contrast, he noted, the U.S. enclaves in Central America featured strict racial segregation. This was true of not only the Panama Canal Zone but also the region's Caribbean lowlands, where United Fruit and other U.S. enterprises were "the great employers of labour and have their own countrymen in all their offices." Having spent time in New Orleans, Bury attributed this rigid color line to the influence of the American South.[2] Some United Fruit managers agreed. In his 1925 master's thesis on the U.S. banana industry, former company official John L. Williams, a New Englander who had likely witnessed the Jamaican uprising in Guatemala, maintained that racial tensions in the firm's enclaves stemmed from "one—and only one fact—the color line, as interpreted and practiced in the Southern states."[3]

But such accounts raise more questions than they answer. How could the racial culture of a Northeastern firm such as United Fruit, which was based in Boston and employed few white Southerners, be attributed to Southern influence? What was the relationship between the company's racial and labor practices and the U.S. government's expansion into Central America and the Caribbean? And how did the attitudes and actions of migrant workers and local peoples influence social relations in U.S. enclaves? Answering such questions requires moving beyond a notion of white Americans transplanting "Southern" race relations to overseas territories. To be sure, United Fruit's enclaves were marked by racial hierarchy, segregation, and violence—ostensible features of the Jim Crow South. But although domestic racial assumptions undeniably shaped the firm's practices, its racial policies did not so much reflect Southern influence as the interplay between West Indians, Central Americans, and corporate labor control strategies in an imperial setting.

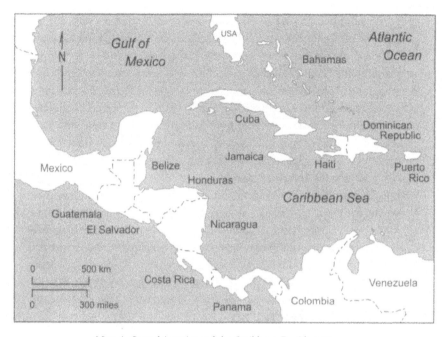

Map 1. Central America and the Caribbean. By Ole J. Heggen

The company's approach to its West Indian workers following the 1909 strike illustrates this difference. Whereas whites in the U.S. South tended to respond to black resistance with community-based violence such as lynching and race riots, United Fruit utilized the tools available to it as a transnational firm. Its primary strategy was to develop a divided workforce through the recruitment and hiring of Hispanic laborers. The resulting system of labor segmentation sought to heighten the cultural and racial tensions already present between Spanish-speaking Central Americans and English-speaking West Indians. This strategy succeeded in dividing United Fruit's laborers, but it also drew the firm into more complex and contested relations with its host nations. By the 1920s, Hispanic laborers and nationalists were denouncing U.S. domination as well as black immigration, and this resistance ultimately spurred the company to mute its imperial rhetoric and abandon its strategy of labor segmentation.

This book is about the intersection of corporate power, U.S. expansion, West Indian migration, and local aspirations in Central America. Historians have long linked business interests to the formation of the American empire in the Hispanic Caribbean, but few acknowledge the profound influence of corporate labor policies and worker responses on U.S. relations with the region. Focus on diplomatic and military policies formulated in Washington misses the foundational importance of transnational capital to American empire building. Between 1848 and 1940, it was far more common for the peoples of Central America and the broader Caribbean to encounter U.S. power and labor practices through interactions with private enterprise than with the American state. And even exceptions to this rule—the U.S. government's interventions in Cuba and construction of the Panama Canal, for example—took shape within a racial and imperial context established, to a large extent, by American capital.

United Fruit lies at the heart of this story. Although not founded until 1899, the firm had its roots in the private ventures and racialized labor practices that characterized post-1848 U.S. expansion into the Hispanic Caribbean. By the early 1910s, the company had become the most powerful economic force in Central America and the largest agricultural enterprise in the world. But although it usually sympathized with official U.S. policies, its primary influence came not from requests for U.S. government assistance, but rather through a corporate colonialism that complemented Washington's activities in the region. This relationship was most visible following the U.S. government's creation of the Panama Canal Zone in 1903. Like United Fruit, the U.S. Isthmian Canal Commission depended heavily upon black immigrant workers, and it was this labor system that served as the clearest link between the private and public components of the U.S. empire. British West Indians, in particular, moved frequently between their home islands, the Canal Zone, and nearby corporate enclaves in their search for opportunity and autonomy. For their part, U.S. government and United Fruit officials drew upon the same regional labor pool and shared racialized understandings of work, authority, and order that undergirded the strategies of domination and division they applied to their enclaves.

Race and Labor in the United States

United Fruit managers and other white Americans carried a complex legacy of race and labor with them to Central America. Ironically, the U.S. conception of black workers had its deepest roots in the Caribbean itself. Spain had first imported Africans to its Caribbean colonies in the early sixteenth century, and by the 1530s Portuguese entrepreneurs were using African slaves to develop a profitable sugar trade in Brazil. By the 1640s, the English sugar colony of Barbados had followed suit, turning to enslaved Africans as its main source of labor, and in the following decades, planters in mainland colonies such as Virginia and Carolina adapted the system to tobacco and rice cultivation. In the process of producing these tropical commodities, black bodies became not only commodified themselves, but also inscribed with the ability to withstand the tropical diseases and the harsh conditions such labor entailed. These racial assumptions gained force in the early nineteenth century as cotton grown on the expanding Southwestern frontier topped the nation's exports and fed Northern textile mills.[4]

In the process, whites across the nation embraced the dehumanized and emasculated vision of blacks that slavery produced. Northerners flocked to stage shows such as the 1828 smash hit *Jump Jim Crow*, which featured a white performer in blackface impersonating a bumbling slave, and such attitudes moved easily across frontiers and blue-water borders. In 1856, for example, New Englander John M. Dow, a skipper for the Pacific Mail and Steamship Company, tried to impress white women in Kingston, Jamaica, by having local "negro boys" perform tricks for money. In a letter to his future wife, he recalled:

> That which amused the ladies most was when I directed the little ebony faced fellows to form themselves into a line against the wall of the yard; to look up, open their eyes and lips wide, and teeth compressed together, that we might see the line of contrast, which their white teeth, and eyes, made, with their darky skins. It was a ludicrous sight.

When he tossed the coins, he noted, "all white had disappeared, [leaving] nothing but a confused jumble of little whooly heads, knocking against, and tumbling over each other."[5] Indeed, by the time of the Civil War, two and a half centuries of slavery had shaped popular views of blacks and their proper "place" in American society. Northern as well as Southern whites associated blackness with menial work, entertainment, and social inferiority. These shared assumptions weakened the nation's commitment to Reconstruction and dampened Northern opposition to the violent reassertion of Southern white supremacy that became synonymous with "Jim Crow."[6]

Equally important in shaping the relationship between race and work in U.S. enclaves in Central America were the labor control strategies developed by Northern industry, among them labor segmentation. Despite their small numbers, black workers in the Northeast were confined to the least-skilled tasks in most shops and factories. By the 1850s, moreover, New England textile barons were using Irish immigrants to divide their workers. Over the following decades, massive immigration from southern and eastern Europe enabled large industries such as steel to refine this strategy. By 1907, economist John R. Commons could claim that "the only device and symptom of originality displayed by American employers in disciplining their labor force has been that of playing one race against the other."[7] This system of labor control featured the manipulation of tensions among immigrant and native-born whites, to be sure; but it also rested upon a shared commitment to racial hierarchy. Despite the cultural differences among them, all workers perceived as "white" drew social and economic benefits from nonwhite subordination, and most objected to the employment of blacks in any but menial positions. For these same reasons, the hiring of African Americans proved an effective means of weakening unions and breaking strikes, particularly with the acceleration of black migration to the North after 1910.[8]

U.S. Enclaves and West Indian Workers

By this time, the influence of domestic racism on U.S. imperial culture was already evident, especially in the construction of the Panama Canal (1904–1914). With its strict racial segregation and predominantly West Indian workforce, the Canal Zone struck many observers as a colonial replication of the Jim Crow South. U.S. government officials usually denied this connection, claiming they were simply adapting to practices already in place. As Colonel George W. Goethals, chief engineer of the Panama Canal, explained in 1915, not only was it "customary in these tropical countries for white men to direct the work and for Negroes to do the harder parts of the manual and semiskilled labor," but it was "not compatible with the white man's pride of race to do the work which it is traditional for the Negroes to do."[9] But such a statement begs the question: who or what had made this hierarchy "customary" and "traditional"? The answer, to a great extent, was private U.S. enterprise, which had been remaking the landscapes and labor systems of Central America for decades before the U.S. canal project broke ground. Indeed, the racialized labor system of the Canal Zone represented not a "unique American creation for a unique enterprise," as one scholar has argued, but rather a U.S. government expansion upon a model developed by business interests, including the progenitors of United Fruit.[10]

The system had its origins in the post-1848 confluence of U.S. expansionism, private enterprise, and West Indian immigration into Central America. Following its victory over Mexico, the United States began the long process of supplanting Great Britain as the dominant power in the Caribbean. The main agents of this shift were private entrepreneurs and contractors, most of them Northerners, who came to Central America first to build railroads and later to buy and grow bananas. But therein lay a paradox: although eager to displace British influence, these private U.S. interests were forced to rely on the British Empire for their labor needs. Unable to secure sufficient numbers of workers among Hispanic or indigenous Central Americans, they turned to West Indians. The vast majority of these black immigrants hailed from Jamaica and other British colonies, which offered an ample supply of mobile, English-speaking labor. Between 1850 and 1914, some 300,000 West Indians traveled to the Central American rimlands, providing critical labor to foreign enterprises, above all United Fruit and the French and American canal projects. In the process, Jamaicans and other migrant workers became an integral part of U.S. expansion into Central America.

British West Indians brought with them a distinctive racial culture rooted in a history of struggle. A Jamaican slave revolt in 1831 had helped pushed Great Britain toward emancipation, and over the following decades West Indian ex-slaves sought to define their newly won freedom in terms of personal autonomy and economic independence. The collapse of the colonial sugar economy created some opportunity, as thousands managed to acquire land and grow subsistence and cash crops. But the quest for autonomy led tens of thousands more to U.S. enclaves in Central America, where most hoped to save enough money to buy land in their home islands. For their part, British officials generally encouraged this emigration as a means of relieving pressure on the island economies. At the same time, in an effort to strengthen their rule, British colonial officials extended opportunities to lighter-skinned "colored" residents while espousing an inclusive rhetoric that often contrasted race relations in the British Caribbean to those in the United States.[11]

The resulting social order was hardly free of racial tension, as evidenced by the outbreak and repression of the Morant Bay Rebellion in Jamaica in

1865. In the eyes of U.S. visitors, however, the postemancipation British Caribbean seemed to lack color lines. During his 1850 visit to Jamaica, for example, *New York Evening Post* editor John Bigelow was initially skeptical of British Governor Charles E. Grey's assertions that "we are amalgamated, we do not recognize any distinctions of color." But Bigelow soon came to agree. In addition to holding jobs in the customs and police services, he noted, Jamaicans of African descent could practice law and serve on juries. Further, U.S. forms of racial deference did not seem to apply. During one church service, Bigelow recorded that "a very black woman about fifty years of age entered . . . and advanced towards some seats on one of which a beautiful little white child was sitting. She motioned to the child to find another seat and [the child moved] into a neighboring pew without showing the slightest discontent."[12] Bigelow's observations likely revealed more about him than about life in Jamaica. But they hinted at a critical distinction between race relations in the United States and the British Caribbean. Although the memory of slavery in the British colonies was still raw and racial hierarchy remained in place, black residents faced little of the populist racism that confronted African Americans following emancipation. Largely free of the daily humiliations and threats of violence that underpinned Jim Crow in the United States, blacks in the British colonies were less accustomed to daily displays of racial deference.[13]

British West Indians carried this sensibility with them to Central America. Although they welcomed the economic opportunities that the U.S. empire offered, they often rejected its racial culture, which they usually attributed to domestic American racism. Their resistance took many forms, including verbal sparring, violent confrontation, and support of race-based movements such as Marcus Garvey's Universal Negro Improvement Association (UNIA). West Indians also looked to Great Britain for protection, often forcing British officials to mediate between black subjects and white American employers. It was this West Indian resistance that convinced United Fruit to expand its hiring of Hispanic workers. The resulting system of labor segmentation continued to be structured by racial hierarchy, but it bore only a superficial resemblance to the Jim Crow South. Despite their prejudice toward blacks, white American managers by the 1920s had come to view West Indians as their most competent laborers and assigned them most of the skilled positions within their workforce. This labor structure in turn contributed to fierce anti-black sentiment among Hispanic workers and nationalists. U.S. capital may have drawn British West

Indians to Central America, but they were not accepted as part of Central American society.

Central American Host Nations

Contrary to the claims of observers such as John Williams, racial tensions in host nations did not stem from U.S. influence alone. Slavery and Spanish colonial rule left a powerful legacy of hierarchy and inequality in Central America; and although racial identities in the region often proved more fluid and complex than in the United States, Hispanic elites generally shared white American prejudice toward peoples of African and indigenous descent. From the beginning, moreover, racial anxieties were tied to questions of national sovereignty. By 1840, the Federal Republic of Central America had dissolved into five small nations (Guatemala, El Salvador, Honduras, Nicaragua, and Costa Rica) whose leaders struggled to maintain political order and territorial integrity. Among their greatest challenges was the assertion of control over their Caribbean coasts, whose black and indigenous residents had long enjoyed autonomy and close ties to British interests. Partly for this reason, leaders in Central America initially welcomed U.S. influence as a counterbalance to Great Britain. Although Southern slave expansionism and attacks by American "filibusters" in the 1850s tempered this enthusiasm, Central American elites continued to view U.S. entrepreneurs as a key source of technical expertise and commercial dynamism. By the late nineteenth century, however, many began to realize that private U.S. enterprises posed potential threats to national sovereignty and identity: not only could American business open the door to U.S. government interventions, but its reliance on black immigrant labor raised fears of racial degradation. Such anxieties only grew with the formation of United Fruit, which drew tens of thousands of West Indians to its enclaves and continued to employ them long after it expanded its hiring of Hispanics. For these reasons, nationalist critiques of the firm in the 1920s and 1930s reflected more than simply a debate over jobs and immigration: they signified a struggle over racial identity and national sovereignty.

Although this book is regional in scope, examining trends throughout Central America and the broader Caribbean, it focuses particularly on Costa Rica and Guatemala. These nations provide compelling case studies for two key reasons. First, both played central roles in the formation and expansion of United Fruit. Second, they pose strikingly divergent political cultures and racial alchemies. In Costa Rica, the early development of small-scale coffee agriculture, combined with the lack of racialized labor coercion, resulted in less political turmoil and violence than in other Central American nations. By the end of the nineteenth century, this economic and political stability had contributed to a sense of national exceptionalism that hinged upon the claim that Costa Rica was the only "white" country in Central America. In contrast, racial anxiety and labor coercion shaped Guatemala's development. From the beginning, Guatemalan elites anguished over their nation's indigenous majority. Initially, they focused on maintaining political order, but by the 1870s and 1880s liberal leaders passed laws designed to force Mayan Indians into wage labor on coffee plantations. To justify its policies and maintain its authority, the Guatemalan state encouraged Hispanicized Guatemalans, or *ladinos,* to think of themselves as separate from and superior to the indigenous population. The result was an economy based on racial coercion and violence, and a political culture susceptible to authoritarian rule.

Despite these differences, Costa Rica and Guatemala pursued similar development strategies, which opened the door to United Fruit. In 1870s and 1880s, both countries signed contracts with U.S. railroad entrepreneurs, who brought black immigrant laborers to their Caribbean coasts. The resulting rail lines and labor systems laid the foundation for United Fruit's power in Central America. But the distinct political and racial cultures of Costa Rica and Guatemala had tremendous influence on the firm's operations. Particularly after it made its transition to a segmented workforce in the 1910s, United Fruit found it difficult to isolate its enclaves from the political currents of its host nations. In Costa Rica, a free press and open political system allowed nationalists to voice concerns about the threat the company posed to national sovereignty and racial identity. In Guatemala, while dictatorial rule enabled United Fruit to secure some key concessions, the brutality of local authorities toward black immigrants often disrupted work on the company's farms. By the 1920s, moreover, Hispanic workers in both nations were pushing to limit the employment of West Indians. Although Costa Rican and Guatemalan laborers accepted the presence of Hispanic immigrants from elsewhere in Central America, they denounced the firm's employment of English-speaking blacks. Their grievances contributed to a wave of Hispanic nationalism that swept Central America in the 1920s and 1930s and ultimately forced

United Fruit to accommodate the anti-black xenophobia it had helped incite.

United Fruit and the U.S. Empire

This book builds upon a rich body of scholarship on both United Fruit and the U.S. empire. Studies of the company have long noted its influence on the migration and trade patterns of the broader Caribbean, and a number of scholars have examined its operations in Central America. Most of these works are locally focused, however, and tend to ascribe the tensions in and around United Fruit's enclaves primarily to Central American racial and economic anxieties.[14] While the internal dynamics of host nations are a critical part of United Fruit's story, they must be examined in conjunction with the broader formation and transformation of the U.S. empire. Only then can we appreciate the profound impact of American racial practices and labor control strategies on the social landscape of Central America.

For their part, U.S. diplomatic historians have yet to integrate corporate expansion and labor migration fully into U.S. imperial history. Recent studies of working people in the Panama Canal Zone and the American naval base at Guantánamo Bay, Cuba, have paved the way for a new social history of the American empire. Yet, this scholarship focuses almost entirely on lands annexed or occupied by the U.S. government, implicitly excluding corporations and their client states from the imperial framework.[15] This is not to argue that diplomatic historians have ignored private interests—far from it. But even the best surveys of U.S. foreign relations tend to treat transnational firms superficially.[16] In studies of U.S. expansion into the Caribbean, United Fruit usually appears only episodically, and even books offering accounts of "banana wars" and "banana men" have little to say about the banana industry.[17] This gap stems partly from sources. With notable exceptions, scholarship on U.S. relations with the Hispanic Caribbean continues to rely on documents produced by the U.S. government. Such an approach obscures United Fruit's pivotal influence on U.S. interactions with the region. It also elides the role of migrant workers and local peoples in shaping the American empire.

This book offers a reinterpretation of that empire by drawing upon a wide range of public and private sources in Costa Rica, Guatemala, and Great Britain, as well as the United States. Although focusing to a great extent on labor, it makes no claim to having captured workers' experiences adequately. Their voices in the historical record are limited. U.S. government documents offer some insight on American race and labor relations, mostly in the Panama Canal Zone; but they rarely convey the views of West Indian and Hispanic workers. In fact, the best sources on workers within the U.S. empire reside in the British National Archives. Because American enterprises employed West Indian subjects in such large numbers, British officials took an interest in working conditions and labor practices within U.S. enclaves. In addition, many West Indians sent letters and petitions to the Colonial and Foreign Offices. Although the vast majority of the workers who built the U.S. empire remain silenced, these sources provide an unparalleled view of working life, particularly in United Fruit's enclaves.

Finding sources from the firm itself is an even more daunting task. Although United Fruit has been the subject of numerous studies, internal documentation is notoriously scarce. Like all corporations, the company had little incentive for transparency or archival preservation. Indeed, in the late 1970s and early 1980s, its successor, United Brands, ordered most of the records of its Latin American divisions destroyed. In the following years, only anthropologist Philippe Bourgois managed to obtain documents from one of United Fruit's operations in Central America—the Bocas del Toro Division in Panama.[18] As such, I assumed that my research into the firm's racial and labor policies would entail digging around the edges of the corporate wall, gleaning insight from visitors' accounts and the private papers of company officials.

My time in the Archivo General de Centro-América in Guatemala City gave me little reason to think otherwise. Leafing through moldering, worm-eaten documents as bus exhaust blew into the reading room, I encountered United Fruit frequently—in the form of ship manifests, passenger lists, and telegraph messages to Guatemalan officials. But such sources revealed little about the firm's corporate culture. As a result, I focused my attention on Guatemalan government correspondence as well as legal cases involving black immigrants. As I began my research in the Archivo Nacional de Costa Rica, I took a similar approach. After several days of work, however, an archivist suggested that I look at the records of the Northern Railway. Knowing that the railroad had been a thinly disguised subsidiary of United Fruit, I took her advice. As I dug into the massive collection, however, I soon realized that it was not limited to the railroad: it included the entire correspondence of United Fruit's Costa Rican Division. For a historian of United Fruit, this was the mother lode. In addition to confirming the centrality of race to United Fruit's corporate culture, these records revealed the process by which the firm shifted toward labor segmentation in the face of resistance by its West Indian workforce. They also documented the company's ties to the broader U.S. empire in the Caribbean.

The inclusion of United Fruit and its Central American client states alters our view of that empire in at least three critical ways. First, it allows for recognition that transnational American firms, like the U.S. imperial state, were cultural as well as institutional constructs influenced by both the domestic U.S. racial context and the global framework of imperialism. Second, it opens the way for an exploration of the connections between U.S. government and corporate colonialism. These include not only the exchange of managerial personnel and laborers, but the transfer of the ideas and assumptions that shaped U.S. business and government officials' views of hierarchy, order, and work in the Caribbean. Finally, a focus on corporate expansion and labor control strategies allows for the examination of nations that may have avoided Washington's intervention but experienced U.S. imperial domination nonetheless.

Organization

The organization of this book reflects the interwoven history of United Fruit and the U.S. empire in the Caribbean. Part I traces the foundations of that empire. Chapter 1 examines the shifting forms of U.S. expansion and their impact on Central America between 1848 and 1885. In the wake of the U.S.-Mexican War, Americans experimented with a number of imperial schemes, including attempts by filibusters to seize Central American territory. But it was the Panama Railroad that augured the future of the U.S. empire in the region. Completed by Northeastern capital and migrant labor, the project tied Panama to the United States and established a model for future ventures in the region. This was evident in Costa Rica and Guatemala in the 1870s and 1880s, when liberal reformers invited foreign contractors, including U.S. entrepreneur Minor C. Keith, to build rail lines to their Caribbean coasts. The ensuing construction brought the first West Indian laborers to Costa Rica. Chapter 2 analyzes the relationship between U.S. business expansion and Washington's leap into overseas empire. In the 1880s and 1890s, American investment in tropical commodities as well as railroad construction helped spur the U.S. government to take a more aggressive role in the Hispanic Caribbean. Washington's imperial surge of 1898–1903 in turn shifted the context in which Central American leaders, as well as U.S. entrepreneurs, made key decisions. Eager to avoid dependent status, Costa Rican elites grew ever more determined to assert their nation's whiteness. In order to pursue their dreams of development, however, they allowed Keith to employ black immigrants and adopted policies that enabled him to cofound the United Fruit Company. In Guatemala, a similar push to establish national autonomy through a Caribbean railway brought the first influx of black immigrant laborers—African Americans from the U.S. South—and opened the door to United Fruit's influence.

Part II focuses on the implementation and contestation of U.S. labor control strategies in Central America. Chapter 3 explores the formation of United Fruit's enclaves in the context of Washington's own colonial ventures between 1904 and 1912. Initially, United Fruit and U.S. government officials attempted to impose familiar forms of racial hierarchy on their predominantly West Indian workforces. By the early 1910s, however, West Indian resistance, along with rising labor needs, pushed the company toward the recruitment of Hispanic workers. Chapter 4 analyzes the development of this labor segmentation system in the 1912–1921 period. In these years, United Fruit expanded its hiring of Central Americans, routinely placing them below black immigrants in the labor hierarchy. In addition to fomenting divisions within the workforce, this strategy contributed to heightened anti-black sentiment in host nations, as well as the growing popularity of Garvey's UNIA among West Indian workers.

Part III examines the interplay between racial tensions on the ground and wider changes within the U.S. empire. Chapter 5 explores the link between Hispanic nationalism and anti-black agitation in the 1920s. As region-wide resentment toward Washington's interventions grew, Central American workers and nationalists denounced United Fruit and West Indians alike as agents of U.S. imperialism, and governments throughout the Hispanic Caribbean moved to restrict black immigration. Chapter 6 examines how that Hispanic nationalism, along with the economic crisis of the 1930s, pushed both the U.S. government and United Fruit to adopt "Good Neighbor" policies. In Washington's case, this entailed renouncing military intervention and dismantling its imperial protectorates over Cuba and Panama. For United Fruit, it meant, among other things, agreeing to exclude black workers from its new Pacific Coast enclaves in Costa Rica and Guatemala and thus limiting its labor control options. Such a shift highlights the role social relations on the ground played in driving U.S. government and corporate policy changes.

In recent years, the influence of transnational capital has come under increased scrutiny. In addition to debating the human and ecological costs of "globalization," many observers have asserted that the U.S. government's use of corporate contractors such as Halliburton and Blackwater in its occupations of Afghanistan and Iraq has resulted in an unprecedented privatization of the U.S. empire. But such arrangements are embedded in the long, intertwined history of U.S. government and corporate expansion that stretches back into the nineteenth-century Caribbean. In the case of Central America, the influence of United Fruit extended far beyond making investments that U.S. government officials felt compelled to protect. The company and its predecessors did not merely contribute to the expansion of U.S. power: they *made* much of the empire Washington would inherit and seek to manage. That empire entailed corporate attempts to impose familiar conceptions of racial hierarchy and labor discipline, to be sure. But those policies were questioned and contested by black immigrants, Hispanic workers, and Central American nationalists in a process that transformed the U.S. empire.

Part I

FOUNDATIONS OF EMPIRE

Chapter 1

Enterprise and Expansion, 1848–1885

In February 1855, the Panama Railroad Company announced the official opening of the world's first transcontinental railway. Located within what would become the Panama Canal Zone a half century later, the line connected Aspinwall (present-day Colón) on the Caribbean to Panama City on the Pacific. At the time, it represented the largest American investment outside the borders of the United States. In the weeks following its opening, stockholders of the New York–based company, including William Aspinwall himself, gathered in Panama, then a province of New Granada (Colombia), to celebrate. They drank toasts to the late John L. Stephens, a diplomat, writer, and prominent promoter of the project; they predicted a new age of commerce and progress. Above all, they cheered the railroad's role in linking the United States to its new territories on the Pacific Coast. Yet they said little about the Colombian and immigrant laborers who had built the railway. Like the "natives" of Panama, the workers were silenced in the firm's imperial narrative.[1] The company itself suffered a similar fate in the United States. Although newspapers across the country celebrated the railroad, news of its completion soon gave way to other headlines. These featured not only the controversy over slavery in the Western territories but also the recent exploits of U.S. filibusters in Central America. Just four months after the Panama Railroad's completion, a band of adventurers led by William Walker seized control of Nicaragua. When Walker reinstituted slavery in the conquered nation the following year, he thrust Central America into the domestic debate over slavery and territorial expansion.

Both filibustering and the Panama Railroad had their immediate roots in the U.S.–Mexican War. The 1848 victory over Mexico left thousands of young American men enthralled with conquest and convinced of their racial supremacy. It also yielded Pacific territories that lacked transportation links to the rest of the nation, a deficiency that became apparent when the discovery of gold in California brought a stampede of American prospectors. Although most made their way across the plains and deserts of the West, thousands more traveled via Nicaragua and Panama. That migration in turn drew the attention of U.S. adventurers, entrepreneurs, and policy makers to Central America. Whether they welcomed it or not, the region's residents were about to be drawn into the process of U.S. expansion.

After 1848, that expansion would be shaped, to an extraordinary degree, by private interests. The most spectacular examples were the filibusters, whose campaigns to seize new territories by force received some encouragement from Washington. But the impulse for landed expansion slowed with the coming of the Civil War. Emancipation ended all talk of new slave states, and in the following years the U.S. government focused on domestic issues such as Reconstruction and railroad building. The completion of the transcontinental railroad to San Francisco in 1869 rendered the U.S.-owned railway across Panama virtually obsolete. But the same debates over race and citizenship that stalled further territorial acquisitions made the Panama Railroad Company a useful model for U.S. expansion. Indeed, although Washington's attempts at formal overseas empire in the 1870s and 1880s proved halting, private American interests continued to entrench themselves throughout Central America and the rest of the Hispanic Caribbean. In the process, other U.S. enterprises experimented with their own versions of the business model and labor system first established by the Panama Railroad.

This connection was especially evident in Costa Rica and Guatemala. By the 1850s and 1860s, the coffee exports of both countries were growing quickly, due in part to new markets in California. In addition to reshaping regional land use and labor systems, this rising coffee sector brought to power ambitious "liberal" leaders who were determined to promote economic development at any cost. In both Costa Rica and Guatemala, their visions of progress hinged upon the construction of Caribbean railroads that could carry coffee to Atlantic markets. To build these lines, they turned to U.S. contractors, the most successful of whom was Minor Keith. Throughout the 1870s, Keith experimented with a number of labor sources in his quest to complete Costa Rica's railroad. By the early 1880s, however, he had come to rely primarily on British West Indians. And just as the Panama Railroad prefigured aspects of the Canal Zone, Keith's efforts in Costa Rica established the strategies of racial domination and labor control that would later characterize United Fruit's enclaves.

Competing Empires and Contested Sovereignty

The Caribbean coast of Central America had become a contact zone between the Hispanic and British Caribbean long before U.S. business interests appeared. Since the seventeenth century, English merchants had dominated trade along the coast by establishing ties to local black and indigenous communities. The most important of these were the Miskito Indians, who lived under a British protectorate that stretched across much of the Honduran and Nicaraguan coasts. In the 1830s, however, such arrangements began to clash with the efforts of the new Central American states to establish their territorial sovereignty. In addition to the Miskito protectorate, British settlers and black Creoles controlled Nicaragua's Caribbean port of San Juan del Norte, without which Nicaraguan officials could neither collect customs duties nor regulate commerce. Farther to the north, Great Britain ruled Belize, a predominantly black mahogany colony that Guatemala claimed was part of its national territory. From the beginning, then, the Central American states associated dark-skinned populations on the Caribbean coast with foreign threats to their sovereignty.[2]

A revealing glimpse of this British influence appeared in John L. Stephens's famous account *Incidents of Travel in Central America* (1841). Arriving in 1839 to take up his post as U.S. minister to the collapsing Central American Federation, Stephens was struck by the West Indian character of the Caribbean coast. In Belize, he observed, "I might have fancied myself in the capital of a negro republic." Along with the black majority came relaxed views toward interracial sex: in this British colony, he learned, "the great work of practical amalgamation, the subject of so much angry controversy at home, had been going on quietly for generations, . . . [and] some of the most respectable inhabitants had black wives and mongrel children whom they educated with as much care . . . as if their skins were perfectly white." Equally shocking was the sight of black men in positions of authority. At the Grand Court, for example, he found that one of the judges was "a mulatto" and one of the jurors a "Sambo"—of mixed indigenous and African descent. Stephens admitted that he "hardly knew whether to be shocked or amused at this condition of society."[3]

The U.S.-Mexican War transformed this British presence from curiosity to threat in the eyes of Americans. Following Washington's seizure of California, many Americans came to view Central America, and particularly a future Nicaraguan canal, as integral to their new empire. It was in this context that the British navy formally seized San Juan in early 1848, renaming it "Greytown" in honor of Jamaica's governor and attaching it to the Miskito protectorate. Americans bitterly denounced the move, with some U.S. newspapers accusing Great Britain of holding territory in the name of "drunken savages." For its part, the Nicaraguan government promoted its own version of the Monroe Doctrine, declaring that "the extension and propagation of monarchical institutions whether by conquest, colonization, or the sovereignty of wandering tribes . . . on the American Continent, is contrary to the interests of the Republican States of America, and menaces their peace and independence."[4] By aligning itself with Washington, Nicaragua hoped to play the two powers against each other and reassert control over Greytown.

In April 1850, U.S. and British diplomats ended the impasse by signing the Clayton–Bulwer Treaty, which provided for mutual control and non-fortification of any Central American canal. In addition to preventing an imperial clash, the agreement likely facilitated the recruitment of British West Indian laborers for the recently begun construction of the Panama Railroad. Nevertheless, the treaty brought howls of protest from U.S. expansionists, in part because it failed to annul Miskito sovereignty. One American in Nicaragua complained that the United States was "playing 'second fiddle' to John Bull" by allowing London to retain Greytown in the name of a few hundred "shoeless naked Indians."[5] Such comments were hardly surprising. Americans had long accused Britain of sponsoring Indian resistance to U.S. expansion in the West; it now seemed to be doing the same in Nicaragua. But Secretary of State John Clayton expressed hope that Great Britain would soon "extinguish the Indian title . . . within what we consider to be the limits of Nicaragua," adding that "we have never acknowledged, and never can acknowledge the existence of any claim of sovereignty by the Mosquito King or any other Indian in America."[6] In doing so, Clayton implicitly recognized Nicaragua as a "civilized" nation entitled to sovereignty. Soon, however, U.S. expansionists would challenge that status of the Central American states.

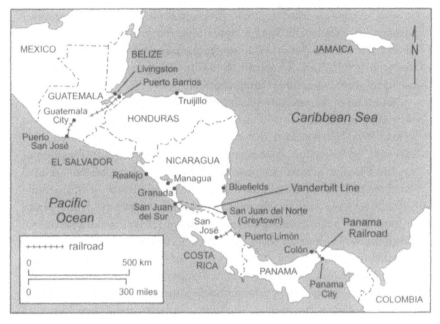

Map 2. Central American Transit Routes prior to 1904. By Ole J. Heggen

Isthmian Crossings

As U.S. and British diplomats sparred, California-bound prospectors brought changes to Central America. In Nicaragua, hotels, restaurants, and whole towns sprang up along the route from Greytown to Realejo, and prices soared as demand outstripped goods and services. The migration also began the process of reorienting Central American commerce toward the United States. Previously, regional trade had been limited to intermittent visits by British vessels. With the gold rush, however, U.S. merchant ships began arriving on the Pacific and Caribbean coasts, and the population boom in California provided a new market for regional exports, particularly coffee.[7] The gold rush also had a significant social impact on Central America. American migrants carried with them domestic prejudices that often contributed to the abuse of local residents. This sometimes took an anti-Catholic bent. In June 1849, for example, a U.S. traveler refused to doff his hat during a religious procession in Chinandega, Nicaragua, and drew a pistol on a priest who tried to remove it for him. Other Americans viewed Central America as an outlet for their sexual desires, forcing themselves on local women or marrying under false pretenses. In 1853, for example, former U.S. diplomat E. George Squier reported that in Granada, a man named Walcott had "married a very respectable girl of the country, & afterward left her, having a wife or two in the States."[8] Such incidents inevitably stirred anti-American resentment.

Americans in Central America, like U.S. visitors to the British Caribbean, were often flummoxed by the racial complexity of local society. When informed by a Nicaraguan that local rebels "want to kill all the white inhabitants" of the nation, for example, gold prospector William Denniston mocked Hispanic pretensions to whiteness, asking how it would be possible "to draw the line of distinction between white and black in this country."[9] Other travelers fell back upon domestic class and racial assumptions. In June 1850, while traveling through Nicaragua, Michigan native Albert Chapman Wells observed that "the Negro Indian portion of the people resemble in character and disposition the *Five Pointers*"—referring to the predominantly black and Irish residents of Manhattan's Lower East Side. In Managua, his group convinced their landlord to "call on the Senoritas for our benefit during the evening," but Wells claimed to recoil from "the half dressed—half brown half black and half white sooty faced damsels." One girl agreed to dance with one of the Americans "upon condition that he paid her $2." After much consideration, the man (who may have been Wells himself) declared he "would not pay a 'nigger' $2 to dance with him."[10] Sometimes the racial certainties of home could cushion a bruised ego.

These tensions only grew as U.S. capitalists consolidated their control over travel across Nicaragua. In January 1851, Cornelius Vanderbilt opened a transit line that utilized steamships, riverboats, and carriages to convey passengers from New York to San Francisco via Nicaragua. In its first four years of operation, the enterprise carried as many as 2,000 people per month. Although most Americans crossed quickly, a significant number remained in Nicaragua. Inspired by visions of Manifest Destiny, many predicted U.S. settlers would supplant native Nicaraguans or at least establish familiar color lines in place of the racial disorder they perceived. In October 1851, Wells, now living in Granada, asserted that American residents "look forward to the time when black blood will be forced to take the position that nature designed it should occupy."[11]

U.S. influence was especially noticeable in Greytown, where British interests were giving way to both the transit company and a growing number of American settlers. Visiting in 1853, Squier declared it "in all respects & wholly a fine *American* town" destined to be controlled by the

United States.[12] But this U.S. influence brought tragic results. In May 1854, local residents attacked Vanderbilt's property after one of the company's American captains shot a black boatman. Determined to protect a U.S. firm in a strategically vital region, President Franklin Pierce dispatched the U.S. warship *Cyane*, which bombarded and virtually destroyed Greytown. To justify the destruction, Pierce cited the offenses committed by "a heterogeneous assemblage gathered from various countries, and composed for the most part of blacks and persons of mixed blood" with "mischievous and dangerous propensities."[13] It was not the last time a racialized threat to U.S. capital would spur Washington to imperial violence.

The impact of the gold rush was even more profound in Panama. Between 1848 and 1860, more than 200,000 Americans crossed the narrow Colombian province. Although racial inequality and conflict were hardly new to Panama's diverse population, U.S. migration generated new tensions. Initially, American travelers crossed by river and trail, relying on Afro-Panamanian guides and boatmen. Such dependence on black labor was familiar to Southern whites, but for many Northerners it was their first significant contact with people of African descent. Even without firsthand experience, however, they drew upon familiar racial assumptions. When he crossed in December 1849, for example, Wells complained bitterly about prices in Chagres and fantasized about murdering one "old thief of a Negress"; and, upon arriving in Panama City, he pronounced "the natives" "a gambling Cock Fighting Roman Catholic race—made up of the blood of the Indian Negro Spaniard & Frenchman."[14] Such comments underscored the racial disorientation many Americans experienced in this unfamiliar setting. As historian Aims McGuinness observes, "while many recognized that color mattered in Panamanian society, they were often unsure how it mattered."[15]

Racial tensions only grew with the construction of the Panama Railroad. The project was the brainchild of William H. Aspinwall, owner of the Pacific Mail Steamship Company. Recognizing the need for interoceanic transit following the U.S. seizure of California, Aspinwall, partnering with former diplomat John L. Stephens, won a concession from the Colombian government. With Stephens serving as its first president, the new Panama Railroad Company began surveying in 1849, and the following year it set up headquarters at the mouth of the Chagres River. Like the many enterprises that followed throughout Central America, the company soon recognized labor supply as its most pressing problem. Unable to hire sufficient numbers of local Panamanians, who enjoyed opportunities in the local transit economy, the company searched for alternative labor sources.

In addition to recruiting workers from elsewhere in Colombia, it experimented with contracted white American and Irish laborers, indentured Chinese workers, and Jamaican immigrants. Although company officials shared the common assumption of black immunity to tropical disease, they worried that laborers from post-emancipation Jamaica would prove difficult to manage. In September 1850, chief engineer George Totten warned Stephens that the Jamaicans would "require driving or tasking" and might clash with Irish coworkers. He also noted that the higher wages promised to Jamaican workers could stir tension with Colombian workers.[16]

Even as it struggled to maintain an adequate workforce, the Panama Railroad Company began reshaping the physical and social landscape of Panama. In labor camps along the rail route, Colombian, Irish, West Indian, and Chinese workers cleared brush, graded land, and laid track. Meanwhile, at the termini of the railroad, the company carved out its own private enclaves. On the Pacific side, it controlled the area around the rail depot just north of Panama City. On the Caribbean coast, it built the new company town of "Aspinwall" (called "Colón" by Panamanians). Although the firm ostensibly operated under Colombian sovereignty, it enforced its own rules within its holdings and even formed a private police force to maintain order along the rail line. The result of these arrangements by the time of the railroad's completion in 1855 was not unlike the Panama Canal Zone fifty years later: an American-owned transit corridor marked by migrant labor and racial hierarchy.[17]

The combination of U.S. corporate power and the imperious behavior of U.S. migrants stirred anti-American sentiment among Panamanians, most famously during the April 1856 "Watermelon Slice Riot" in Panama City. Although the incident began with the refusal of an American traveler to pay a local vender for fruit he had sampled, it quickly escalated into mob violence that targeted company property as well as U.S. migrants. After sixteen Americans were killed, the Pierce administration dispatched naval vessels. By September, with tensions continuing to mount, U.S. marines briefly landed in Panama City to guard the rail depot.[18] As in the destruction of Greytown two years earlier, resentment toward an American company had sparked racially charged resistance, which in turn prompted Washington's intervention. Although the American press denounced the riot as mindless savagery, many Panamanians considered it patriotic resistance to U.S. expansionism. They had good reasons for such views. Not only was the railroad company gaining control over Panama, but American filibusters had recently conquered Nicaragua. Indeed, at the time of the Watermelon

Slice Riot, Central Americans were engaged in a desperate struggle with the invaders that would soon involve the slave debate in the United States.

Slavery and the Filibuster Wars

The late 1840s and 1850s witnessed a series of private attempts to seize territory in the Hispanic Caribbean. Most of the early filibustering schemes focused on Cuba. Americans had long coveted the Spanish colony, and following the war with Mexico, many Southern planters considered it critical to the survival of the slave states. Drawing upon the arguments of Cuban slaveholders themselves, they asserted that annexation would help contain British abolitionism. Early attempts to conquer the island coincided with the gold rush and drew wide support among the many prospectors who stopped in Havana on their way to Central America. Soon, Washington took up this call. In 1853, Pierce's minister to Madrid, Louisianan Pierre Soulé, offered to purchase Cuba. When Spain refused, Soulé helped draft the Ostend Manifesto, which asserted U.S. claims to the colony and warned that emancipation would transform Cuba into another Haiti, bringing "horrors to the white race" and possibly "consum[ing] the fair fabric of our Union."[19] Meanwhile, U.S. capital was making inroads into Cuba. By the 1850s, for example, Boston merchant Elisha Atkins controlled much of the sugar trade in the port of Cienfuegos and had begun to finance Cuban planters. Although the filibusters were making headlines, it was businessmen such as Atkins who were laying the foundation for U.S. control of Cuba.

By the mid-1850s, Mexico and Central America had surpassed Cuba as targets for conquest. Initially, their encounters with filibustering grew more out of U.S. westward expansion rather than Southern slavery. In the wake of the gold rush, as Anglo-American men pushed to assert their authority over California's indigenous and Hispanic population, they also sought further outlets for their aggression.[20] Among the U.S. migrants who espoused this spirit of Manifest Destiny was William Walker, a Kentuckian who led a band of Americans into northwestern Mexico in late 1853. After terrorizing locals, Walker proclaimed himself president of the new "Republic of Sonora." His reign was cut short by Cocopa Indians and Mexican residents, who routed his small army and sent it limping back across the border. Nevertheless, the adventure made Walker one of California's first celebrities.[21]

He soon found another opportunity, this time in Nicaragua. Locked in a losing struggle with the rival Conservative Party, Nicaraguan Liberals contacted Walker, who along with fifty-five men boarded a leaky brig in San Francisco in May 1855 and sailed for the Pacific port of Realejo. Contrary to the hopes of his local allies, however, Walker planned not to restore Liberal rule but to conquer Nicaragua and its neighbors. After defeating the Conservatives and setting up a puppet regime in Granada, he called for American immigration. He received an enthusiastic response: in two months alone, Vanderbilt's transit company carried 2,000 recruits to join Walker's crusade. Pierce promptly recognized Walker's regime, and the Democratic Party inserted a plank into its 1856 platform endorsing "American ascendancy in the Gulf of Mexico."[22] But despite Washington's approval, the filibusters faced fierce resistance within Central America. Fearing that Walker planned to conquer the entire region, Costa Rican troops invaded Nicaragua in spring 1856, and, soon after, Vanderbilt turned against him. Hoping to rally support in the United States, Walker played the race card. In addition to doling out land and mining concessions to white settlers, he reinstituted slavery in September 1856. Such policies aimed to make Nicaragua a "home for Southern men," he later explained. "With the negro-slave as his companion, the white man would become fixed to the soil; and they together would destroy the power of the mixed race which is the bane of the country."[23] But the restoration of slavery only increased opposition to Walker, and by early 1857 Central American armies were besieging his regime. Defeated in battle and weakened by disease, the surviving filibusters were rescued by a U.S. naval vessel.

Walker was not finished, however. Over the following months he sought help reclaiming his empire by stoking sectional tensions in the United States. In 1857–1858, he undertook a speaking tour through the South, proclaiming that his policies had been "calculated to bind the Southern States to Nicaragua, as if she were one of themselves."[24] In response, many Southerners took up his cause. In March 1858, the New Orleans *Crescent* called for Southern conquest of Central America, not only because "our own peculiar form of society [is] best suited for renovating the tropical regions of this continent," but to "prevent Abolition fanaticism from getting the first foothold in Nicaragua." Such efforts, it added, would provide a "national method by which to heal the social and political disorder of Spanish America, and to restore the choicest portions of the continent to the uses and purposes of civilization."[25]

Over the following decades, several U.S. writers would echo these sentiments, blaming Central America's woes on its rejection of Walker's "civilizing" mission.[26] In reality, the filibuster wars devastated the region, with deaths from gunfire and disease numbering in the tens of thousands. In the wake of these conflicts, Central American leaders realized the United States posed a threat to their sovereignty; and many moved to limit the influence of Americans, particularly those who had supported Walker. Albert Wells, for example, had his new mine and home in Segovia, Nicaragua, confiscated. For a man who had welcomed Walker's new racial order, it was a bitter pill to swallow. "They have robbed me of a large fortune," he complained to his brother in December 1858. "To be forced by a set of d[amne]d 'niggers' to look on with folded arms while they eat the soup is too hard for a white man to bear." Complaining of Washington's failure to defend American interests abroad, he longed to be protected "in the old fashioned English way."[27]

By this time, however, even Great Britain was moving to recognize Central American sovereignty. Although they refused to transfer Belize to Guatemala, British officials signed a treaty with Nicaragua in 1860 to replace the Miskito protectorate with an indigenous reserve. That same year, London transferred control of the Bay Islands and Miskito Coast of Honduras to the Honduran government. The latter agreement in turn brought a fitting end to William Walker. Following announcement of the treaty, British and Creole residents of the Bay Islands asked Walker to help them remain independent of Honduras. When the overeager adventurer invaded the mainland port of Trujillo, however, the British navy captured his small force. British officers then turned Walker over to Honduran authorities, who executed him in September 1860.[28]

From Black Colonization to Reconstruction

By the fall of 1860, few Americans were concerned with the fate of William Walker, but dreams of a Caribbean empire continued to influence the domestic slave controversy. Amid the secessionist stampede following Abraham Lincoln's election, Southerners promised to carry on the filibusters' legacy, with one Georgia newspaper proclaiming that Central America was the "birthright of the new nation."[29] For their part, many Northern leaders, too, gazed southward, proposing black colonization as a solution to the sectional crisis. Despite their differences, both imperial visions assumed the biological suitability of blacks to the tropics. During one meeting with prominent African American leaders in August 1862, for example, Lincoln himself recommended Central America as an ideal refuge "because of the similarity of climate with your native land."[30] Such reasoning reflected not only the limits of Republican thought, but the racial assumptions that had already nudged U.S. enterprises in the region to recruit black laborers.

Some enthusiasts viewed colonization as a tool to spread U.S. influence. Postmaster General Montgomery Blair predicted that black settlers would create "rich colonies under our protection" and transform all of Central America into "our India."[31] The New York *Independent* agreed: in addition to spreading U.S. Protestantism to lands "where Papal dogmas and ceremonies engrafted upon old Indian superstitions have so long held sway," colonization would ensure that "the problem of the future development of the negro race, under conditions of freedom and self-government, may be solved in part in Central America."[32] To Washington's chagrin, however, only Haiti and Colombia agreed to accept black colonies, the latter in the Panama province. In contrast, the Central American states refused all proposals for African American settlement. Considering their ongoing efforts to rein in foreign interests and dark-skinned residents on their Caribbean coasts, it was a predictable response.[33]

Although black colonization proved irrelevant to the Civil War's outcome, U.S. visions of Caribbean racial disorder persisted into the era of Reconstruction. For many white Southerners, the sight of black men in uniform and positions of authority recalled the British West Indies. In 1867, former Confederate general Josiah Gorgas, father of famed Panama Canal medical officer William Gorgas, responded to the sight of a black policeman in Selma, Alabama, by warning that Washington planned "to convert the Southern States into a Jamaica."[34] Equally troubling was the creeping lack of deference on the part of the freedmen. This concern puzzled many newcomers to the South. As one Northerner observed, whites in North Carolina "perceive insolence in a tone, a glance, a gesture, or failure to yield enough by two or three inches in meeting on the sidewalk."[35] Yet these were no small matters, for white and black Southerners alike understood the importance of gesture and personal bearing to the fragile fabric of white supremacy.

Like their West Indian counterparts, African American freedmen sought personal and economic autonomy. Their most immediate expression of independence came through mobility, leading Southern planters to complain that blacks were "wandering" from place to place. Such rhetoric echoed that of British colonial officials and, later, United Fruit managers, who bemoaned the restlessness of black workers. Unlike ex-slaves in Jamaica, however, African American freedmen had little opportunity to purchase land.

Convinced that black landownership would hamper Southern recovery, Republican leaders refused to break up Southern estates. As a result, even before the withdrawal of U.S. troops from the South in 1877, most freedmen found themselves trapped in rental and sharecropping arrangements that amounted to debt peonage.[36]

This outcome reflected not only the process of sectional reconciliation but also the values of the Gilded Age. By the late 1870s, Northern elites were more interested in investing in the South than in protecting black rights, and many welcomed the political stability that white supremacy provided. Along with that stability came a revived Northern acceptance of black subordination as critical to social order and national progress. Indeed, even many former abolitionists agreed with the sentiment, voiced by Virginia railroad magnate and ex-Confederate general Thomas Logan, that blacks should be trained to perform their "caste allotment of social duties . . . on the principle of a division of labor applied to races."[37] Not coincidentally, a growing number of white Northerners echoed Southern misgivings toward black citizenship.

The New Empire and the New Liberalism

These domestic developments powerfully influenced the U.S. approach to the Hispanic Caribbean. Despite emancipation, the American impulse for empire remained strong. Yet with the nation embroiled in debates over race and citizenship, the form of that empire remained an open question. Prior to the Civil War, shared assumptions of white supremacy had hastened the conquest of new territories, whose nonwhite residents were killed, displaced, or subjugated to the U.S. racial order. But in the wake of Reconstruction's liberal reforms, which implied full citizenship for all men brought into the republic, racism became a strong buffer against the annexation of further territories. This shift had little impact on business interests, however. Indeed, even as Washington focused its attention inward, American investors and entrepreneurs in the Caribbean were laying the foundation for a new U.S. empire focused on commerce and driven by private enterprise.[38]

The racial constraints on formal expansion became evident with the failed annexation of Santo Domingo (the present-day Dominican Republic). In late 1869, President Ulysses S. Grant approved two treaties with the Dominican government: the first provided for annexation of Santo Domingo and American citizenship for its people; the second allowed for purchase of the strategically valuable Samaná Bay if the Senate rejected the first. Echoing earlier advocates of black colonization, Grant argued that possession of Santo Domingo would ease U.S. racial tensions by providing a refuge for ex-slaves. In the midst of Reconstruction, however, few white Americans welcomed the incorporation of more nonwhites into the nation. As Missouri Senator Carl Schurz warned, "fancy ten or twelve tropical States added to the Southern States we already possess," with millions of tropical people "of the Latin race mixed with Indian and African blood ... [who] have neither language nor traditions nor habits nor political institutions nor morals in common with us."[39] Such anxieties contributed to the Senate's rejection of both treaties.

Yet even as formal attempts at empire floundered, trends in Latin America enhanced the influence of U.S. business interests, particularly in the Hispanic Caribbean. In the wake of independence, most Latin American nations had struggled with poverty and instability, and by the 1860s many elites had concluded that their racially mixed societies were ill suited to representative government. As a result, they turned increasingly to liberal models that focused on economic growth. Influenced by European doctrines such as Positivism, they argued that only firm rule by enlightened elites could bring order and progress. The most striking example of this new liberalism occurred just south of the Rio Grande. In 1876, after decades of civil war and foreign intervention, Mexico came under the dictatorial rule of Porfirio Díaz. Surrounding himself with liberal advisers, Díaz broke up indigenous and communal lands and courted foreign investment. But while these policies brought impressive economic growth, they opened the door to foreign domination. By the mid-1880s, U.S. and British interests controlled large portions of Mexico's mining economy and most of its expanding rail network.[40]

Compared to Mexico, the Central American nations remained isolated from the world economy. Although the gold rush had awoken elites to commercial opportunities, particularly in the coffee trade, scarce capital and poor infrastructure limited their production. Like their Mexican counterparts, Central American liberals seized upon railroads as the key to progress, and turned to Great Britain for construction loans. But poor credit forced them to accept onerous terms, laying the seeds for the debt crises that later spurred U.S. interventions. Liberals also focused on the problem of labor. Although most Central America nations had large potential pools of workers, the vitality of indigenous communities and subsistence farming hampered efforts to recruit them into commercial agriculture. Many light-skinned elites interpreted this resistance racially, declaring Indians and dark-skinned *mestizos* too backward to grasp the benefits of wage labor. Like their counterparts throughout the Americas, Central American leaders initially hoped to fill this void through European immigration, which would have the added benefit of "whitening" their populations. But they soon realized they could not compete with large nations for European immigrants and grew more determined to utilize local sources of labor. By the 1870s and 1880s, most of the Central American states had turned to both authoritarian rule and coercive labor policies, all in the name of progress.[41]

Coffee and Costa Rican Exceptionalism

Costa Rican tradition holds it apart from these regional trends. According to the nation's exceptionalist narrative, the virtual absence of indigenous peoples enabled Spanish settlers and their descendants to construct an egalitarian society free of the race mixing and political violence that plagued the rest of Central America. Like most nationalist mythologies, this tale contains elements of truth. Compared to Guatemala or El Salvador, for example, Costa Rica did have a small indigenous population, which prevented the development of a large-scale, racialized labor system. Along with the early adoption of coffee cultivation, this lack of labor coercion afforded the nation relative stability. But Costa Rica also had much in common with its neighbors. As in the other Central American states, its social relations and national identity grew out of colonial racial hierarchies, and its liberal reformers of the 1870s and 1880s faced the same challenges as their counterparts throughout the region.[42]

Exceptionalist claims aside, nonwhites were hardly absent from Costa Rican history. The territory's pre-Columbian population was actually quite dense, perhaps as high as 400,000 at the time of European contact. When Spanish settlers arrived in the Central Valley in the 1560s, however, epidemics and slave raiding had decimated all but the most remote indigenous communities.[43] In addition to facilitating the myth of an empty land, this demographic collapse prevented colonists from forming the large, forced-labor estates that marked much of Spanish America. African slavery also remained limited. Although some slaves worked cattle ranches in the northwestern region of Guanacaste, the cacao plantations of the Matina Valley represented the only concentration of slave labor. Located in the future banana belt, the cacao sector never reached a large scale, but it did bring the first significant African presence to Costa Rica's Caribbean lowlands.[44]

Despite pockets of prosperity, Costa Rica remained a provincial back-water throughout the colonial era. Even its break with Madrid came with a whimper: like the other Central American states, it hosted no battles and boasted no heroes in the struggle for independence. From the early 1820s until the late 1830s, Costa Rica was a nominal member of the Central American Federation but remained isolated from its conflicts. Nevertheless, the tiny state suffered its share of coups and dictatorships. It was one such dictator, Braulio Carrillo (1838–1842), who helped foster the coffee sector, which formed the economic basis for Costa Rican stability.[45]

Elite landholders began planting coffee trees around the capital of San José in the 1810s, and by the 1830s they were exporting their small crop to Europe. Although early returns were modest, planters recognized the potential of coffee cultivation, which spread quickly through the Central Valley. According to John L. Stephens, coffee farming set Costa Rica apart from its neighbors. Unlike the rest of Central America, which was "retro-grading and going to ruin," he concluded that Costa Rica's Central Valley was "smiling as the reward of industry." In a mere seven years, Costa Rican planters had transformed the area from "an open waste" to a thriving coffee center, and although San José lacked the "grandeur or architectural beauty" of other Latin American capitals, it exhibited a businesslike air unusual in "lethargic" Central America.[46] Such comments introduced U.S. readers to an early version of Costa Rican exceptionalism. Unlike later writers, however, Stephens made little racial distinction between Costa Rica and its neighbors. At this point, the nation's exceptionalism hinged less upon whiteness than upon its thriving coffee industry.

The structure of the new export economy contributed to this sense of uniqueness. Unlike their counterparts in Guatemala and El Salvador, Costa Rican elites never dominated coffee farming. Sparsely populated and lack-ing an exploitable racial group, Costa Rica suffered from chronic labor shortages. As a result, large landholders encouraged cultivation by selling land and extending credit to small farmers. This arrangement enabled the elite to control the marketing of coffee without monopolizing cultiva-tion. The government, too, encouraged small-scale farming by distributing seed and selling public lands. The result was broad landownership, little labor coercion, and an incipient sense of racial and national unity. While its neighbors languished in internal conflict, Costa Rica quietly built an ex-port economy that incorporated a large number of its citizens as producers. Rising customs receipts and land sales in turn placed the Costa Rican state on sound financial footing.[47]

In these same years, foreign interests made steady inroads. Like its neighbors, Costa Rica depended on Europe, particularly Great Britain, for markets, credit, and manufactured goods. By the 1850s, this relationship had given rise to a local merchant elite as well as the founding of the Banco Anglo-Costarricense—Central America's first commercial bank. U.S. influence also grew. Although few gold speculators crossed Costa Rica, the nation's leaders noted the rising American interest in the region, and especially in a Nicaraguan canal. Because the canal's Caribbean entryway would be the San Juan River, which formed part of Costa Rica's border with Nicaragua, any canal concession or seizure of Nicaragua would threaten Costa Rican sovereignty.[48] That danger became very real when the U.S. filibusters invaded Nicaragua in 1855. Costa Ricans watched nervously as Walker added recruits and reinstituted slavery. Convinced the Americans would soon target his nation, Costa Rican President Juan Rafael Mora rallied his countrymen to war by declaring that "a band of adventurers, the scum of all the earth . . . not succeeding in satisfying their voracity where they now are, are planning to invade Costa Rica and seek in our wives and daughters, our houses and lands, satisfaction for their fierce passions."[49] Supported by Great Britain, Mora's army marched into Nicaragua, defeating Walker at the Battle of Rivas. During the fighting, however, cholera swept through the Costa Rican ranks, and when the troops returned home the disease killed approximately 10 percent of the population. Nevertheless, the conflict added a key component to the Costa Rican narrative. Spared the conflicts of independence, Costa Ricans had lacked a unifying nationalist struggle. The defeat of Walker filled that void. In the following decades, Costa Rican leaders built monuments to the *Campaña Nacional* ("National Campaign"), as the war came to be called, and celebrated their effort to rescue Nicaragua and the rest of Central America from slavery and foreign aggression. That their forces had defeated white Americans made the accomplishment seem all the greater.

Despite this victory, Costa Rican dreams of national development faced formidable challenges. Although global demand for coffee was rising, the country lacked commercial connections. By the early 1850s, the Pacific Mail Steamship Company had begun service between Costa Rica's Pacific port of Puntarenas and the California coast, but it demanded a hefty subsidy in return for unreliable service. Still worse, it failed to offer a solution to the nation's principal dilemma: like its neighbors, Costa Rica was cut off from direct Atlantic trade by its Caribbean lowlands. As a result, coffee bound for Europe or the Eastern United States had to travel over cart roads from the Central Valley to the Pacific port of Puntarenas before shipment around Cape Horn. The completion of the Panama Railroad in 1855 shortened this trip considerably. Nevertheless, the 1860s witnessed the emergence of a new generation of reformers who were determined to accelerate their nation's material progress. Like their counterparts throughout the hemisphere, they called on the state to stimulate commerce, build essential infrastructure, and promote immigration. In 1870, these forces brought General Tomás Guardia to power. A typical liberal dictator, Guardia ruled Costa Rica until his death in 1882, leaving his mark on the nation. In addition to boosting spending on education and social services, he promoted exports to Europe and the United States. But Guardia's most important project was the construction of an "Atlantic Railway," which would link the coffee-growing Central Valley to the Caribbean outlet of Puerto Limón.[50]

The Caribbean Coast and Minor C. Keith

The Caribbean coast held a special place in the hopes and anxieties of the Costa Rican elite. Residents of the Central Valley had long viewed the region as a realm of tropical disease and alien races. Like most of Central America's Caribbean littoral, the humid lowlands hosted a mixed population of indigenous and African descent that lay outside of government control. Since independence, the Costa Rican state had sought to extend its authority to the coast, often by promoting foreign settlement. But its hospitality extended only to Europeans and white North Americans. Like other Central American states, Costa Rica rejected the Lincoln administration's proposals for black colonization, and fears of an African American exodus helped spur the Costa Rican Congress to pass a "Law of Settlement and Colonization" in 1862, which prohibited immigrants of the "Negro and Chinese races."[51] Even at this early point, Costa Rican leaders aimed to limit the racial threats emanating from the Caribbean coast.

The coffee boom of the mid-nineteenth century lent urgency to the development of the region. A rail connection would give the Central Valley direct access to Atlantic markets and open vast tracts of land for settlement. But San José found it difficult to attract capital for the project. By the late 1860s, the government had declared Puerto Limón a customs-free port and even discussed the possibility of granting rights for a naval base to either the U.S. or Prussian governments in return for construction of the railroad. But most Costa Rican leaders feared that control of the railway by a foreign state would threaten national sovereignty. As a result, when speculator and former U.S. presidential candidate John C. Frémont attempted to transfer his railroad concession to the U.S. government, San José scotched the deal.[52]

Upon rising to power, Guardia seized upon the construction of the Atlantic Railway as his personal mission. He hoped to pay private contractors directly for the work, thereby maintaining national ownership of the line. From the beginning, however, this plan was on shaky ground. Although Guardia's regime managed to secure financing in London, crafty creditors skimmed off most of the loan in commissions, netting San José $900,000 in return for a $3 million obligation.[53] To build the railroad, Guardia turned to U.S. entrepreneur Henry Meiggs. Despite recently completing Peru's Andean railway, Meiggs was more of a dealmaker than a railroad builder. After organizing the Atlantic Railway Company in 1871, he transferred the contract to his nephew, Henry Meiggs Keith. Like Guardia, the U.S. contractors had high hopes for the railroad's impact on Costa Rica. As one of Keith's associates, William Nanne, declared in 1872, "all we want is the Capital and Immigrants and we will be able to make this Country another California."[54] Such optimism helped lure Keith's younger brother, Minor Cooper Keith, to manage the rail company's commissary in Puerto Limón. Twenty-three-year-old Minor soon proved himself adept at commercial affairs, establishing a brisk trade in imported American goods as well as local commodities such as turtle meat and sarsaparilla—used to make root beer. Over the following years, he opened trading posts in Bluefields, Nicaragua, and Bocas del Toro, Panama, two future centers of banana exports, even as he took a lead role in the rail construction itself.

The Keiths soon realized that their greatest challenge was labor supply. Because Costa Rican laborers in the Central Valley refused to migrate to the diseased lowlands, the contractors were forced to import workers. Minor first tried New Orleans, where he scoured the docks, alleys, and prisons for laborers. But these recruits, most of them white Americans, deserted and died off in such high numbers that he soon convinced San José to let him import immigrants banned under the 1862 law. His decision was rooted in the racial assumptions of the time. Like most white Americans, Keith and his colleagues believed that blacks and most Asians were immune to tropical diseases such as yellow fever and malaria. As one of the railroad managers observed, "I was always of opinion, that it was a mistake to bring white laborers for that work on the coast. The negroes and Chinese seem to do better than any others."[55] Initially, the American managers favored Asian contract laborers, whom the company began importing in early 1873. Like contemporary railroad builders in the American West, Keith and his colleagues viewed these workers as company-owned servants. In a February letter acknowledging the arrival of "562 China-men," for example, Nanne promised the railroad company's New York supplier, W. R. Grace, to "pay the value of these slaves by monthly installments."[56] Such language was apt, for when Asian contract laborers proved just as susceptible to tropical disease as white workers, the company simply sold them as servants and farm laborers to Costa Rican planters in the interior. The Chinese were "sold as if they are . . . slaves for a certain term of years," observed U.S. diplomat George Williamson. "The value of each Chinaman is computed according to the period he is still obliged to labor. When sold, it is agreed that he shall serve his new master only for said balance."[57] This trade in Asians proved profitable for the contractors, but it did little to resolve their labor shortage.

Keith and his associates soon came to view the British Caribbean as the most promising source of workers, for three main reasons. First, in contrast to the Asian contract laborers, West Indians indeed seemed more resistant to tropical diseases. Although they remained susceptible to malaria, as well as the respiratory illnesses common in the railroad's squalid labor camps, many enjoyed immunity to yellow fever due to childhood exposure. Second, the contractors found British West Indians relatively easy to manage. Not only did they speak English, but many had experience in rail construction, including a number of former employees of the Panama Railroad. Finally, they were available in large numbers. As early as September 1873, Minor Keith happily reported that "621 men arrived from Jamaica last month, and 200 more [were] expected."[58] Over the following years, West Indians came to dominate the railroad's workforce. To control these black laborers, Keith and his fellow white managers attempted to impose a familiar system of racial hierarchy. In addition to monopolizing supervisory and engineering positions, they utilized intimidation and violence to enforce black deference. In this effort, they received firm support from the Guardia regime, which maintained military rule in the newly organized province of Limón. Indeed, while the Costa Rican state eschewed labor coercion in the Central Valley, it enforced vagrancy laws against West Indians who refused to work, thereby encouraging the abuse of black immigrants by local authorities.[59]

Even at this early stage, U.S. racial ideology and labor practices seemed to influence Costa Rican attitudes. One revealing anecdote emerges from Minor Keith's efforts to court his future wife, the daughter of former Costa Rican president José María Castro, in the early 1880s. Knowing little Spanish, Keith memorized a joke to break the ice:

Un negrito	A darkey
llegó al infierno	Arrived in hell
y pegó un grito	And let out a yell
El diablo salió	The devil appeared
y le contestó	And answered him
"Aquí no se aceptan negros."	"Here Negroes are not admitted."

Keith's weak Spanish caused him to botch the punch line, but the Castros laughed nonetheless.[60] The exchange reveals much about the transnational dynamics of race in Costa Rica. In the process of building a bond with an elite family, Keith drew upon racial stereotypes and practices from the United States. That the Castros joined in the joke hinted at an incipient anti-black consensus between Costa Rica's elite and its preeminent foreign entrepreneur.

At the time of this episode, the completion of the Atlantic Railway was very much in doubt. Because Guardia had insisted that the railway be built from both ends simultaneously, his government quickly depleted its funds. The resulting suspension of payments to the contractors in 1876 led to a rupture between the Keiths and W. R. Grace, spurring the disgusted Henry to turn the entire enterprise over to Minor.[61] The financial shortfall also undercut the railroad's labor system. Because most of its West Indians workers had traveled to Costa Rica freely, they were under no obligation to remain, and many began drifting away. As a result, throughout the late 1870s and early 1880s, Minor struggled to maintain a sufficient workforce as he waited for San José to resolve its debt crisis. For their part, Costa Rican leaders grew increasingly desperate to complete the rail line. If their nation was to maintain its exceptional character, they believed, it needed access to U.S. and European markets, which only the Atlantic Railway could provide. In order to have that railroad, however, they would have to compromise their vision for the Limón province. Having already accepted black immigration as a necessary (though, they hoped, temporary) evil, they would soon enter an agreement that ended their dream of national control of the railroad and granted Keith a private empire on the Caribbean coast.

Race and Labor in Guatemala

Unlike Costa Rica, Guatemala could never claim to lie outside of Central American history. As the region's political and economic epicenter, it represented everything Costa Ricans defined themselves against. Since the conquest, Spanish settlers and their descendants had sought to dominate the large Mayan population, and the resulting racial divisions and forced-labor practices shaped elite views of hierarchy, order, and state power. As a result, Guatemalan liberals took a very different approach to labor scarcity than their Costa Rican counterparts. This included a series of coercive policies in the 1870s and 1880s. Nevertheless, Guatemala faced the same obstacles to railroad construction, and it, too, turned to U.S. entrepreneurs for solutions.

The relationship between race and labor lay at the heart of Guatemalan history. Although African slavery played an important role in the colonial economy, indigenous peoples provided the main source of labor. In the colonial era, Spanish officials had resettled the Mayan population into several thousand village communities. They defined the residents of these towns as "Indians" and subjected them to tribute labor, known after 1800 as *mandamientos*. As was true throughout Spanish America, however, the definition of "Indian" proved mutable, for two key reasons. First, sexual contact between Europeans, indigenous, and Africans produced a large mixed group, often called *"ladinos,"* who were not subject to tribute labor. Second, many Maya left their communities and adopted Spanish language and dress, in the process blurring the line between Indian and *ladino*. In addition to undermining the colonial labor system, these demographics shaped the outlook of Guatemalan elites, who became obsessed with both their own "purity of blood" and the "dangers posed by the dark-skinned masses."[62]

These racial anxieties were driven home by a popular uprising in the late 1830s, which dismantled the Central American Federation and led to the rise to power of a *ladino* named Rafael Carrera, who ruled Guatemala until his death in 1865. While some conservative elites welcomed Carrera, most viewed him as a symbol of dark-skinned barbarism, and many foreign visitors agreed. John L. Stephens described Carrera's followers as "a tumultuous mass of half-naked savages," and a decade later one British diplomat dismissed Carrera's Guatemala as "a country whose ignorant and savage inhabitants do not respect or understand the rights of diplomatic agents."[63] Despite such assertions, Carrera hardly ushered in an age of savagery. Instead, he adopted a careful mixture of policies, drawn from both colonial and liberal traditions. Above all, he prevented conflict in his racially divided nation by limiting the imposition of *mandamientos* on Mayan communities. This approach served Guatemala well through the 1840s and 1850s, providing political stability in an era of limited commerce and low labor demands. As a result, domestic tensions remained muted, enabling Carrera and his advisers to focus on external threats.[64]

Much of their concern centered on the Caribbean lowlands, which would later be organized as the Department of Izabal. As in other Central American countries, the loosely controlled Caribbean coast was home to most of Guatemala's black residents. In addition to former slaves and their descendants, these included a large number of Garífuna. Often called "black Caribs," the Garífuna had their origins in a shipload of rebellious slaves who were deposited on the coast by the British in 1797. Most of Guatemala's Garífuna resided in the town of Livingston, at the mouth of the Dulce River, where they practiced a blend of African and indigenous culture.[65] When Stephens visited Livingston in the late 1830s, he found a population of "about fifteen hundred Indians, negroes, mulattoes, mesti[z]os, and mixed blood of every degree, with a few Spaniards." He even met a runaway American slave who had lived in Livingston for eight years and become a man of "considerable standing."[66] These unique demographics contributed to the Caribbean coast's isolation from the rest of Guatemala. Despite efforts by the Guatemalan state to assert its authority, often through white colonization schemes, the region had closer ties to British-controlled Belize than to Guatemala City.[67]

Under Carrera, the Guatemalan government sought to contain perceived racial perils on the Caribbean coast, which were often associated with foreign threats to sovereignty. These anxieties shaped its response to the U.S. expansionism of the 1850s and early 1860s. In 1856, Guatemala joined the war against Walker, and it publicly sided with the Union during the U.S. Civil War. According to the American minister to Guatemala, E. O. Crosby, Carrera and his advisers worried that if the Confederacy survived, it would absorb Mexico, Central America, and Cuba, thereby making the Gulf of Mexico "a great inland sea surrounded by a slave empire." But Guatemalan officials also recoiled from the U.S. government's proposals for black colonization of the Caribbean lowlands. As Crosby recalled, "they put the question to me: 'If the U.S. want[s] to colonize the free blacks on territory by themselves, why don't they appropriate some of their own sparsely populated territory to this purpose and keep them themselves?'—a question which I must confess I found very difficult to answer."[68] Carrera and his advisers understood that Southerners had no monopoly on expansionism and that African American settlement could open the door to U.S. domination.

Such fears were hardly frivolous. Crosby himself longed for Guatemala to be "under the U.S. flag, and populated by the Anglo-Saxon race," and he criticized Washington for being "so tardy or indifferent to the acquisition of tropical possessions." But Guatemalan officials had a more pressing concern: black colonization would enhance the racial distinctiveness of the Caribbean lowlands and further undermine national cohesion. According to Crosby, Carrera and his advisers worried that "English speaking negroes . . . could not be assimilated with their already mixed population" and that the black newcomers "would gradually introduce a new order of things that would eventually lead to an open rupture between them and the native races."[69] In later decades, such concerns would prove prophetic, as black immigration indeed sparked racial tensions.

By the late 1860s, however, Guatemalan elites were focused on other issues. The success of Costa Rica convinced many landowners to try their hand at coffee. As they pushed to expand cultivation, however, they confronted persistent labor shortages. This proved particularly frustrating because, in contrast to Costa Rica, Guatemala had a vast potential workforce in the Mayan highlands. But indigenous Guatemalans were hardly eager to leave their communities for the harsh treatment, low wages, and humid climate of coffee plantations. Planters dismissed this as racial backwardness rooted in the colonial past and reinforced by Carrera's conservatism. As one elite asserted in 1867, "these Indians, divided into or belonging to different tribes, and speaking different dialects, are peaceful, docile, and generally inclined to work, but strongly addicted to their own habits, ways and customs."[70] Such men concluded that only a forceful state willing to adopt coercive labor policies could ensure the nation's progress.

Barrios and the Liberal State

These were the seeds of the new liberal movement. In 1871, ambitious coffee planters, organized around the Liberal Party and led by Justo Rufino Barrios, overthrew the conservative government and ushered in a new era of Guatemalan history. The ensuing Barrios dictatorship (1873–1885) pushed aggressively to expand the coffee industry. One key step was a sweeping land reform that required plots to be placed under individual title. By breaking up Mayan communal lands, the law aimed not only to open new lands to coffee planters, but also to undermine subsistence farming and thereby force highland Maya to labor for those planters. This same logic led to the revived use of the *mandamiento* and the passage of vagrancy laws. To bolster this labor regime, the Liberal state promoted a racialized national identity that divided *ladinos* from Indians. In the process, "*ladino*" lost much of its mixed-race stigma and came simply to signify "non-Indian." Over time, the term expanded to include all, whether light- or dark-skinned, who spoke Spanish, wore non-Indian clothing, and lived outside of indigenous villages. This identity offered concrete benefits, for coercive labor laws applied mostly to Indians. In this way, Barrios and his successors encouraged *ladinos* to identify with the state and set themselves apart from the Mayan majority.[71]

Like other reformers throughout Latin America, Guatemalan Liberals also tried to attract white immigrants, who they hoped would counteract their nation's racial shortcomings. In 1877, for example, the members of Guatemala's Immigration Society called for greater recruitment in European and U.S. cities, declaring white immigration an "immense fountain of progress."[72] Although such efforts fell short, pockets of foreign settlers did appear. In 1878, for example, when a ship carrying 340 Italians arrived at the Guatemalan coast, the government invited them to settle. Far more important, however, were German immigrants, who played a critical role in developing the coffee industry. By the 1880s, they had transformed the town of Cobán, Verapaz, into their own coffee enclave. With their efficient trade through Livingston and close connections to European markets and commercial banks, German coffee farmers boasted an early form of the vertical integration that United Fruit would later perfect in the banana industry. Indeed, by the late nineteenth century, the Germans of Verapaz were a formidable economic and political force in Guatemala. In contrast, American influence remained limited primarily to the Protestant missionaries whom Barrios welcomed to the Mayan highlands.[73]

Nevertheless, a small number of Americans travelers visited Guatemala during Barrios's reign and recorded their impressions. Among the richest accounts was that of New Englander William Brigham. Like most visitors, Brigham depended on Guatemala's forced-labor system to move about the country. "Indios are obliged to carry burdens," he explained. "The person hiring pays the authorities with whom the men are registered." Brigham found the system "very convenient" and boasted that in one highland town, "we went to the Plaza, [and] captured a mozo[laborer] without the intervention of the authorities." Despite such enthusiasm, however, he did not wholly accept Guatemala's state-sponsored racial hierarchy. Indeed, he found much to admire in the Maya, whom he considered "neater in their persons and garb than the ladino population."[74] But like most foreign visitors, Brigham admired Barrios and his policies. While admitting the regime was "republican in name only," he concluded that a dictatorship "is perhaps a political necessity of the country and race, however repugnant to Anglo-Saxon ideas"; after all, he asserted, Guatemala had "made more material progress in the ten years of his administration than the other Central American Republics have made in half a century." In order to continue its development, however, Guatemala needed foreign capital and immigrants. An infusion of U.S. investment, Brigham predicted with startling prescience, could transform the Caribbean coast into a "great fruit-producing orchard of the United States . . . not necessarily by political annexation, but by commercial intercourse."[75]

Barrios and his supporters largely agreed with Brigham's analysis, and like their Costa Rican counterparts they turned to U.S. contractors to build the railroads needed for this development. They began with rail lines on the Pacific Coast, which could carry coffee from inland plantations to the expanding markets of California. After several failed ventures, Barrios succeeded in luring William Nanne away from Keith's enterprise in Costa Rica. In 1877, Nanne signed a contract to lay track from Puerto San José on the Pacific to the town of Escuintla. Having completed that segment in 1880, he agreed to extend the line to Guatemala City in return for a 99-year lease on the railway. But soon after, he sold the concession to California rail titan Collis P. Huntington. Although Barrios worried that this West Coast monopoly could pose a threat to his nation, a hefty bribe put his patriotism at bay. Even before the railway was completed in 1884, however, it was clear that it would not solve Guatemala's problems. Like other ports on Central America's Pacific Coast, Puerto San José was too shallow for efficient commerce, and steamship service remained unreliable. Moreover, Barrios and his Liberal Party still hoped to prevent a foreign monopoly from controlling their nation's trade.[76]

As a result, they increasingly focused their attention on the development of the Caribbean coast. In addition to declaring Livingston a tariff-free port, Barrios opened public lands to settlers and pressed for the construction of a "Northern Railway," which would link Guatemala City and the western coffee lands to Atlantic commerce, thereby circumventing the Pacific line. Like their counterparts in Costa Rica, Guatemalan Liberals came to view the railroad as the key to national autonomy and progress. "The railroad to the north . . . carries within it the resolution of the great problems that stand before all who are interested in the future of the Republic," declared Barrios's minister of development in 1880; not only would it "stimulate in an incalculable way the agricultural and mercantile interests," but it would "create a spontaneous current of honorable and hard working immigrants" and "call to the attention of European and American capitalists the almost inexhaustible resources of this privileged soil."[77]

Also like Costa Rican leaders, Guatemalan Liberals hoped to retain national ownership of the railroad. In 1884, after imposing a domestic tax to pay for the construction, Barrios signed an agreement with Tennessee-based contractors to build the Northern Railway. Confident of success, he ordered that its Caribbean terminus be named "Puerto Barrios." But construction of the nearly 200-mile railway proceeded slowly. As in Costa Rica, labor shortages exacerbated the challenges of climate and landscape. The local population of Garífuna and *ladinos* was too small to provide adequate labor, and coffee planters resisted the transfer of Mayan workers to the railroad. As a result, the Guatemalan state looked abroad for laborers. At first, Barrios hoped to attract white immigrants with promises of land grants following the railroad's completion. When that strategy failed, he accepted the U.S. contractors' requests to import nonwhite labor. Although they initially looked to the British Caribbean, canal excavation by a French company in Panama had drained the West Indian labor pool. As a result, the contractors turned to the American South, and particularly to U.S. blacks. Beginning in the summer of 1884, hundreds of African Americans arrived on Guatemala's Caribbean coast. Despite assumptions of black immunity, many quickly fell victim to yellow fever and malaria. By March 1885, the situation of railroad workers in Guatemala had grown so desperate that the U.S. Navy sent a warship to rescue Americans in Livingston and Puerto Barrios, including a number of African Americans.[78]

By this time, Barrios's other ambitions had brought rail construction to a halt. Since coming to power, the dictator had dreamed of reunifying Central America under his leadership, and by the early 1880s he was courting U.S. support. In return for Washington's help, he hinted at his willingness to grant the rights to build a canal and naval bases in the region.[79] In addition to draining the Northern Railway of its funding, Barrios's ensuing attempt to unify Central America by force led to his death on a Salvadoran battlefield in April 1885. But his vision for Guatemala lived on. Over the following years, his successors continued to strengthen the nation's coercive labor system and pushed for completion of the Northern Railway. As in Costa Rica, however, these policies brought unintended consequences. Although progress-minded elites viewed the Northern Railway as a means of safeguarding national autonomy and even improving Guatemala's racial character, its construction would open the way to the foreign domination and black immigration they had long sought to avoid.

Those trends in Guatemala reflected broader changes in the U.S. relationship with Central America and the Hispanic Caribbean. The U.S.-Mexican War and subsequent gold rush had drawn Central America into the process of U.S. expansion. As prospectors poured across the region, American officials and entrepreneurs sought to displace British interests and assert control over isthmian transit routes. By the mid-1850s, private enterprises such as the Panama Railroad had not only shifted the commercial patterns of the region, but introduced racial and labor practices that would characterize U.S. enclaves. At the same time, notions of Manifest Destiny and rising sectional tensions drove Americans to support various expansionist schemes, including Walker's devastating war in Central America. The Civil War brought an end to most territorial expansion, however, and by the 1870s and 1880s, business interests had become the most important agents of American influence in the Hispanic Caribbean.

This growing prominence of private enterprise coincided with the rise of a new Latin American liberalism. Determined to promote progress and prosperity, elite reformers throughout the region coupled authoritarian rule with commercial expansion and railroad construction. Liberals in Costa Rica and Guatemala followed this pattern, but labor shortages limited their options. In their thriving coffee sectors, the two nations could hardly have been more different. While Costa Rica's lack of an exploitable racial group resulted in a broad-based system of small farming, Liberal Party leaders in Guatemala revived coercive labor practices from the colonial era to force indigenous peoples to work on coffee plantations. In the area of infrastructure and trade, however, Costa Rica and Guatemala faced comparable obstacles and adopted similar solutions. In order to achieve their development goals, both needed railroads to the Caribbean, and both turned to U.S. entrepreneurs to build them. By the late 1880s, moreover, the leaders of both nations had accepted black foreign workers as necessary for the completion of their rail lines. Over the following decades, however, this combination of private U.S. influence and black immigration would clash with Central American visions of national sovereignty and identity.

Chapter 2

Joining the Imperial World, 1885-1904

In late 1874, seventeen-year-old Konrad Korzeniowski stepped off a
Marseilles pier and boarded the merchant ship *Mont-Blanc*. After living
with an uncle in Krakow for five years, he had decided to try life at sea.
This first voyage, to the French colony of Martinique, convinced him he
had found his calling, and he returned aboard another vessel in July 1876.
After stopping in Martinique, this ship spent a month along the coasts of
Colombia and Venezuela, likely running guns to local rebels. It next sailed
to the Danish West Indies, then on to Haiti, reaching Port-au-Prince in
late October. There, as the rest of the crew completed maintenance and
loaded a cargo of sugar and logwood, Korzeniowski took time to explore.
Although it was his last voyage to the Caribbean, the region left a powerful
impression on him.[1]

Other adventures beckoned. In 1878, he joined the British merchant
marine, which took him to the exotic corners of the world, from Istanbul
to Malaya, Bombay to Borneo. But in 1889, at the height of his maritime
career, he resigned and settled into a London flat to write. Still, one had to
eat, so in May 1890 he signed on as skipper of a Congo River steamer. The
job took him deep inside the colonial domain of Belgian King Leopold II.
The Congo railway was not yet completed, forcing Korzeniowski and his

porters to trek to Kinshasa by foot. The following six months proved a revelation to Korzeniowski, who soon realized that, despite talk of a "civilizing
mission," violence and ivory profits ruled the Congo Free State. And the
worst was yet to come. Soon after his departure, the forced labor demands
of the rubber boom killed hundreds of thousands of Congolese. In other
colonies, he had noted the gap between promise and practice, but here it
seemed a chasm. As he later admitted to a friend, before the Congo, he had
"not a thought in his head."[2]

In 1895, Korzeniowski published *Almayer's Folly,* a novel set in Malaya,
and he followed up with *An Outcast of the Islands* (1896) and *The Nigger
of the 'Narcissus'* (1897). Then came *Heart of Darkness* (1899), published under
the name Joseph Conrad. The layered narrative of the novella conveyed the
experiences of Conrad's alter ego, Marlow, an employee of the Belgian
company sent up the Congo River to retrieve a rogue agent named Kurtz.
Over the course of Marlow's long journey, colonial greed and brutality blur
the line between civilization and savagery. As Marlow himself reflects, "The
conquest of the earth, which mostly means the taking it away from those
who have a different complexion or slightly flatter noses than ourselves, is
not a pretty thing when you look into it too much."[3]

When Conrad began writing *Heart of Darkness* in 1898, he was well
aware of the U.S. leap into overseas empire that same year, and he ex-
plored it directly in *Nostromo* (1904). Set in the fictional Latin American
republic of Costaguana, the novel draws its title from an Italian foreman of
a foreign-owned railroad who commands the "outcast lot of very mixed
blood, mainly negroes" employed by the company. But the story centers on
Charles Gould, a Costaguana-born Englishman who inherits a silver mine
in the nation's western coastal province. With the help of U.S. investors,
he revives the mine, declaring that foreign capital will uplift the troubled
nation. "Only let the material interests once get a firm footing," Gould
explains, "and they are bound to impose . . . law, good faith, order, [and]
security."[4] Yet instead of progress and order, the mine spawns racial tensions and political chaos—described at one point as the "clamour of *Negro
Liberalism.*"[5] In response, Gould's financiers cooperate with ambitious local
elites to sever the province from the rest of the country. The presence
of U.S. naval vessels ensures the independence of this new "Occidental
Republic," which seems destined to become an American satellite. And according to the principal U.S. investor, Holroyd, Costaguana is only a hint of
the commercial expansion to come. Revealing his "insatiable imagination
of conquest," he predicts that Americans "shall run the world's business

whether the world likes it or not. The world can't help it—and neither can we, I guess."[6]

Conrad's plot had much basis in reality. Set in the 1880s and 1890s, *Nostromo* reflected a key shift in imperial power. At the beginning of this period, British interests still controlled much of Latin America's economy. By the late 1890s, however, American capital was gaining predominance in the Hispanic Caribbean. Not coincidentally, Washington's efforts to protect American interests grew more aggressive. This included not only the 1898 occupation of Cuba but also the U.S.-sponsored secession of Panama from Colombia in 1903, which took place even as Conrad wrote. Within days of this "revolution," U.S. officials imposed a canal treaty on the new republic, making it a colony in all but name. "[W]hat do you think of the Yankee Conquistadores in Panama?" Conrad asked a friend in December 1903; "Pretty, isn't it?"[7]

Like their real-life Latin American counterparts, the Costaguanans are hardly helpless victims in *Nostromo,* and many eagerly collaborate with foreign interests. Despite the potential threat to their national sovereignty, Costaguanan elites welcome the "progressive" influence of foreign capital while deploring their country's racial backwardness, and some ultimately contribute to its dismemberment. Throughout the novel, Conrad explores these tangled ties of race, empire, and Latin American liberalism, but he makes clear that foreign business drives the colonial encounter. In *Nostromo,* as in *Heart of Darkness,* the demands of capital shape the course and culture of empire.[8]

This insight is crucial to understanding the process by which the United States joined the imperial world. In the late 1880s and 1890s, the combination of Europe's global expansion and domestic U.S. anxieties led many Americans to call for overseas empire. But because American politics remained focused on domestic issues, U.S. influence in Central America and the rest of the Hispanic Caribbean continued to be spread primarily through private interests. This included mining and railroad enterprises akin to those in *Nostromo* as well as a growing trade in tropical commodities, above all sugar and bananas. In addition to reshaping commercial and labor patterns, these business interests helped draw Washington into a more active role in the region. Indeed, it was primarily the attacks on U.S. sugar properties by Cuban rebels that precipitated the War of 1898. The ensuing imperial occupations, especially in Cuba, further racialized U.S. public and private interactions with the peoples of the Hispanic Caribbean. By the time Washington seized Panama in late 1903, the nations of the region found themselves in a tenuous position: even as they struggled to lift themselves to Western standards of civilization, the United States seemed determined to push them into the ranks of the colonized tropics.

Costa Rica and Guatemala could not help but be affected by these trends. Like other countries in the region, they sought to navigate the perilous seas of race and imperialism. By the 1890s, both were asserting their claims as civilized nation-states, with Costa Rica stressing its singular whiteness. At the same time, however, the two countries continued to depend on U.S. entrepreneurs and English-speaking black immigrants to develop their Caribbean coasts. Far from securing progress and sovereignty, such policies opened the way to corporate domination by the United Fruit Company, a private empire that was taking shape even as Washington built its own public empire.

European Imperialism and the French Canal

Joseph Conrad's was indeed an imperial world. But as his fiction made clear, imperialism did not always come in the form of territorial annexation. Although European expansion in the late nineteenth century certainly involved the extension of state authority over foreign peoples, it made its greatest impact through the economic changes that it wrought. As they fell under European financial and political control, societies in Africa, Asia, and the Middle East shifted to the production of mine products and cash crops for export to imperial centers. At the same time, European officials and entrepreneurs undertook large infrastructure projects, especially railroads and canals, in order to facilitate this trade. Together, these efforts brought profound changes to the work experiences and migration patterns of local peoples. Although the Congo was an extreme example, most imperial regimes practiced some form of coerced labor, and European officials frequently imported nonwhite workers and soldiers from other colonies and regions. In addition, colonial subjects themselves migrated within and between colonies in search of greater opportunity or autonomy, and they often faced local hostility. In sum, the global experience of colonialism involved not only political and economic domination but also labor migrations and demographic transformation.[9]

The United States responded to Europe's expansion with a mixture of admiration and angst. Although most white Americans shared the racial assumptions behind European imperialism, they had a long tradition of distrusting any expansion other than their own. Amid a series of economic downturns, moreover, many Americans worried that the European powers were closing future outlets for U.S. exports and enterprises. They also realized that the threat was not limited to state-driven expansion, for private European investment often preceded moves toward annexation and protectorates. Examples included not only the famous British East India Company but also the Suez Canal, the construction of which in the 1860s led to a British protectorate over Egypt in 1882. A similar turn of events seemed possible in the Hispanic Caribbean, where European investors controlled most of the region's debt and infrastructure.[10]

These fears came into sharp focus in the early 1880s, when the French-owned Compagnie Universelle du Canal Interocéanique began canal excavation in Panama. Headed by Ferdinand de Lesseps, father of the Suez Canal, the enterprise represented a direct challenge to future U.S. control of the region. Since at least the gold rush, Americans had assumed that any Central American canal would be built by U.S. interests, and in 1876 Washington's Interoceanic Canal Commission had thrown its support behind the Nicaraguan route. By the time the French company appeared, however, private U.S. attempts to build a Nicaraguan canal had faltered. In 1884, President Chester Arthur attempted to revive these efforts and undercut de Lesseps by signing a canal treaty with Nicaragua, which would have replicated the British protectorate in Egypt. But the U.S. Senate, leery of opening the way to annexation or violating the Clayton-Bulwer Treaty with Great Britain, rejected the agreement.[11]

Meanwhile, Americans watched nervously as the French canal project got underway. By the mid-1880s, the Compagnie Universelle employed about 19,000 people, some 16,000 of whom were West Indians. Although most of these laborers came directly from their home colonies, the high wages of canal work also lured hundreds, perhaps thousands, away from U.S. enterprises in Central America, including the railroad construction in Costa Rica and Guatemala.[12] Still, the company's challenge to U.S. influence was not nearly as ominous as it appeared. Although the French firm purchased the Panama Railroad, it kept many of the rail line's personnel and hired more Americans for the excavation itself. In the process, the Compagnie Universelle adapted many of the railroad's labor practices to its own purposes. In addition, the French company utilized a divided pay structure in which white, foreign employees were paid in gold coin and laborers, most of them British West Indian, were paid in silver.[13] Despite this racialized labor hierarchy, canal workers faced few restrictions on their movement and personal freedom. Like the Panama Railroad, the French firm asserted little of the imperial authority and social control later wielded by the U.S. government in the Canal Zone.

Also like the Panama Railroad, the Compagnie Universelle ultimately depended on U.S. military power to maintain order on the isthmus. This became apparent when a civil war between Liberal rebels and Colombia's Conservative government broke out. By early 1885, the conflict had spread to Colón, where the Liberals were led by an Afro-Panamanian lawyer and politician named Pedro Prestan. In addition to disrupting trade and canal construction, the rebellion raised racial tensions. Soon American residents were calling for the use of "Judge Lynch" to cow the rebels, and Prestan was threatening to kill all whites in Colón. The flash point came in March, when the Pacific Mail Steamship Company refused to release a cargo of arms to the rebels. In response, Prestan seized several Americans hostages, including Pacific Mail agent John M. Dow—the same man who had used "negro boys" to entertain white women in Jamaica thirty years earlier.[14] Soon after, Prestan's followers started a fire that consumed much of Colón. As it had during the 1856 Watermelon Slice Riot, Washington dispatched warships to restore order. Over the following months, U.S. marines helped Colombian troops hunt down and hang Prestan and his followers, some of whom were Jamaican migrants.[15]

In the wake of the rebellion, shortages of labor and capital hampered the French canal effort. Despite racialized assumptions of West Indian immunity, blacks as well as whites fell victim to tropical and respiratory illnesses. In all, some 22,000 employees died, forcing the Compagnie Universelle to search continually for workers, often in the same places as U.S. railroad contractors in Central America. In a March 1886 letter, for example, one of the company's American managers suggested it might find workers among "our Southern negroes" as well as Chinese immigrants being turned away by the 1882 Exclusion Act.[16] Even more crippling than the insufficient labor supply were cost overruns, which forced the company to shut down in late 1888. The collapse of the canal effort was disastrous for the thousands of West Indians left stranded and unemployed in Panama. In the eyes of most Americans, however, the French failure removed what had seemed a serious threat to U.S. power in the Caribbean.

Bananas and Sugar

In reality, U.S. economic control had continued to grow, especially in Central America, despite the French challenge. Although the bulk of U.S. overseas investment remained concentrated in Mexican mines and railroads, commerce in tropical commodities became increasingly important in the 1880s and 1890s. This included the burgeoning banana trade. American merchant ships had purchased bananas sporadically since the 1860s, mostly from the British West Indies. By the 1880s, however, the U.S. appetite for the oddly phallic fruit had brought a banana boom to many parts of the broader Caribbean. In addition to West Indian farmers in Jamaica and other British colonies, a growing number of locals and foreign settlers on Central America's Caribbean coast, including Minor Keith, turned to banana cultivation. Initially, dozens of merchant houses and shipping lines competed to buy and market these bananas, but large firms soon appeared. In 1885, Boston entrepreneur Andrew W. Preston organized the Boston Fruit Company, which came to dominate the banana trade between the West Indies and the Northeastern United States. By the early 1890s, moreover, Keith's Tropical Trading and Transport Company handled most of Central America's rising banana exports.[17]

In this early era, the majority of Central American bananas entered through New Orleans. With steamship lines connecting it to ports throughout the Caribbean, the Crescent City played a role akin to Miami in later decades. Hispanic elites visited to shop and sample cultural venues while American adventurers used New Orleans as a launching pad for various schemes in the region. At times, the economic and political worlds of Louisiana and Central America seemed to blur. In the mid-1880s, for example, Louisiana state treasurer and former Confederate officer E. A. Burke hopped a ship to Honduras after embezzling nearly two million dollars from the state lottery fund; when Louisiana banned the lottery, he reestablished it in the Honduran port of Cortés.[18] A more famous connection was writer William Sydney Porter, better known as O. Henry, who fled from New Orleans to Honduras in 1896 to avoid prosecution. Living in Trujillo, where William Walker had been executed decades earlier, Porter gathered material for his collection of short stories *Cabbages and Kings* (1904), which introduced the term "banana republic." Set in the fictional nation of Anchuria, the stories lampooned the "comic opera" nations of Central America and the American ne'er-do-wells who sought their fortunes there. But Porter also hinted at the increasingly imperial bearing of American banana firms, describing his fictional "Vesuvius Fruit Company," based perhaps on United Fruit itself, as "the power that forever stood with a chiding smile and uplifted finger to keep Anchuria in the class of good children."[19]

This early banana commerce had an especially striking impact on Honduras's southern neighbor, Nicaragua. In the 1880s, as canal schemes swirled around Greytown, the port of Bluefields to the north enjoyed a banana boom. Like Greytown, Bluefields had long been governed by black Creoles closely tied to British merchants. By the early 1890s, however, U.S. investors, including Keith, had gained control of the port's trade and most of the nearby banana plantations, for which they imported hundreds of black laborers from Jamaica and Panama. This incipient American enclave came under threat in 1894, when President José Santos Zelaya moved to incorporate the entire Miskito Reserve into the Nicaraguan state. After Zelaya's representatives toppled Bluefields's Creole government and imposed a banana export tax, U.S. settlers joined with local blacks and Miskitos to reject Nicaraguan rule. To the American planters' surprise, however, the U.S. government supported Zelaya. From Washington's perspective, it seemed a prudent move: by bolstering Zelaya, it could secure Nicaraguan control over the Caribbean coast in anticipation of canal construction while still fostering U.S. banana interests. Soon after, the emboldened Zelaya expelled the British consul in Bluefields. When Great Britain responded by occupying the Pacific port of Corinto in retaliation, Washington again came to Zelaya's aid, pressing London to withdraw. As U.S. commercial interests in Central America grew, the U.S. government was becoming ever more determined to assert its hegemony in the region.[20]

The connection between private investment and U.S. government policy was even more evident in the Cuban sugar industry. By the 1880s, the combination of global competition and a long nationalist rebellion had brought many Cuban sugar planters to financial collapse. To help boost the island's recovery, Spain negotiated a reciprocity treaty with the United States in 1884. Reflecting the commercial rather than territorial focus of American expansion, U.S. Ambassador John W. Foster predicted the agreement would give the United States an "almost complete commercial monopoly," thereby "annexing Cuba in the most desirable way."[21] Although the Senate failed to ratify the treaty, it approved a similar one in 1891. By that time, U.S. capital had already begun to "annex" Cuba, gaining control of the sugar trade as well as much of the production on the island itself.

Among the most prominent of the new U.S. sugar planters was Edwin F. Atkins. The son of Boston sugar merchant Elisha Atkins, he took control of the foreclosed Soledad estate, near the southwestern port of Cienfuegos, in the early 1880s. Like the proud New Englanders who would later manage United Fruit, Atkins envisioned himself bringing Yankee progress to the backward tropics. But race and labor relations at Soledad often seemed to more closely resemble the U.S. South. In fact, by purchasing the estate,

Atkins temporarily became a slaveholder. After visiting his new plantation in 1882, he wrote his mother, "Imagine me the centre of a crowd of over two hundred negroes, each one of whom kneeled down on passing me, saying, 'Your blessing, Master.'"[22] As the plantation's slaves passed into freedom in 1885–1886, however, Atkins confronted problems of labor supply and discipline. As it did throughout the broader Caribbean, the French canal project in Panama drew workers away from rural Cuba, making labor recruitment more difficult at Soledad and other plantations. At the same time, Afro-Cuban workers proved increasingly determined to claim a greater measure of autonomy.[23]

For their part, Atkins and his plantation managers adopted several strategies of labor control. Initially, they looked primarily to the Spanish colonial state to repress Afro-Cuban threats to their authority or property. In response to the theft of cattle by black locals, for example, Atkins called in the civil guard who, he recalled, "went into the woods looking for negroes" and later reported that "they would give no more trouble, as [the guardsmen] had hanged them all on trees."[24] In the following years, Atkins hired veterans of the Spanish army to serve as private guards on the estate. But despite the resemblance of such practices to the U.S. South, the labor regime at Soledad and other U.S.-owned properties had more in common with Northern industrialism. In addition to their construction of a massive new mill to enhance the efficiency of sugar processing, Atkins and his managers utilized a system of labor segmentation to promote racial divisions and reinforce their own authority. Although slaves had previously worked in Cuban sugar mills, Soledad confined blacks largely to fieldwork while Spanish and Chinese immigrants filled other niches in the loading and milling of cane.[25] Atkins's modernized mill in turn reflected the vertically integrated control U.S. capital was gaining over the sugar industry. Just as the planters and small farmers around Soledad relied on Atkins for the processing and shipment of their cane, Cuba itself depended on the U.S. sugar market for its economic and political stability.[26]

That dependence became apparent in 1894, when the U.S. Congress raised tariffs on foreign sugar, sending Cuba's economy into a tailspin. Cuban nationalists seized upon the downturn to renew their struggle. Among them was the Afro-Cuban leader Antonio Maceo, who had spent the previous years working in Louisiana, Panama, and Costa Rica. Indeed, when he and fellow insurgent leader Agustín Cebreco embarked for Cuba in early 1895, they did so from the latter's farm near Puerto Limón, Costa Rica, not far from Minor Keith's operations.[27] Spanish officials seized upon the prominence of black leaders such as Maceo to discredit the insurgency. In a September 1895 interview with the *New York Herald,* for example, Spanish Ambassador Enrique Dupuy de Lôme asserted that "many negroes of Cuba, like those in the South, do not want to work" and warned that insurgent victory would replicate the horrors of the Haitian Revolution.[28] U.S. investors echoed these warnings. In January 1896, after insurgents had burned portions of Soledad's cane fields, Atkins informed a journalist that the culprits were "colored men," and in a letter to his wife two months later he reported that the rebels were predominantly black and that their numbers included "a few negroes supposed to have come from Haiti or Santo Domingo."[29]

Race and the Imperial Leap

Historians have offered many explanations for why Washington went to war in 1898, but few have emphasized the interwoven economic and racial threats posed by the Cuban rebels themselves. Without doubt, other factors were in play: the quest for markets, imperial ambition, masculine anxiety, and humanitarian sentiment all contributed to the U.S. decision for war.[30] But had Spain crushed the rebels quickly, there would have been little outcry in the United States. It was only as the conflict dragged on, and insurgents turned to burning sugar estates and recruiting black laborers, that U.S. officials' patience waned.[31] This is not to argue that white supremacy drove U.S. expansion. Although these years witnessed the nationwide acceptance of Southern Jim Crow, symbolized by the Supreme Court's 1896 *Plessy v. Ferguson* decision, domestic racism remained primarily an obstacle to overseas empire. Nevertheless, by the 1890s political and business elites throughout the nation generally agreed that dark-skinned peoples were incapable of maintaining public order and protecting private property, which were the hallmarks of responsible government. Informed by both global imperial rhetoric and the distorted memory of Reconstruction, this assumption helped shape the U.S. approach toward not only the Cuban revolution but also the Caribbean interventions that followed.

By the time William McKinley took office in March 1897, American attention was focused on Cuba. Although the new president sympathized with Spanish efforts to restore order, the destruction of American investments, along with the public outcry against Spanish abuses, proved impossible to ignore. After the sinking of the USS *Maine* in February 1898, the clamor for intervention became overwhelming. In his April 1898 war message to Congress, McKinley declared that "humanity," "civilization," and "endangered American interests" compelled the nation to war, but he made no mention of Cuban independence and sought no alliance with the insurgents. Despite the pro-Cuban sympathies of the American public and press, both of which tended to depict the rebels as white, U.S. officials had no intention of turning Cuba over to an interracial insurgency that had targeted America property. McKinley's policy options were reduced by the passage of Senator Henry M. Teller's amendment to the war bill, which disclaimed "any disposition or intention to exercise sovereignty, jurisdiction, or control" over Cuba. The amendment reflected a compromise among several interests. Sugar-producing states such as Teller's Colorado hoped to avoid competition from an annexed Cuba, and many Americans continued to oppose the incorporation of dark-skinned peoples. For their part, most expansionists viewed the amendment as a temporary measure that would enable them to assuage domestic opponents while pursuing a "large" imperial policy.[32]

The U.S. occupation of Spain's former colonies brought these tensions into stark relief. Many Americans welcomed their overseas conquests as proof the United States had joined the imperial world. Campaigning in September 1898, future Senator Albert J. Beveridge proclaimed, "Hawaii is ours, Porto Rico is to be ours; at the prayer of her people Cuba finally will be ours," while "the flag of a liberal government is to float over the Philippines." If any man doubted the commercial benefits of colonialism, he declared, "ask him why England does not abandon South Africa, Egypt, India." Yet skeptics of empire also made their voices heard. As he had in the 1870s, Senator Carl Schurz railed against the incorporation of "Spanish-Americans, with all the mixture of Indian and negro blood," as well as "Malays and other unspeakable Asiatics."[33] Meanwhile, the small but vocal Anti-Imperialist League warned that colonial rule was contrary to both the U.S. Constitution and the nation's republican values.

Imperialists dismissed such arguments. The United States had long governed dependent peoples, they reasoned, and territorial conquest hardly implied full citizenship for nonwhites. After all, Beveridge observed, representative government applied only to those capable of self-rule: "We govern the Indians without their consent, we govern our territories without their consent, we govern our children without their consent."[34] The Supreme Court agreed. In its landmark Insular Cases of 1900–1901, it resolved these Constitutional tensions by inventing the concept of "unincorporated territory." This ensured that new possessions such as Puerto Rico and the Philippines, though subject to U.S. sovereignty, would have no path to statehood. In doing so, the Court implicitly denied the nation's new subjects the right of self-determination.[35]

By this time, the bloody implications of such logic were already becoming apparent in the Philippines. Fighting between U.S. troops and Filipino nationalists broke out in February 1899, and it quickly assumed the characteristics of a race war. During the ensuing three-year "pacification," approximately 220,000 Filipinos died, the majority of them noncombatants.[36] For many African Americans, the domestic roots of the bloodshed were clear. "All this never would have occurred if the army of occupation would have treated them as people," observed one black soldier stationed in Manila; but whites had tried to "apply home treatment for colored peoples," robbing, ravishing, and cursing them as "damned niggers."[37] Indeed, many ascribed the conflict to the exportation of Jim Crow. A black army sergeant stationed in Cuba warned that "American rule in the Philippines would be only a repetition of White rule in the south and American rule on this island today. The sole aim and cry would be to 'Keep the nigger down!'"[38]

The violence troubled imperial enthusiasts as well. In 1899, colonial scholar Poultney Bigelow, son of John Bigelow, expressed concern that, up to this point in their history, Americans had proved capable only of "exterminating the inferior race" and "administering territory for the white man only." Two years later, at the height of the bloodshed in the Philippines, he reminded Americans that they had "a Colonial Empire to administer" and suggested that Congress establish a "Colonial West Point" to train officials for responsible government of subject peoples, "whether they be Spanish or Tagalog; Chinese or Malay; . . . East or West Indian." If matters remained unchanged, he warned, racial violence would undermine the U.S. empire's civilizing potential.[39] Many officials shared these concerns. In 1901, as gruesome reports from the Philippines emerged, Washington moved to rein in the military's race war. By the following year, civilian officials such as Governor-General William Howard Taft had adopted a subtler approach to colonial rule aimed at working with Hispanicized elites.[40]

The Occupation of Cuba

Similar factors shaped the U.S. occupation of Cuba. Even before the war with Spain had ended, the United States was moving to assert its authority over the Cuban rebels. On the ground, this entailed treating Afro-Cuban insurgents much like black U.S. troops. One veteran rebel later recalled that American soldiers "used to shout 'Nigger, nigger,' and burst out laughing."[41] From a policy perspective, it meant denying insurgents the right to rule Cuba. As Major General William R. Shafter put it, "we have taken Spain's war upon ourselves."[42] Still, U.S. officials worried that any move to overturn the Teller Amendment would spur Cuban resistance, a fear that only grew after the fighting broke out in the Philippines. As Theodore Roosevelt warned Secretary of State John Hay in July 1899, "a series of disasters at the very beginning of our colonial policy would shake this administration" and possibly lead to the "abandonment of the course upon which we have embarked—the only course I think fit for a really great nation."[43] As a result, U.S. officials walked a thin line in Cuba, attempting to avoid conflict with nationalist rebels while pushing for Americanization and possible annexation.

Initially, the U.S. occupation focused on public health. During the war, far more American troops had fallen to yellow fever, malaria, and typhoid than to enemy bullets; if the United States hoped to control Cuba, it had to keep its soldiers alive. This struggle against tropical pathogens provided one justification for U.S. rule, as Americans increasingly described their efforts in terms of "uplifting" the population. Some sanitation policies indeed improved Cuban health conditions. In Havana, for example, army disease specialists William Gorgas and Walter Reed eradicated yellow fever. Yet U.S. officials focused almost exclusively on areas where Americans, Spaniards, and elite Cubans resided. Conversely, they viewed Afro-Cubans primarily as obstacles to, rather than beneficiaries of, their healthy policies. One U.S. sanitary commissioner in the eastern city of Santiago, for example, complained that most of the population was "extremely ignorant, careless, superstitious and filthy."[44]

U.S. policy and rhetoric mapped closely onto the racial and regional divisions already present within Cuba. Since the colonial era, residents of western Cuba had viewed the eastern Oriente province much as elite Costa Ricans and Guatemalans did their Caribbean coasts. Impoverished, predominately black, and geographically close to Haiti and Jamaica, Oriente symbolized the Afro-Caribbean threat to Hispanic civilization. During the struggle with Spain, Cuban rebels had tried to end these divisions by promoting raceless nationalism, but the U.S. intervention scotched this possibility.[45] Like Cuban conservatives and U.S. investors, moreover, Washington placed most of the blame for Cuba's economic collapse on the insurgents' decision to disrupt the sugar industry and destroy private property. As a result, U.S. officials pushed to muster out the rebels by paying them to turn over their guns. Although Cubans of all backgrounds had participated in the insurgency, the thrust of the policy was clearly to get Afro-Cubans out of politics and back into the cane fields.[46]

This effort to demobilize the rebels was closely tied to the goal of protecting private property. U.S. expansionists had long coveted Cuba, and many Americans now viewed annexation as the only means of safeguarding U.S. investments. After interviewing Atkins in June 1899, for example, the *Boston Transcript* warned that a U.S. withdrawal would allow "unscrupulous politicians and ignorant black Cubans" to take control, "leaving no voice in the Government to the large holders of property who are Spaniards and Americans, and who constitute the most progressive element of the population."[47] General Leonard Wood, governor of the Santiago province, agreed, declaring that "all the foreigners, including the Spaniards, and the property holding Cubans, favor annexation to the United States" because independence would lead to "the establishment of another Haitian Republic."[48] The problem was that most Cubans opposed annexation, and the fiercest resistance came from black veteran insurgents.

Upon his appointment as governor-general in late 1899, Wood tried to resolve this dilemma. Among his top priorities were ending banditry and preventing labor unrest, both of which carried racial implications. In the new rural guard, he encouraged summary justice against bandits, which often resembled lynch law. Not coincidentally, he urged that security forces be as light-skinned as possible: advertisements for enlistment often welcomed only white Cubans to apply. Such requirements seemed logical to U.S. officials, who knew Cuban guardsmen would have to police black workers as well as deter bandits.[49] Wood also sought political solutions. Although fear of resistance prevented him from disfranchising Afro-Cuban veterans, he used property and literacy requirements to strike at black voting rights, observing that such measures would restrict the suffrage of those elements "which have brought ruin to Hayti and San Domingo."[50] The resulting electoral suppression rivaled that of the Jim Crow South, with two-thirds of adult males excluded from voting. Secretary of War Elihu Root approved of these measures in both racial and sexual terms. By ensuring "a conservative and thoughtful control of Cuba by Cubans," he predicted, suffrage restriction would open the way for consensual annexation; after all, "It is better to have the favors of a lady with her consent than to ravish her."[51] But despite these hopes, a groundswell for annexation failed to materialize either in the United States or in Cuba. In addition, the Cuban Constitutional Convention of 1901, which included a number of insurgent veterans, insisted on universal male suffrage.

With their initial plans thwarted, U.S. officials opted for an imperial protectorate. The so-called Platt Amendment offered Cuba nominal independence in return for accepting Washington's right to intervene in order to maintain "a government adequate for the protection of life, property, and individual liberty." Root proudly observed that the amendment mirrored Great Britain's protectorate over Egypt, which had allowed "England to retire and still maintain her moral control."[52] Indeed, the arrangement hardly signified an abandonment of U.S. imperial objectives. "There is, of course, little or no independence left in Cuba under the Platt Amendment," observed Wood. "The more sensible Cubans realize this and feel that the only consistent thing to do now is to seek annexation."[53] Equally important, it allowed U.S. capital to continue its expansion into Cuba. Wood signaled this in March 1902, when, in one of his last acts as Cuba's governor, he opened public lands to U.S. investors. Among them was the recently formed United Fruit Company, which quickly acquired vast tracts in northeastern Cuba. There it would develop a modern sugar complex similar to its banana enclaves in Central America.[54]

Taking Panama

Even as Washington withdrew from Cuba, it set its sights on a Central American canal. With a two-ocean empire to administer, U.S. policy makers now viewed the waterway as a strategic necessity, but the route and means remained in question. Nicaragua had long been the favored choice, and President Zelaya seemed a likely partner for the enterprise. Despite his earlier tiff with American settlers in Bluefields, he welcomed canal construction and in October 1898 granted a concession to the Nicaraguan Canal Syndicate, controlled by W. R. Grace & Co. Although Costa Rica protested that the agreement infringed upon its sovereignty, the Nicaraguan route enjoyed broad support in the United States, especially among commercially minded Southerners. Its most outspoken champion was Alabama Senator John Tyler Morgan, who called on policy makers to support the effort while admitting that it might lead to U.S. imperial rule in Central America. In response to suggestions that this would violate the Monroe Doctrine, he maintained that the doctrine "doesn't inhibit us from acquiring foreign possessions.... There is nothing in it to retard our advancement."[55] Louisiana Senator Samuel McEnery was equally blunt:

If Costa Rica and Nicaragua object, then I would have the Government take forcible possession of enough territory for the purposes of the canal. If it should be necessary, I would advocate sending a sufficient army to the disputed territory, seize it, put 30,000 men to work and have the work supervised under United States engineer officers. The canal should be dug at once, peacefully if we can, but dug regardless of all obstacles.[56]

Such rhetoric reflected two interrelated shifts in the U.S. approach to Central America following the War of 1898. First, it revealed that many Americans now believed that construction of an interoceanic canal was too important to be left to private capital. Second, it hinted at the increasingly imperial and racialized bearing of the United States toward the region. Amid their decisions to deny self-determination to Cuba and Puerto Rico, many Americans seemed ready to apply similar logic to Central America. Not surprisingly, such language alarmed the region's leaders, including Zelaya himself. Although not opposed to subsidies from Washington, Zelaya wanted the canal built by private interests that could be regulated, at least to some degree, by the Nicaraguan state; outright control by the U.S. government, he feared, would lead to imperial domination. His dilemma deepened in 1902, when a new canal commission confirmed Washington's preference for the Nicaraguan route. While Zelaya welcomed the verdict, he resisted pressure to transfer the Grace concession to the U.S. government.[57]

In this context, U.S. officials turned their attention to Panama. Hoping to profit from American canal fever, the representative of the defunct French canal firm, Philippe Bunau-Varilla, offered to sell his company's concession to Washington. Colombian leaders in Bogotá were receptive to the idea. They had recently welcomed United Fruit's arrival on their nation's Caribbean coast, and they seemed willing to accept U.S. government control of a waterway through Panama. By 1903, however, Colombia badly needed funds to rebuild after a devastating civil war, and officials in Bogotá demanded adequate compensation for the canal route. With his profits in peril, Bunau-Varilla warned the Colombians not to get greedy. "[I]t would be extremely dangerous for your government to demand more than six million dollars," he cautioned," for the United States was "now a global power and could still choose Nicaragua or seize Panama if it desired."[58] At first, these seemed idle threats, but when the Colombian Congress rejected the canal treaty, President Theodore Roosevelt threw his support behind a separatist rebellion in Panama. In November 1903, even before the Panamanian conspirators had proclaimed independence, Roosevelt dispatched warships to the isthmus, where they blocked Colombian attempts to put down the revolt. Meanwhile, Bunau-Varilla and Secretary of State Hay drafted a treaty akin to the Platt Amendment that granted Washington control over the Canal Zone and the right to intervene in Panama. Dependent on the U.S. government for survival, Panamanian leaders had little choice but to accept.[59]

Roosevelt justified this land grab in terms familiar throughout the imperial world. In addition to denouncing the Colombians as "dagoes" and "jack-rabbits," he claimed that, "if ever a government could be said to have received a mandate from civilization, the United States holds that position with regard to the interoceanic canal." Privately, he was more candid, admitting that the Panamanian revolution was "an ordinary filibustering expedition."[60] It was an apt metaphor, for Washington had seized Panama by means William Walker might have applauded. Such parallels were not lost on Central American leaders. Although Panama was not considered part of Central America, its early encounters with U.S. expansion had much in common with those of neighboring nations, and the U.S. protectorate over the new republic, along with Washington's broader imperial surge, was a troubling omen for the countries of Central America.[61]

Whiteness and Progress in Costa Rica

In this context, it is hardly surprising that Costa Rican elites pushed whiteness to the center of their national identity. Like their counterparts throughout the hemisphere, they accepted the linkage between progress and racial purity. Moreover, it was clear that in a world ruled by empires, the status of legitimate nation-states hinged to a great extend upon whiteness. Determined to assert their place among the civilized and sovereign, Costa Rican leaders sought to distinguish their nation from its neighbors. In addition to celebrating its thriving coffee sector, they promoted a narrative of racial exceptionalism. Costa Rica was distinct from the rest of Central America, they claimed: its Spanish settlers had neither enslaved nor interbred with Indians, and the nation therefore represented a progressive white outpost in a mixed and degraded region. At times, this rhetoric resembled that of the American West. By the late 1880s and 1890s, the white yeoman farmer on his coffee homestead had become the symbol of national identity. As Costa Rican diplomat Manuel Aragón asserted in late 1892, Costa Ricans "are all hardworking, enterprising and full of noble ambition to acquire a piece of land and keep it cultivated in the most productive scale." What made this possible, he explained, was the "absence of the indolent Indians, common in many other countries," which ensured the "homogeneity of our race."[62]

These exceptionalist claims seemed to convince most American visitors. In response to a 4th of July toast from Costa Rican President Bernardo Soto in 1887, for example, U.S. Minister John R. Wingfield praised Costa Rica as a land "so like our own, where there is a resolute, industrious people, every man owning and loving his own land and homestead."[63] Three years later, American travel writer Frank Vincent reported that, in contrast to the "pure Indians," "negroes," and "curiously mixed races" found elsewhere in Central America, the "chalky white . . . hill-dwellers of Costa-Rica" possessed "the purest native blood."[64] By the time future U.S. diplomat Dana G. Munro published his influential *Five Republics of Central America* in 1918, the racial basis of Costa Rican exceptionalism was unquestioned. Noting that the inhabitants of the Central Valley were "distinctly Spanish in race and civilization," Munro explained:

> The political development of this compact community of white peasants has necessarily been very different from that of the neighboring countries, where a small upper class of Spanish descent had ruled and exploited many times its number of ignorant Indians and half-breeds. In Costa Rica the fact that nearly all of the inhabitants were of the same stock and had inherited the same civilization has always made the country more democratic, and has forced the class which controlled the government to consider to some extent the wishes and interests of the masses.[65]

Munro's emphasis on the Central Valley pointed to a critical aspect of Costa Rican national identity. Most observers agreed that the residents of the coffee-rich Central Valley were lighter-skinned than most Central Americans. But like its neighbors, Costa Rica contained striking demographic diversity within its borders. In addition to the predominantly *mestizo* Guanacaste province and the increasingly West Indian Caribbean coast, the nation possessed a number of indigenous communities, particularly near the Panamanian border. By the 1880s and 1890s, however, Costa Rican elites were projecting the carefully cultivated image of the "white" Central Valley onto the nation as a whole, identifying the coffee heartland as the "real" Costa Rica. In the process, they sought to exclude dark-skinned regions from Costa Rican identity and erase nonwhites from their national history. This included, for example, concerted efforts to whiten the memory of the Costa Rican troops who had fought William Walker, many of whom were *mestizo* residents of Guanacaste and the Pacific coast.[66] It also influenced various schemes to develop the Caribbean coast. When two promoters—one American and one Costa Rican—proposed an agrarian colony near the port of Cahuita in June 1895, for example, they promised to settle "15 families of the white race."[67]

This racialization of Costa Rican nationhood also emerged in elite efforts to attract immigrants. In his 1890 guidebook, Costa Rica's minister to the United States, Joaquín Bernardo Calvo, depicted his country's racial landscape in terms familiar to white Americans. "In Costa Rica," he explained, "while a primitive people still exists, its numbers are few, and it is completely separate from the civilized race," which was "white, homogeneous, healthy, and robust." Although he acknowledged the presence of blacks on the Caribbean coast, he stressed the region's similarity to the U.S. South. Upon arrival at Puerto Limón, he explained, the visitor to Costa Rica could have his bags carried by the "darkey boys" who "are always to be found lounging about the pier."[68] Such language sought to assure Americans that emigration to Costa Rica would require few adjustments in racial practices.

Costa Rican diplomat Ricardo Villafranca stressed similar themes in his pamphlet *Costa Rica: The Gem of the American Republics,* written for the 1895 Cotton States and International Exposition in Atlanta. In his quest for American immigrants, Villafranca attempted to tap into U.S. economic anxieties, particularly toward the closing frontier. Pointing to the settlers "now struggling [in] many of the western American states and territories," he emphasized that these same Americans would find rich opportunities in Costa Rica, where land was abundant and fertile and the few remaining Indians were "quiet and peaceable, looking upon the encroaching civilization with an air of resignation, and honoring white men with almost a spirit of worship." Although this might sound like Western boosterism, Villafranca assured his readers that it was not a "land-booming scheme"; rather, Costa Rica was a promising new frontier waiting for Americans to transform it into "a thrifty garden spot." To illustrate his sincerity, he quoted one of his own letters describing foreign immigration as that "most potent instrument of progress" and calling on his government to "gather in those who are honest and industrious, that they may unite to form one people with our own."[69]

Of course, it was white immigrants only that elites such as Villafranca wanted to "unite with our own," for they assumed that only whites could contribute to Costa Rica's progress and development. Unlike their counterparts in Guatemala, however, Costa Rican leaders viewed immigration as a means of preserving rather than transforming their nation's racial identity. Indeed, it was no coincidence that their assertions of whiteness and calls for white immigration increased as the number of West Indians on the Caribbean coast grew. Ironically, on the back cover of Villafranca's pamphlet appeared an advertisement for the main employer of those black immigrants: it read, "Minor C. Keith ... Land Dealer and Producer and Exporter of Bananas."[70]

Bananas, Labor, and the Rise of United Fruit

The fact that Keith characterized himself as a banana exporter reflected a critical development on the Caribbean coast. Beginning in the mid-1870s, Keith had become intrigued with the commercial potential of the fruit trade. His West Indians workers had cultivated plantains and other food crops in garden plots since their arrival in Costa Rica. During the funding delays of the late 1870s and early 1880s, however, Keith encouraged them to grow commercial varieties of bananas. This led to the earliest form of the contract farming system that came to define much of United Fruit's operations in Costa Rica. In return for leasing land to West Indians, most of whom were former or current rail construction laborers, Keith required that they cultivate bananas and sell only to him.[71] It was an appealing option for these immigrants, most of whom had come to Central America in the hopes of attaining economic autonomy. Now Keith was promising them access to land and markets in return for growing a crop with which many were familiar from their home islands. With economic opportunities becoming increasingly scarce in the British Caribbean, many West Indians responded enthusiastically. In June 1887, for example, Jamaican Abraham Noah declared that Keith offered "great facilities" for people to settle near Puerto Limón and claimed that "any man coming with determination to work can in time realize a competency."[72] The arrangement also served Keith well: in addition to keeping West Indian workers in Limón province, it enabled him to become a major player in the banana trade while providing the unfinished Atlantic Railroad with much-needed cargo.

The latter proved particularly important because, by the late 1880s, it was his railroad. In 1884, with little hope of resuming national financing of the rail construction, San José had agreed to a momentous contract with Keith. In return for renegotiating Costa Rica's British-held debt and completing the Atlantic Railroad, Keith would receive a 99-year lease on the railway and 800,000 acres of land in Limón province—roughly 7 percent of the national territory. These concessions laid the foundation for Keith's, and later United Fruit's, power in Costa Rica.[73] Despite this potential windfall, however, Keith faced the difficult task of obtaining new loans in London's competitive credit market. For more than two years, he wrangled with Costa Rica's British lenders while searching for new funding for himself. If only he could find the capital, he knew he could transform the Caribbean coast virtually into his own colonial domain. It was appropriate, then, that in these same years, Belgium's King Leopold II himself was seeking British capital for his Congo railroad. Although the two men would secure financing and succeed in parlaying their railroads into private empires, the construction of those railways took so many lives that local tradition in both the Congo and Costa Rica told of a black body buried beneath each rail tie. Such colonial comparisons were not lost on Keith's contemporaries, who would soon dub him the "Cecil Rhodes of Central America." But all that lay in the future. In October 1886, Keith reached an accord with Costa Rica's creditors, who agreed to restructure the nation's debt and extend him funding to complete his railroad.[74]

No sooner had Keith returned to Costa Rica than he faced another crisis. The Compagnie Universelle's operations in Panama had drained the British Caribbean labor pool, and he could not hope to match the French firm's high wages. For their part, many West Indian banana farmers in Limón proved reluctant to return to rail construction. In desperation, Keith turned to southern Europe, importing over 1,500 Italian workers in 1887. Although representing a tiny fraction of the European immigration then flowing to the Western Hemisphere, the newcomers made a memorable impression on Costa Rica. Aware of the racial anxieties of the Costa Rican elite, Keith assured the Costa Rican Congress that the immigrants were "good humble thrifty workers . . . of a superior race which will do the country good as they mix in with the rest of the natives."[75] But the Italians proceeded to "mix in" more than Keith expected. In October 1888 they went on strike, complaining of tropical disease, poor working conditions, and delayed pay. About six hundred made their way to San José and asked to be returned home. Keith demanded that Costa Rican authorities force the men back to work, but in stark contrast to its treatment of West Indians, the government invited the strikers to settle in Costa Rica. Some seven hundred accepted; the rest sailed for Italy.[76]

This state response was consistent with Costa Rica's racialized approach to immigration. Although the nation's leaders had initially accepted the necessity of using Asian and black laborers to complete the railroad, by the late 1880s many worried that Keith's reliance on West Indians threatened Costa Rica's status as a white nation. As yet, those anxieties remained confined to the elite, for few Costa Rican laborers coveted West Indians' jobs. But the combination of nonwhite immigration and U.S. racial practices was drawing out more virulent forms of Costa Rican racism. Indeed, although some scholars have suggested that widespread anti-black sentiment emerged only in the 1930s, evidence indicates it appeared much earlier.[77] In December 1888, for example, U.S. Consul W. R. Bross reported that Costa Rican officials' harassment of black immigrants had grown so rampant that "throughout the British possessions in the West Indies, the Governments have issued proclamations warning people not to come here," making it "difficult to obtain laborers for our [railroad] work."[78]

In the same letter, Bross revealed the potential for racialized clashes between Americans and Hispanics as Costa Rican resentment of U.S. influence grew. In a recent incident, he reported, the newly appointed governor of Limón province, named Escobar, had quarreled with a white American aboard a train. According to Bross, Escobar had "engaged an American named James in conversation, in which he roundly abused Americans." When James asked him if he liked Americans, Escobar retorted, "No! Better Niggers!" James responded that, compared to Costa Ricans, blacks were a "superior race," prompting Escobar to draw his pistol and threaten to kill the American.[79] The incident illustrated Costa Rican sensitivity to racial slights from white foreigners. In a nation pushing to claim its membership in the white world amid rising nonwhite immigration, comments that placed Hispanics on a level equal to or lower than blacks hit a very raw nerve.

For his part, Keith was little concerned with Costa Rican feelings or racial purity. His main priority was building the Atlantic Railroad, and he viewed West Indians as the laborers best suited to the job. Years of experience had convinced him, moreover, that he knew how to handle such workers. Over the following decades, he never tired of telling the story of 1,500 faithful Jamaicans who had worked for him without pay for nine months in the late 1870s. With the collapse of the French canal effort in

1888, moreover, such laborers were again in ample supply, and in December 1890 Keith's black workforce finished the Atlantic Railroad. The human costs were high: in nearly two decades of construction, some 4,000 laborers had perished, most of them Jamaican. In addition, dozens of white managers had died, including three of Keith's brothers. Nevertheless, Minor had fulfilled his promise to complete the railroad, and now he stood poised to reap the reward.[80]

He had come a long way from his turtle-trading days of the early 1870s. The 1884 contract made Keith Costa Rica's largest landholder and de facto owner of its principal railway. Government concessions also gave him authority over Puerto Limón's sanitation infrastructure, as well as control over much of its steamship traffic. In addition, he enjoyed a virtual monopoly on Costa Rica's banana trade. By the early 1890s, his Tropical Trading and Transport Company annually exported a million stems of bananas from Puerto Limón, many of which were grown on Keith's own plantations. He was also developing plantations in Nicaragua, Panama, and Colombia.[81] This access to reliable sources of bananas made him a dominant force in the New Orleans banana market and a formidable rival of the Boston Fruit Company. Although the New England firm dwarfed the Tropical Trading and Transport Company, Keith's operations in Costa Rica posed a unique challenge to his larger competitor. Boston Fruit was attempting to grow its own bananas in Cuba and the Dominican Republic, but it still depended on Jamaican farmers for most of its fruit. Rising market demands and unpredictable weather in the West Indies placed Boston Fruit in an increasingly perilous position. As company president Andrew Preston admitted as early as 1891, "It is very plain to my mind that the successful company of the future is the one that controls the growing of its own fruit."[82]

Financial crises and a critical decision by the Costa Rican government soon spurred these competitors to join forces. In 1898, tropical hurricanes decimated Boston Fruit's main banana suppliers in Jamaica. Soon after, Keith's New Orleans creditors unexpectedly declared bankruptcy, calling in his debts of nearly $1,500,000. Facing ruin, Keith turned to Costa Rican President Rafael Yglesias Castro who granted the harried entrepreneur an unconstitutional loan. This decision stemmed from perceived national interests as well as good will: Castro had no desire to see his country's most dynamic economic force collapse. Yet by allowing Keith to retain his assets, Castro's decision had a profound effect on the future of Costa Rica and the rest of Central America: just months later, in March 1899, Keith joined with Boston Fruit to found the United Fruit Company. Preston became president of the new corporation and Keith vice president. Although few Americans took notice of the new company's formation, it reflected the same impulse toward vertical integration that drove the larger industrial mergers in these years. Combining Boston Fruit's Northeastern market dominance with Keith's control of production and transportation, United Fruit immediately wielded vast power in Central America and especially Costa Rica. By 1904, Keith had transferred some of his Costa Rican lands directly to the new firm and folded the Atlantic Railroad into a thinly veiled United Fruit subsidiary—the Northern Railway Company. In rescuing Keith, the Costa Rican state had helped create the corporate giant that would come to control much of its national life.[83]

Making a Ladino *Nation in Guatemala*

In these same years, similar patterns took shape in Guatemala. As in Costa Rica, the elite depiction of the nation grew more racialized in the late 1880s and 1890s. In Guatemala, however, racial rhetoric remained directly tied to the nation's labor system. Following Justo Rufino Barrios's death in 1885, Guatemalan Liberals continued to refine their labor control strategies. In addition to the *mandamiento* and vagrancy laws, they supported a developing system of debt peonage. Using manipulative offerings of alcohol and pay advances, *ladino* labor recruiters lured highland Maya into debt, while planters used devious bookkeeping to trap them in an intergenerational cycle of servitude that provided cheap workers for the coffee harvest.[84] For its part, the Guatemalan state required that all potential workers carry account books proving their indebtedness to a coffee planter, and local authorities ensured that they worked off their debts rather than fleeing. Partly for this reason, the nation's expanding police and military forces remained entirely *ladino.* During crises, the state impressed Maya into military service, but they were usually mustered out quickly. Following an 1890 conflict with El Salvador, for example, the government immediately demobilized all indigenous men, who, it claimed, "lack the capacity to understand what it is to be a soldier and the very important mission [they have] to fulfill in the defense of the country and in the maintenance of internal order."[85] Because the army was, above all, an arm of labor control, the permanent inclusion of Maya was unthinkable.

This labor regime went hand in hand with racial abuses. In addition to the arbitrary power of planters and local authorities, indigenous Guatemalans regularly faced racial discrimination akin to that in the Jim Crow South. While Guatemalan elites depicted the Maya as natural servants unfit for citizenship, working-class *ladinos* sought to maintain their privileged social status by emphasizing their differences from the Maya. In the 1890s and early 1900s, for example, American missionaries found themselves forced to offer segregated services for *ladinos* and indigenous converts, not simply for linguistic reasons but because the *ladinos* refused to associate with *"indios."*[86] In 1915, Dana Munro observed similar attitudes aboard a steam launch on Lake Atitlán in the western highlands. Initially, Munro was concerned with the safety of the overloaded craft, which appeared "top-heavy." But just prior to departure, he recalled, the captain "ordered all of the Indians into the hold where the horses and mules already were, and closed the hatch. The ladino passengers stayed on deck."[87]

Equally revealing was the experience of Byron and Bella Tunnell, a white American couple from California. In early 1894, the Tunnells had fled economic turmoil in the United States in search of opportunity in Guatemala. Although Byron hoped eventually to "buy a small piece of new land and start a finca of our own," he took a job on an estate in Colomba, in the western heartland of Guatemala's coffee boom. Working as an overseer, he soon learned the racial structure of work on a coffee plantation. "Indians do all the field and servile labor," he explained in a July 1894 letter, "and we few Americans fill special niches or oversee the plantation gangs on these 700 acres or so."[88] Bella, too, emphasized the racial hierarchy of plantation life. In response to her mother-in-law's query of whether "the colored people eat [with us]," Bella reassured her that "they all live on the finca in houses built by the owner."[89] Even as Byron and Bella adapted to Guatemalan racial norms, however, they applied their own, particularly to blacks. In March 1895, Bella wrote that "Sherman Taylor a colored man they have here . . . got [to] telling me about his wife and child in the States, and as he is a good fellow I felt that I must listen to him." After witnessing Taylor arguing with the farm's owner two weeks later, however, she reported that "the boss had a fuss with the big niger [*sic*] Sherman this morning and [paid] him off."[90] In Bella's eyes, Taylor's dispute with his employer had transformed him from "a good fellow" into "the big niger."

Yet the largest U.S. influence on Guatemala came not from the small number of immigrants such as the Tunnells, but from the growing power of American capital. By the early 1890s, Collis Huntington was tightening his hold on the country. Along with the rail line between Puerto San José and the capital, his Guatemala Central Railroad Company had acquired the newly built railway to the nation's other Pacific port of Champerico.[91] In addition, Huntington controlled the Pacific Mail Steamship Company, which provided the only service to Guatemala's Pacific coast. This interlocking monopoly of land and sea transportation enabled him to skim off much of the nation's export revenue. According to one U.S. diplomat, Huntington's rail line was "the most remunerative piece of railroad in the world, of its length."[92] This corporate domination made Guatemalan leaders even more eager to complete the Northern Railway, which they increasingly viewed as the key to national autonomy.

The Northern Railway and Racial Hierarchy

In the mid-1890s, the Guatemalan government renewed its push for the Northern Railway. The new U.S. contractors found labor far more available than their predecessors a decade before. In the wake of the French canal company's collapse and the Costa Rican railroad's completion, British West Indians found their way to Guatemala's Caribbean coast. Even more important to the construction effort were U.S. blacks, who came in much larger numbers than in the 1880s. By the time of the railroad's completion in 1908, perhaps as many as 5,000 had come to Izabal.[93] Hailing mostly from the Gulf Coast, these African American migrants viewed rail work in Guatemala as a potential escape from shrinking opportunities and racial violence at home.

Unfortunately, the life awaiting them often proved all too familiar. Labor recruiters lied to immigrants about wages and living conditions, and managers confined blacks to menial positions and maintained segregation in labor camps. Whites also demanded racial deference, requiring blacks to address them as "mister," and enforced the color line with daily abuse and deadly violence. In April 1896, for example, a mob of white Americans dragged an African American man named Harper from a prison and lynched him.[94] White railroad contractors also called on the Guatemalan state to hunt down runaway workers and break strikes, encouraging local authorities to engage in anti-black violence.[95] Such practices helped establish the pattern of black-*ladino* relations in the Caribbean lowlands, but official abuses also grew out of Guatemala's political culture. The growing numbers of English-speaking blacks in Izabal unnerved many elites, who already distrusted the region's Garífuna community. These anxieties were rooted in not only the racial hierarchy inherited from the colonial era, but also elite conceptions of national identity. Having asserted *ladino* dominance over the Mayan majority, Guatemalan officials were hardly eager to increase their dark-skinned population, particularly because they assumed only white immigrants could contribute to Guatemala's progress. Like their Costa Rican counterparts, Guatemalan officials accepted the necessity of black foreign workers, and in an 1897 agreement the government placed no limits on the contractors' ability to import laborers.[96] But the Guatemalan elite viewed black immigrants as sojourners: they might help build the railroad, but they could never become part of the nation.

Also like their Costa Rican counterparts, Guatemalan leaders found it difficult to finance their Caribbean railroad. Although they had hoped to retain national ownership of the line, the collapse of international coffee prices in 1897 brought financial as well as political turmoil. The following year, Manuel Estrada Cabrera seized power. A liberal dictator in the mold of Justo Rufino Barrios, Estrada Cabrera was determined to complete the Northern Railway not only to promote exports but also to press Guatemalan claims to neighboring Belize. With the nation's economy in crisis, however, his regime found it increasingly difficult to fund the rail contractors, who were in turn unable to pay their laborers. After several months of delayed wages, the rail workers, most of them African American, declared a strike in September 1898. In response, the frustrated Estrada Cabrera took control of the construction away from the contractors.[97] Over the following years, rail laborers found themselves treated as employees of the Guatemalan government. Those who refused to work risked the same official repression that was common in the coffee sector. Indeed, by 1903, local judges were applying vagrancy laws designed for the highland Maya to discipline black immigrant railroad workers.

By the early 1900s, Estrada Cabrera had concluded that only foreign capital could complete the Northern Railway and develop the Caribbean coast. In 1901, he signed the nation's first contract with United Fruit, which provided for the carrying of mail from Puerto Barrios and allowed the company to purchase bananas from local growers.[98] Meanwhile, he was also negotiating with United Fruit Vice President Minor Keith to finish the Northern Railway. To interest the famed builder of Costa Rica's railroad, however, Estrada Cabrera realized he needed to offer an attractive concession. In 1904, the Guatemalan government approved an agreement modeled on Keith's 1884 contract with Costa Rica. In return for completing the railroad, Keith would receive an exclusive 99-year lease on the line, 165,000 acres of land concessions near its route through the Motagua

River valley, and ownership of a large portion of Puerto Barrios, including its wharf. In addition, the contract exempted all agricultural products, with the exception of coffee, from export taxes. These terms laid the foundation for a new banana enclave.[99]

Once again, Keith had parlayed the ambitions and financial vulnerability of a Central American nation into land concessions and control of its principal rail line. At the time, Guatemalan elites viewed the arrangement, quite logically, as the only means of finishing the railway. In retrospect, however, the 1904 contract represented a profound setback for their long-term goals: the railroad they had regarded as the guarantor of national autonomy would now provide an avenue for foreign domination. In the following years, Keith would complete the railroad and open his land concessions to United Fruit. The company and its closely affiliated railway would in turn construct a new order of things on the Caribbean coast.

That new order was already becoming evident in the neighboring British colony coveted by Estrada Cabrera. Soon after United Fruit was founded, it had acquired a monopoly over Belize's banana trade, and residents of the colony soon grew resentful of the firm. In addition to hiking freight rates, United Fruit offered low prices for bananas and often rejected fruit for little reason. When local farmers sought out other buyers, moreover, the company punished them by refusing future purchases.[100] Equally troubling was the racial segregation enforced on United Fruit's steamships. According to one March 1902 petition by three prominent Afro-Belizeans, "black passengers, though paying first class fares, were prevented from sitting at table with the other passengers and were otherwise treated as a class apart." Pointing out that "black taxpayers" contributed to the subsidy paid to United Fruit, the petitioners called on colonial officials to press the company to change its policies. Although the British governor dismissed such concerns, the petition hinted at the coming West Indian resistance to the forms of domination the firm intended to impose.[101]

United Fruit's efforts in Central America were part of the larger story of U.S. empire building between 1885 and 1904. Although many Americans called for the United States to join Europe's imperial scramble, Washington remained focused on domestic affairs for most of this period. As a result, business interests remained the driving force behind U.S. expansion in Central American and the rest of the Hispanic Caribbean. In addition to railroads and mines, this included large investments in tropical commodities such as bananas and sugar. In the process, private enterprise influenced local racial dynamics and immigration patterns and paved the way for the U.S. government's assertions of imperial power, particularly in Cuba and Panama. Those racially charged interventions in turn placed U.S. business activities in an ominous light for the Central America elite, who worried that corporate influence and nonwhite immigration might lead to political subordination.

This was certainly the case in Costa Rica and Guatemala. During the 1880s and 1890s, the combination of railroad construction and banana commerce drew U.S. capital and black immigrants to the Caribbean coasts of both nations. In Costa Rica, the elite responded with assertions of national whiteness, which only grew louder following the War of 1898. At the same time, however, the Costa Rican government adopted policies that enhanced Minor Keith's power and enabled him to help found United Fruit. Guatemalan leaders followed a similar path. Although they hoped a Caribbean railway would secure their national autonomy, economic constraints forced them to turn to Keith, thereby opening the door to United Fruit. For its part, the new firm could not help but be shaped by the imperial context into which it was born. Like its corporate progenitors, United Fruit espoused racial assumptions that buttressed white rule both within the United States and throughout an increasingly colonial world. After 1904, moreover, it operated within the imperial sphere of a U.S. government that was engaged in similar efforts to remake the social and economic landscape of the Hispanic Caribbean.

Part II

RACE AND LABOR

Chapter 3

Corporate Colonialism, 1904–1912

In early 1912, twenty-six-year-old Hugh Wilson learned of his appointment as U.S. chargé d'affaires in Guatemala City. A Yale classmate of Secretary of State Philander C. Knox's son, Wilson welcomed the news and boarded a New Orleans steamer for Puerto Barrios, Guatemala's busy banana port. There he was met by the general manager of United Fruit's Guatemala Division, Dartmouth-educated Victor M. Cutter. With "a broad grin on a rugged clean-shaved face," Wilson recalled, Cutter was "picturesque . . . a huge figure in tropic white [that] O. Henry would have cherished." As the young diplomat followed Cutter down the gangway, he caught his first glimpse of United Fruit's workforce. In the "black moist night," a "line of negroes stripped to the waist and bare-footed, each bent under the load of a huge bunch [of bananas] strode up the wharf," where they "passed their burden into the hold through a chain gang of handlers." At the head of the line, "the blackest and biggest buck of all smoked a cigarette and whirled a machete," chopping off excess banana stems as they passed. From the pier, the two Americans strolled to the rail depot, where Wilson boarded the dawn train for Guatemala City. Only then did he grasp the scope of United Fruit's empire: the train "ran through jungle for a while," he noted, "then pushed out into the banana lands, a sea of them. They seemed to reach the horizon."[1]

Shortly after Wilson settled into his post, Philander Knox undertook a goodwill tour of Central America and the Caribbean. In Guatemala, the secretary and his retinue rode Collis Huntington's railway from the Pacific coast to the capital, where they were feted by dictator Manual Estrada Cabrera. Afterward, Knox delayed appointment of a new minister, leaving young Wilson in charge. "In those days of 'Dollar Diplomacy,' the voice of the United States was the voice of Jove," Wilson recalled. "My lightest word . . . was debated and discussed. Hidden meanings were searched out and a degree of cunning and omniscience attributed."[2]

Despite this responsibility, Wilson found time to visit the banana lands and became close friends with Cutter, who was only four years his senior. During Wilson's visits, Cutter schooled his friend in the racial culture of United Fruit's enclave, where company officials not only maintained racial segregation but also emphasized the performance of white superiority common to colonial settings. Indeed, assertions of white masculinity were integral to the enforcement of nonwhite deference. Cutter's "handling of negroes was remarkable," Wilson observed: "He excelled in everything they admired. He could fight the wildest of them, he could outshoot them, his endurance was unlimited and his occasional flash of ferocious temper kept them cowed." Such qualities were essential, he explained: "These negroes from Jamaica were cheerful and reasonably industrious, but full of liquor they became dangerous. Cutter would face them down in their worst moments."[3] Yet mention of those "worst moments" suggests that West Indian acceptance of U.S. imperial culture was hardly complete. In fact, in late 1909, less than three years before Wilson's arrival, black workers had briefly risen up against their white supervisors. In this light, Cutter's displays of skill and aggression seemed calculated to bolster a racial hierarchy that appeared perilously fragile.

A rail excursion with Cutter and three West Indian laborers illustrated this reality for Wilson. "Cutter and I sat on the front bench with our guns, and the negroes set the gasoline engine in movement," he recalled. "Suddenly a great black turkey–cock soared across the track. Simultaneously we raised our guns and fired. The turkey dropped on the track so close the negroes nearly threw us out of the car by the violence with which they jammed on the brake." When another turkey appeared, Wilson again took aim, but Cutter "savagely" whispered, "don't shoot," explaining in a hushed tone, "didn't you see those niggers' eyes bulge at the first shot? They never

Figure 1. Victor M. Cutter (left) and fellow United Fruit official G. M. Shaw, Guatemala, 1914. Courtesy of Dartmouth College Library

before saw anyone hit a bird on the wing when moving along a railroad. We would probably miss the second shot and spoil the whole thing." "I didn't fire another shot," Wilson noted, "and our prestige was saved."[4] Such constraints on action were familiar to whites throughout the colonial world, and they hinted at both the U.S. effort to impose a familiar racial order and West Indian resistance to that order.

The friendship between Wilson and Cutter is revealing on other levels as well. In addition to highlighting the elite, Northern, and often Ivy League background of many U.S. empire builders, it points to the close relationship between the U.S. government and private business as U.S. imperial culture took shape in Central America. Between 1904 and 1912, amid rising racial anxieties at home, Washington asserted its hegemony in the Hispanic Caribbean and undertook the profound reorganization of life and labor in the Panama Canal Zone. In these same years, United Fruit rapidly expanded its Central American operations, particularly in Costa Rica and Guatemala. Despite their distinct purposes, the efforts of the U.S. government and United Fruit had much in common. Both relied primarily upon West Indian labor in their enclaves, and both enforced strict racial hierarchy and segregation to manage their workforces. These similarities stemmed in part from the considerable exchange of ideas and personnel between the two, but the confluence ran much deeper than that. U.S. government and United Fruit officials alike saw themselves as part of a larger American effort to bring order and progress to Central America and the rest of the Hispanic Caribbean, and they shared key assumptions about race and labor, drawn from domestic practices and corporate precedents, that shaped the vision they sought to impose on the ground. Racial views among Americans varied, to be sure, and white Southerners often proved more confrontational than their Northern counterparts. More apparent than regional differences, however, was the general consensus among Americans on the need for white authority and nonwhite deference.

To the surprise and annoyance of U.S. employers, however, West Indians workers often refused to play the deferential roles assigned them. Their resistance was rooted to a great extent in the culture and history of struggle within the British Caribbean. Equally important, however, was the labor structure of the enclaves themselves. Because menial work in these early years was largely confined to blacks, labor militancy tended to form along racial lines. But local circumstances and degrees of imperial control circumscribed the forms of resistance. In the Canal Zone, although British West Indians provided the bulk of the labor, the Isthmian Canal Commission initially maintained a more diverse and segmented workforce than United Fruit. Along with authoritarian U.S. military rule, this system limited overt labor resistance. In contrast, on the Caribbean coasts of Costa Rica and Guatemala, United Fruit's workforce in its first decade of operations was almost entirely West Indian; as a result, racial and class resentments powerfully reinforced one another. This danger became evident in 1909–1910, when strikes led by Jamaican laborers shook the company's enclaves in both nations. Lacking the coercive force of the U.S. government, United Fruit turned to other means of control, including repression by its host states and the recruitment of Hispanic workers.

Race and Empire

The push to establish a familiar racial order in U.S. enclaves partly reflected domestic American anxieties. By the early 1900s, the influx of southern and eastern European immigrants had raised fears, particularly among the Anglo-American elite, that the nation's racial identity was being diluted. In addition to calls for immigration restriction, debate over the racial and ethnic parameters of U.S. citizenship contributed to a growing reluctance among Northern whites to criticize Southern race relations. Indeed, even many "progressives" argued that black disfranchisement and segregation were necessary to prevent race mixing and social conflict. Such thinking was evident at the highest levels of government. In the mid-1900s, for example, even as he was implementing key features of Jim Crow in the Panama Canal Zone, President Theodore Roosevelt backed away from support of black rights in the United States. Indeed, just prior to departing for his famous visit to Panama in late 1906, he summarily discharged an entire African American army regiment following its clash with white residents in Brownsville, Texas. Such policies reflected the widely held assumption among political and business leaders, in the North as well as the South, that social order required strict racial hierarchy and separation.[5]

The growing black presence in the North contributed to this white consensus. Although African Americans remained excluded from most industrial jobs in the early decades of the twentieth century, they performed menial tasks in many factories and shops and were often used to break strikes by white workers. This strategy of labor segmentation was hardly new to Northern workers, but in the context of rising black migration, it heightened racial anxieties. Not coincidentally, in these same years large numbers of whites attended speeches by visiting Southern ideologues, some of whom used images of Caribbean racial disorder to emphasize the dangers of black equality and race mixing. In January 1908, for example, South Carolina Senator Ben "Pitchfork" Tillman warned one Northern crowd that future visitors would soon find "a breed of mongrels here! Cuba! ...All over the North big buck negroes marrying white women and no law to prevent it!"[6] That many Northerners shared these fears became evident the following July, when whites in Abraham Lincoln's hometown of Springfield, Illinois, attacked the homes and businesses of local blacks, killing at least seven. The riot convinced many Northern leaders that the "Negro Problem" had become a national issue.[7]

Racially charged developments at home in turn reverberated throughout the U.S. empire. One striking example was Jack Johnson. Hailing from the Gulf of Mexico port of Galveston, Texas, Johnson defeated Canadian Tommy Burns in December 1908 to become the first black heavyweight boxing champion. African Americans throughout the nation cheered this victory over white masculinity and power, which came just five months after the Springfield Riot. For their part, white Americans came to see Johnson, who flouted dominant racial and sexual norms, as the embodiment of the "bad nigger."[8] But Johnson's influence reached beyond American shores and into U.S. enclaves in Central America. As John Williams recalled, in United Fruit's Guatemala Division, "Jack Johnson's picture was, in many of the negro huts, an object of far more adoration than that of the crucifix in the huts of the Spanish," and his example proved a "very disturbing feature in the relations of blacks and whites." Each victory in the ring "had its effect on the black race, making them very arrogant, and exhibiting signs of superiority."[9] Indeed, Johnson's image may have helped inspire the 1909 uprising.

It was against this backdrop of transnational racial tensions that the U.S. government asserted its hegemony in the Hispanic Caribbean. The seizure of Panama spurred Washington toward imperial supervision of the region, which U.S. officials considered essential to promoting American business interests as well as protecting the future canal. "The inevitable effect of our building the canal must be to require us to police the surrounding premises," explained Secretary of War Elihu Root. "In the nature of things, trade and control, and the obligation to keep order which goes with them, must come our way."[10] Roosevelt announced this shift in December 1904, with his corollary to the Monroe Doctrine. Although promising that responsible nations "need fear no interference from the United States," he warned that governments that failed to maintain order or pay their obligations would force the United States "to exercise an international police power."[11] Implicit in the policy was the assumption that the region's debts should be transferred to U.S. creditors, thereby precluding European intervention and giving Washington leverage over the nations near the Panama Canal.

This Dollar Diplomacy framed a decade of U.S. policy toward the Hispanic Caribbean. Although Roosevelt initiated it with interventions in the Dominican Republic and Cuba, his successor, William Howard Taft, sought to apply an expansive version of the policy to Central America. Prior to becoming president, Taft had extensive experience in colonial administration, including service as governor of the Philippines, secretary of war during the Panama Canal's early construction, and, briefly, provisional governor of Cuba during the reoccupation of that island in 1906—all experiences that deepened his commitment to his nation's imperial mission. His secretary of state, Philander Knox, held similar views, claiming at one point that U.S. supervision of the Hispanic Caribbean would "reflect credit upon the hegemony of our race and further advance the influence of Anglo-Saxon civilization."[12] As a longtime corporate lawyer, Knox viewed U.S. business as the primary agent of order and progress.

The full implications of this approach became apparent in Nicaragua. Following the U.S. decision to build the canal in Panama, President Zelaya had infuriated Washington by inviting foreign powers such as Japan to build a rival canal. The breaking point came in late 1909, when U.S. investors in Bluefields sponsored another rebellion. After Nicaraguan troops executed two American mercenaries assisting the rebels, Taft and Knox pushed Zelaya out of power. By May 1911, they had installed Adolfo Díaz, a former employee of a U.S. mining company. The new president immediately signed a protectorate treaty granting Washington control over Nicaraguan finances, rights to a naval base, and an exclusive option on the Nicaraguan canal—which U.S. officials had no intention of exercising.[13]

With its resemblance to the Platt Amendment and the Panama Canal treaty, the proposed protectorate heightened fears of U.S. imperialism throughout Central America. Seeking to dispel these anxieties, Knox embarked on his six-week goodwill tour in early 1912. But he encountered anti-American sentiment in much of the region. For many U.S. observers, this hostility only confirmed the assumptions behind Washington's policies. Journalist William Hale attributed Central American distrust to the region's chaotic racial mixtures. Declaring that the protectorate was the only way to govern the "sad-faced, dull-witted Indians" of Nicaragua, he asserted that, "for these people and for this country as much can be done as we did for Cuba."[14] That was, of course, precisely the comparison that alarmed many Central Americans.

The treaty also faced opposition at home. While most U.S. senators shared the administration's racial assumptions, many worried the protectorate would lead to the annexation of Nicaragua. According to State Department official and former U.S. minister to Costa Rica Lewis Einstein:

> A justifiable fear exists that with the problems of internal order confronting us and the difficulty of assimilating the millions of [imm]igrants at home, any further extension of our responsibilities in the direction of bringing new people, the great majority of whom are inferior in civilization, within our control ought strenuously to be resisted.

Despite this reluctance, Einstein argued, the combination of American investment and racial disorder in Central America required a firm hand from Washington. "[T]he heterogeneous nature of [the region's] population, apart from Costa Rica, and the existence in the other countries of a majority of Indian and Negro Indian blood" inevitably spawned instability, he explained, which in turn threatened U.S. enterprises, including not only the Panama Canal, but U.S.-owned railroads, mines, and "banana plantations . . . close to the coast."[15] The White House apparently agreed. When a rebellion threatened to topple Díaz in the summer of 1912, Taft dispatched U.S. marines, initiating a two-decade U.S. military presence in Nicaragua.

Remaking Panama

Even as Washington sought to impose order on the broader Caribbean, it channeled immense resources into the construction of the Panama Canal. Since the gold rush, Panama had conjured images of tropical peril, and the French company's failure was still fresh in the minds of many. In 1896, famed journalist Richard Harding Davis had declared the isthmus "a narrow strip of swamp land [that] has blocked the progress of the world."[16] The U.S. effort to conquer that obstacle entailed massive excavation in the ten-mile-wide Canal Zone as well as extensive efforts in Panama itself, including sanitation and port construction in Colón and Panama City. In the process, the project assumed vast importance for U.S. national and imperial identity: in addition to boosting global commerce and connecting their two-ocean empire, the canal would signify white Americans' triumph over tropical disorder.[17]

Like the French effort before it, however, U.S. canal construction would depend heavily upon black workers. Despite the range of immigrants crossing the Atlantic, British West Indians offered the most convenient labor supply. Not only did they speak English, but they were available in large numbers; in fact, some two thousand, many of them veterans of the French effort, still resided in the Canal Zone. Moreover, like most whites at the time, U.S. government officials assumed blacks were immune to yellow fever and other tropical diseases. Nevertheless, the Canal Commission did not want to rely exclusively on Jamaicans, who had a reputation for assertiveness. Drawing upon domestic labor control strategies in the U.S. industrial economy, American officials sought to build a segmented workforce. As Canal Commission chairman Theodore P. Shonts explained, "a labor force composed of different races and nationalities would minimize, if not prevent," labor resistance.[18] Consequently, they recruited workers from southern Europe and also considered hiring Chinese contract laborers, although the latter were banned under both U.S. and Panamanian law. As in the case of other U.S. enterprises in Central America, however, West Indians, particularly Barbadians and Jamaicans, came to dominate the canal workforce, with some 200,000 traveling to Panama during the construction.[19]

Although these black migrants were happy to find work in the Canal Zone, many resisted the racial hierarchy taking shape there. Hailing from black-majority societies, where most had grown up relatively free from fear of white violence, they often scorned American expectations of black deference.[20] The results were frequently explosive. In early 1906, for example, Poultney Bigelow reported that one white American foreman who called a Barbadian an "impertinent, stinking black [bastard]" had received a mouthful of fist in reply.[21] U.S. officials usually attributed such incidents to lower-class racism among American employees. As the first governor of the Canal Zone, General George Davis, observed in May 1905, "some of our foremen are free and unlicensed in the use of language toward these Jamaicans, just as I have seen foremen in the United States use with respect to Negroes . . . [and] in fact, everybody with a dark skin. According to the ideas of some of our tougher class of Americans, among whom I fear are a good many of our foremen and overseers on the Isthmus, all such people are designated as 'niggers.'"[22]

Yet the U.S. government itself set the tone for life in the Canal Zone. The Canal Commission established a comprehensive system of racial segregation justified by widely shared notions of hierarchy and order. In May 1906 testimony to the U.S. Senate, for example, Secretary of War Taft declared the Canal Zone "one of the best conducted governments I know . . . largely due to the ease with which the tropical negro may be governed." The West Indian had his faults, Taft noted: "[H]e is lazy, and he does loaf about a good deal; but he is amenable to law, and it does not take a large police force to keep him in order." Such comments pleased Senator Morgan, who quipped that "the negro loves nothing in the world so much as he does a master."[23] For top officials, as for the "tougher class," racial hierarchy was the only acceptable form of social order in the Canal Zone.

Equally revealing was the U.S. approach to the health of the canal workforce. As in Cuba, American officials' top priority was to control the tropical diseases that had doomed the French enterprise. In charge of this effort was Colonel William Gorgas, veteran of the sanitation efforts in Cuba. Under his direction, West Indian workers poisoned mosquito breeding grounds and constructed modern new settlements for whites. But U.S. officials initially made little provision for black housing, forcing West Indians to crowd into shantytowns. As a result, although yellow fever vanished from the Canal Zone, lung ailments such as tuberculosis and pneumonia took a heavy toll on black workers. From mid-1906 to mid-1907 alone, 466 canal workers died of pneumonia, 90 percent of whom were classified as "colored."[24]

U.S. officials attributed these casualties to racial inferiority rather than living conditions. Following his 1906 visit to Panama, for example, Roosevelt declared that the "white and colored" cafeterias and schools were adequate and that whites and blacks were "treated exactly alike" in the segregated U.S. hospitals. In other words, life in the Canal Zone was separate but equal. And while he acknowledged the high rate of pneumonia among West Indians, he stressed "the difficulty of exercising a thorough supervision over the colored laborers" who were "less competent to take care of themselves."[25] Such assertions reflected the views of canal authorities, who, like their colonial counterparts throughout the world, viewed dark bodies primarily as reservoirs of disease that had to be contained. As Dr. W. E. Deeks, a consultant for the Canal Commission and future head of United Fruit's medical department, explained in 1911:

> As elsewhere in the world, the enforcement of sanitation among the negroes is a gigantic task. . . . The European laborer, though he mingles with the natives, does not live with them, but the negro lives and sleeps in their

houses, exposing himself constantly to the endemic malarial infection. As long as he has a roof over his head and a yam or two to eat he is content, and his ideal of personal hygiene is on a par with his conception of marital fidelity.[26]

As in the French canal effort, work in the Canal Zone was organized around the silver and gold system. In theory, this was simply a payroll structure that split canal employees into two tiers—one paid in silver coin, the other in gold. Under the comprehensive authority of the Canal Commission, however, it came to divide nearly all social interaction in the Canal Zone along racial lines. Still, the system represented a colonial adaptation, rather than a wholesale transplantation, of Jim Crow. After all, as in the 1850s, the U.S. obsession with black-white relations did not fit Panama's demographic realities. European laborers, for example, were divided between northern Europeans, who held supervisory positions on the gold roll, and southern Europeans, often Spanish, who were confined to the silver. Equally delicate was the position of Panamanians. Although many Americans dismissed Hispanics as "spiggoties," some light-skinned Panamanians held positions on the gold roll. Despite this confusion, the system enabled U.S. officials to assert some recognizable sense of order in a complex colonial enclave.[27]

At its heart, the silver and gold system was a racialized labor hierarchy. West Indians in the Canal Zone quickly learned that most supervisory and skilled positions were closed to them and that the quality of their work mattered less than the tone of their skin. As one black foreman informed Bigelow, "as a man of color he received no encouragement for his work."[28] Conversely, white Americans who wanted to perform manual labor found themselves denied. Canal Zone policeman Harry Frank had initially traveled to Panama "with the hope of shouldering a shovel and descending into the canal with other workmen," but he soon discovered "the awful gulf that separates the sacred white American from the rest of the Canal Zone world." One symbol of this divide, he noted, was the white "Rough-neck" steam shovel operator, who could "claw away at his hillside as savagely as he chose without any danger whatever, beyond that of killing himself or an odd 'nigger' or two."[29]

Franck's comment was only partly in jest. West Indians performed the most dangerous tasks in the Canal Zone and suffered a disproportionate number of workplace accidents. Most of these involved rockslides and premature detonations, but others resulted from white negligence or malice. In

July 1908, for example, a railroad engine driven by a white operator crushed eighteen-year-old Jamaican Jacob Clifford. The young man's father, J. N. Clifford, petitioned the Canal Commission and the British government for an investigation, claiming it was common practice for Americans to "run [their] Engine over these [colored] men that [are] working with them." But canal officials blamed Jacob's death on his own carelessness.[30] The decision reflected a tendency on the part of U.S. authorities to attribute such incidents to racial deficiencies. As one U.S. medical official asserted, the high number of black deaths revealed a "striking lack of appreciation for a dangerous environment [in] the negro's mental processes."[31]

Crime and punishment followed similar patterns. Not only were judges in the Canal Zone more likely to give long sentences to black offenders, but white crimes against blacks were seldom punished. This became apparent at the trial of Louis Dennison, a white American who in March 1910 shot and killed Jamaican James Brown, apparently at random. Upon his arrest, he exclaimed, "Don't be too hard on me boys, I have only killed a nigger." His peers obliged. Presented with no witnesses for the defense and only black witnesses for the prosecution, two white juries acquitted Dennison. As the disgusted British consul, Claude Mallet, concluded, "it is unlikely a jury composed of Canal employees will ever convict a white American and fellow employee for the murder of a negro."[32]

If life in the Canal Zone often resembled the Deep South for black immigrants, it offered aspects of tropical paradise for whites. In new settlements such Ancon, Cristobal, and Balboa, white residents lived as colonial elites, enjoying modern housing, clean water, schools, restaurants, clubhouses, and cheap servant labor. As conditions improved, moreover, canal officials encouraged white American women to settle in the Canal Zone. While some worked for the Canal Commission, the majority came as housewives, many of whom became notorious for their social pretensions. According to Franck, these wives of railroad engineers and steam shovel drivers, now served by "Jamaican mammies," had forgotten "the rolling-pin days of the past" and become "supercilious ladies." As in other colonial settings, white women also played a key role in enforcing the color line.[33]

U.S. imperial culture inevitably influenced relations with Panama itself. Panamanians had many reasons to resent Americans. In addition to ruling the center of their country as a colony, Washington intervened frequently in local politics, and U.S. government commissaries monopolized trade in the Canal Zone. Most offensive of all, however, was the behavior of white canal employees in Panamanian territory. As U.S. diplomat William

F. Sands recalled, "It seemed impossible to get it into [the Americans'] heads that not only was Panama not American soil, but that the Canal Zone itself was not."[34] The depth of Panamanian anger emerged in 1912, when U.S. soldiers and canal employees celebrating the Fourth of July swaggered into the entertainment district of Panama City. When several broke into local businesses and assaulted a policeman, residents and police, many of them Afro-Panamanian, attacked the Americans, sending them scurrying back to the Canal Zone. For white Americans, it was a terrifying inversion of racial hierarchy, not unlike the Watermelon Slice Riot a half-century earlier.[35]

West Indians played little role in such clashes. Without U.S. or Panamanian citizenship to shield them, they could make few claims on Canal Zone or Panamanian authorities and faced abuses from both. For similar reasons, labor organizing among black workers proved difficult. U.S. authorities deported agitators and used vagrancy laws to force strikers back to work. As a result, West Indians tended to express their discontent in a time-honored way: they left. Although Canal Zone officials attributed this high turnover to a black penchant for transience, Bigelow came closer to the truth when he noted that, despite earning two or three times more than on their home islands, many West Indians thought "more of fair treatment than wages."[36] That search for fair treatment took many beyond Colón and Panama City and into United Fruit's division in Bocas del Toro, Panama. By the late 1900s, the corporate enclave, which stretched into Costa Rica, was one of the company's fastest growing divisions. When British Consul Mallet visited the enclave in May 1910, he found a thriving operation that boasted modern wharf facilities, rail connections to thirteen banana plantations, and a workforce of 7,500, 75 percent of whom were British subjects. Declaring United Fruit's efforts "a revelation to me," he boarded a steamer for Costa Rica, where he found the firm and its West Indian laborers equally hard at work.[37]

United Fruit in Costa Rica

United Fruit's Costa Rican Division grew out of Minor Keith's various enterprises in Limón province. Over the previous three decades, Keith and his West Indian workforce had built Costa Rica's Caribbean rail line, transformed Puerto Limón into a modern port, and established commercial banana farming in the surrounding lowlands. As United Fruit prepared to expand upon this base, however, it confronted the familiar problem of labor supply. Although thousands of West Indians resided in Limón province, many had settled down as farmers. In order to attract new workers to the isolated coast, United Fruit continued Keith's practice of offering relatively high wages—roughly double those of the Costa Rican coffee sector. Although the deadly reputation of the Caribbean lowlands continued to deter most Costa Ricans from migrating, large numbers of West Indians, especially Jamaicans, made their way to the banana enclave. Though the U.S. canal construction diverted most Caribbean migrants to Panama, there were some 20,000 British West Indians residing in Limón province by late 1910.[38] In addition to drawing from the same labor pool as the U.S. government, the firm implemented a similar system to control its workers. These parallels were hardly coincidental. Like the U.S. government in Panama, United Fruit's operations in Costa Rica built upon structures and practices previously put in place by private capital. In the Canal Commission's case, it was the Panama Railroad Company and the Compagnie Universelle. In the case of United Fruit in Costa Rica, this involved the various enterprises established by Keith, who in his new position as company vice president not only gave the firm access to vast tracts of land and preferential treatment on his railroad but also passed along his labor control strategies to a new generation of managers.

United Fruit's operations in Costa Rica followed a clear corporate hierarchy. At the head of the division was the general manager, who reported directly to company headquarters in Boston. Beneath him, a small number of superintendents oversaw "districts," each of which consisted of several banana farms. Each farm was in turn run by a "mandador" who was assisted by two timekeepers in charge of recording the hours worked by the predominantly Jamaican laborers. With the exception of the foremen, often drawn from the workers' ranks, supervisory jobs were restricted to whites. To fill these positions, United Fruit initially hired Americans and Europeans already residing in the region, including a number of former adventurers. As it pushed to professionalize its ranks, however, the company began to recruit more educated American men to staff its growing Costa Rica Division, among them a young New Englander named Victor M. Cutter.[39]

Born in 1881 into a farming family in Dracut, Massachusetts, Cutter came of age in the crosscurrents of U.S. industrialism and imperial expansion. As a boy, he regularly carted his father's produce across the Merrimack

Map 3. The Costa Rica Division of United Fruit. By Ole J. Heggen

River to Lowell, one of the centers of the New England textile industry. The businessmen of Lowell made certain that life and work were strictly regimented, as well as segmented by ethnicity and gender, and it seems plausible that Cutter's time there, including attending Lowell High School, influenced his approach to labor control during his thirty-year career with United Fruit. Entering Dartmouth College in 1899 amid the national debate over the annexation of the Philippines, Cutter imbibed the racial and imperial assumptions of his time, becoming a fervent admirer of Rudyard Kipling and Theodore Roosevelt. After graduating, he enrolled in Dartmouth's new Amos Tuck School of Administration and Finance and received his master's degree in the spring of 1904, just as canal excavation was beginning in Panama. His thesis, which examined private business opportunities in the Philippines, called on the United States to embrace its new role as a colonial power and claimed that "the tropics must be ruled from the temperate zone."[40] Upon leaving Dartmouth, he leapt at the chance to take part in that tropical rule, accepting a job as timekeeper in United Fruit's Costa Rica Division. The starting pay was poor: as he later recalled, timekeeper was "the lowest position in Central America open to a white man." Like other colonial spheres, however, the banana lands offered young white men the chance to rise quickly. By early 1906 the twenty-four-year-old Cutter was superintendent of Zent, the largest district in the enclave.[41]

At the head of their black workforce, Cutter and other white managers lived out their colonial and pioneering fantasies. In addition to clearing lands, draining swamps, and building housing and branch rail lines, they remapped the landscape, christening banana farms with names of American cities—such as "Boston," "Chicago," "New York," and "Buffalo"—as well as with titles resonant of the American empire, such as "Manila" and "Bataan."[42] "Those were good days," Cutter later recalled. "Central America was fairly primitive. I used to sit in a saddle 14 or 15 hours a day. I was as hard as nails, and there was plenty of good shooting and exploring work to be done."[43] There was also community displacement to be done, especially near the Panamanian border. In 1908, the company began developing plantations near the Sixaola River. Although linked by rail to the Bocas del Toro Division, the development encroached on lands belonging to Talamanca Indians and West Indian settlers in Costa Rica. With the support of the government in San José, United Fruit evicted these residents, few of whom had legal title to their land. As one West Indian who lost his property told an interviewer decades later, "because my father [was] dead and I was a little boy" the *comandante* allowed the firm to "take it over . . . and plant bananas."[44]

As in the Canal Zone, opportunity in the enclave hinged upon race. Although Americans filled most managerial posts, a small number of light-skinned, English-speaking Costa Ricans served as timekeepers and even mandadors in these early years. Their placement in such positions indicates that United Fruit officials considered some Costa Ricans sufficiently white to wield authority. Blacks were, of course, excluded from such opportunities. In response to an application for a managerial position from a West Indian named William Harton in July 1909, for example, General Manager R. J. Schweppe bluntly inquired, "What is your nationality, and are you a white man?" In a cable to another company official weeks later, Schweppe

Figure 2. United Fruit's Zent District, 1907. Courtesy of Dartmouth College Library

Figure 3. United Fruit's Buffalo Farm, in the Zent District, 1906. Courtesy of Dartmouth College Library

Figure 4. Victor Cutter (left) on La Luisa farm, Costa Rica, 1905.
Courtesy of Dartmouth College Library

complained that Harton had failed to answer the racial question to his
satisfaction:

> In my letter . . ., I asked him whether he was a white man. In his reply of
> August 5th, he evades that question by saying that he is an Englishman.
> Now, as all Jamaicans call themselves Englishmen, what I wish that you
> would find out for me is whether he be a white Englishman or a colored
> Englishman.[45]

Such a distinction mattered a great deal in an enclave where fitness to
command hinged upon whiteness. Conversely, even among skilled laborers,
race determined pay. In March 1913, for example, Schweppe's successor,
W. E. Mullins, rejected an engineer's request for a raise for one of his West
Indian workers by noting that "the rate you recommend is higher than is
paid colored employees."[46]

Figure 5. Victor Cutter supervising a banana harvest, Costa Rica, ca. 1905.
Courtesy of Dartmouth College Library

Labor hierarchy went hand in hand with racial segregation, which extended to United Fruit's farms, housing, railcars, and even hospitals— where white and nonwhite patients were separated into "first-class" and "second-class" accommodations, respectively. According to one company survey in 1913, of the division's 1,186 structures, 890 were used primarily by blacks and 65 were restricted to whites. The latter buildings included clubs and recreational facilities as well as living quarters.[47] Managers often justified this segregation with a familiar blend of racial and sexual anxieties. When, for example, an American nurse named Ruby Cobben applied for a position in United Fruit's hospital in Puerto Limón in July 1910, Schweppe explained that "in our . . . Hospitals, we do not require the services of female nurses as our patients in the larger majority are negroes and it is quite necessary that we make use of men nurses."[48] That white women could not be allowed to attend to black male patients was self-evident.

Such statements also hinted at United Fruit's approach to the health and safety of its employees. As in the Canal Zone, white managers assigned black workers the most dangerous tasks, but turned a blind eye to the human costs. During his visit to the banana enclave in late 1909, for example, Anglican Bishop Herbert Bury learned from a company official that six Jamaican workers had recently died when a cable carrying them over the Reventazón River snapped. "None of the bodies were ever found," Bury noted, "and my informant didn't seem to care."[49] The company's approach to disease control revealed other similarities to the Canal Commission. Company officials routinely exchanged information and supplies with their counterparts in the Canal Zone, and like canal officials they concerned themselves primarily with white health.[50] As in Panama, this focus was understandable. Over the previous decades, yellow fever and malaria had killed scores of Americans on the Caribbean coast.[51] Moreover, company doctors assumed blacks were immune to such diseases but could serve as carriers. Nevertheless, United Fruit's obsession with white health led it to ignore pneumonia and tuberculosis, which plagued its black workforce, and like the Canal Commission, it attributed such ailments to black inferiority rather than the living conditions within the enclave.[52]

Also like the Canal Commission, United Fruit held a virtual monopoly over consumer goods through its commissary system. The company portrayed its efforts to supply the enclave's residents as a part of its civilizing mission. As John Williams put it, the commissaries:

> put the white man's necessities of life before the native. He can not only buy the cheap calico and the machete, but can purchase luxuries, thus raising his standard of life. It is not long before the native population is working regularly in order to secure needed wants. The proposition is then to create wants—and the once lazy tropical population will eventually strive to possess these wants.[53]

But in these early years, the system was also very profitable. With much of its workforce residing on isolated banana farms, United Fruit was frequently the sole source of food and consumer goods. The company sometimes reinforced this monopoly by adopting Keith's practice of paying laborers in scrip redeemable only at commissaries. As the division grew and workers demanded hard currency, however, the firm focused on preventing merchants from operating on or near its holdings. In June 1906, for example,

United Fruit reminded the Northern Railway not to grant licenses for "commissary or store privileges" along its line.[54]

Modes of Domination

Ultimately, however, United Fruit derived its power not from plantations or commissaries but rather from the control over transportation and commerce previously established by Keith. In fact, the company cultivated on average only 25 percent of the bananas it exported from Costa Rica. The remaining 75 percent were grown by non-company farmers, the vast majority of whom depended on the firm for credit, inputs, and even access to land. Although some owned their own farms, most, particularly West Indians, rented from United Fruit and its affiliates. This enabled the company to dictate the use of land. Squatters who refused to sign banana contracts or pay rent faced eviction, and farmers who attempted to sell fruit to other buyers found themselves unable to transport it.[55] United Fruit's control over the railroad and most of the shipping out of Puerto Limón enabled it both to set fees and to accept or reject bananas based on company needs. Nor were banana growers the only ones dependent on this monopoly. Although the Costa Rican government completed a state-owned railroad to the Pacific port of Puntarenas in October 1910, the Northern Railway continued to carry the vast majority of coffee exports, which provided its most profitable freight.[56] In fact, Costa Rica's banana and coffee industries had much in common. In both sectors, small farmers produced the bulk of the crop while a merchant and financial elite controlled credit, transport, and marketing. The principal difference was the nationality of participants. Although beholden to commercial elites, the majority of coffee farmers were Costa Rican, and their citizenship enabled them to exert some influence on the state as producers and property owners. In contrast, on the Caribbean coast, a U.S. corporate monopoly held sway over banana farmers, most of whom were renters and only some of whom were Costa Rican. As a result, in these early years, San José paid relatively little attention to the plight of independent banana growers.[57]

Yet, Costa Rican leaders were hardly blind to the dangers posed by the company. Although their nation had so far avoided the U.S. military interventions suffered by many of its neighbors, Costa Ricans worried about United Fruit's expanding power, and the country's relative democratic openness enabled them to voice their concerns. As early as 1907, Congressional Deputy Ricardo Jiménez warned fellow Costa Ricans of the linkage between corporate power and imperial domination:

> There are some . . . who make fun of us for thinking that [United Fruit President Andrew] Preston could come and take over Costa Rica for himself. It's a pity that these writers haven't . . . read the history of modern conquests carefully. India did not lose its independence because Great Britain had declared war on the Indian princes. It was a merchant company similar to the United Fruit Company which created English interests there and was the precursor to Great Britain's regular armies.

But why look to India for analogies, he asked, when Costa Rica had faced William Walker's filibusters? "Many Americans are completely in agreement with Walker," Jiménez claimed. "In trying to take over our territories they don't believe they are coming to conquer and prey on us: they are coming to claim their rights . . . to fulfill the manifest destiny of their race."[58]

Keith personified this peril. Since his renegotiation of the Costa Rican debt in the 1880s, he had wielded tremendous influence over the nation. As John Williams observed:

> Keith is a 'regent' in Costa Rica, he controls the railroads, the freight and passenger service from the Atlantic to the Pacific, and the freight and passenger service to the United States and Europe. Even the rate of exchange depends upon him, through his import of gold: he finances the State and his bank underwrites the State debt; he forces a favorable foreign policy toward his native land.[59]

Not coincidentally, Washington adopted a supportive stance toward Keith and his company in these early years. Although most U.S. officials viewed Costa Rica as whiter and hence more stable than its neighbors, they considered United Fruit a progressive force in a volatile region. They also hoped the firm would help supplant British influence. Like many other nations in the Hispanic Caribbean, Costa Rica retained its close commercial ties to Europe, and its foreign debt remained in British hands. By 1905, however, that debt was in default, and Washington offered Dollar Diplomacy as the solution, pressing San José to transfer its loans to a New York bank. Privately, Secretary of State Root stressed the desirability of having "the next door neighbor of Panama under the financial control of Americans, with a power of ultimate control by the United States."[60]

The debt question inevitably became entangled with rising Costa Rican anxiety toward United Fruit. Rather than shift the debt to U.S. creditors, some legislators proposed doubling the banana export tax to two cents per stem and applying those funds to the British loan. It seemed a reasonable plan: after all, Costa Rica had accrued the debt by building the railroad United Fruit now used to dominate the nation. But the company pushed back, warning that the tax would lead to reduced purchases of bananas. In response, worried banana farmers on the Caribbean coast petitioned San José to cancel the increase.[61] Meanwhile, Keith played a double game, offering to represent Costa Rica in loan negotiations with U.S. banks while secretly pressing Washington to help quash the tax increase. U.S. officials complied, to the detriment of their own policy objectives. Bowing to pressure from both Washington and United Fruit, San José agreed not to raise the tax until 1930. But this concession made nationalists even more determined to keep the debt out of American hands, and in October 1909 the Costa Rican Congress rejected the New York loan. Although Secretary of State Knox attributed the defeat to creeping anti-Americanism in Costa Rica, it was United Fruit that had torpedoed Dollar Diplomacy.[62]

The 1910 Strike

No sooner had the firm scotched the tax increase than it faced a bitter strike from its banana workers. The conflict stemmed directly from the enclave's labor structure. By conflating race with class, United Fruit had inadvertently fostered a sense of unity and common grievance among its workers, most of whom already shared the language and culture of the British West Indies. Although the Costa Rica Division experienced a number of work stoppages in its early years, labor militancy reached a new level when workers formed a union in spring 1910. Then, in early July, the organization received a welcome boost with the endorsement of Ricardo Jiménez, now president of Costa Rica. Soon after, union leaders announced that a general strike would commence on 1 August: West Indian Emancipation Day. As the date approached, black unionists reached out to the small but growing numbers of Hispanic coworkers. As West Indian stevedore William Cohen publicly declared, the company "mistreat[s] Jamaicans and Spanish [Hispanics], and because of this we don't want to work."[63] Such calls for class unity initially seemed effective. In late July, a worried Schweppe admitted that the union's ranks exceeded 5,000 and included "not only negro but native Costa Rican members."[64]

Even before the strike commenced, however, United Fruit was working to undercut labor solidarity. One tool was its leverage over West Indian communal institutions. Many black churches and fraternal societies resided on company lands and received funding from the firm; managers now pulled on those strings to weaken support for the strike. In one letter, Schweppe scolded a West Indian reverend named John Henderson for "talking against the Company [that] gives [you] bread and butter" and ordered him to "attend strictly and only to your religious duties." Schweppe also threatened to withhold the firm's annual funding of the West Indian Emancipation Day celebration.[65] At the same time, the company accused Hispanic troublemakers of stirring unrest among supposedly content black workers. Indeed, Schweppe blamed the entire strike on a Honduran labor organizer who "has been exploiting our labor and causing us considerable trouble."[66] In addition to eliding evidence of West Indian and Hispanic cooperation, claims of foreign subversion helped justify calls for state repression. At first this seemed unlikely: after all, the Costa Rican president had recently endorsed the union. After a long meeting with Schweppe on 24 July, however, Jiménez agreed to crack down on the strike. The relieved general manager hailed this reversal as "a great thing for us" that "will put down any insubordination."[67]

The final and most significant component of United Fruit's response was the hiring of Hispanic strikebreakers. Although managers had long sought to recruit Spanish-speaking workers, previous efforts had proved disappointing. By the summer of 1910, however, the company's relatively high wages and sanitation efforts had made the Caribbean coast increasingly attractive to Hispanic laborers throughout Central America. United Fruit viewed these migrants as the key to breaking the strike and dividing its workforce. Schweppe's correspondence provides a revealing register of this strategy. In a 24 July cable to Keith, he explained that he intended to undermine the union "by importing a distinct element from that which we now have on our farms."[68] On 2 August, a day into the strike, he reported his plans to "recruit another gang of 100 Costa Ricans from the interior," predicting that "the old gang [of West Indians] will soon become tired of loafing and come back to work." Four days later, on 6 August, he felt confident enough to decline Keith's offer of transferring workers from the company's Cuba Division, explaining that he had "accumulated a great deal of Spanish speaking labor . . . to take care of the loading and also to form enough gangs to pick up what fruit we had."[69]

But despite such measures, United Fruit was unable to recruit enough Hispanic migrants to break the strike, which dragged on through the fall. By November, Schweppe had grown so desperate that he imported 680 strikebreakers from the British colony of St. Kitts. But the predominantly Jamaican strikers undercut this move by reaching out to their fellow British subjects, informing the newcomers of the poor treatment and wage cuts that had led to the strike. In response, most of the St. Kitts men refused to work, causing the company to threaten them with enforcement of Costa Rica's vagrancy law. Tensions mounted as the hungry newcomers demanded food. Then, on 24 November, a group of St. Kitts men attacked a company commissary after its white clerk struck one of them with an axe handle. In response, United Fruit called in the Costa Rican police, who brawled with the rioters. Clashes continued the following day, as Jamaican workers poured in from outlying banana farms and the Costa Rican government dispatched 250 troops to Limón.[70]

Fearing further bloodshed, United Fruit sought the assistance of British officials in Costa Rica. This proved fairly easy in the case of Vice Consul C. G. McGrigor, who was on the company's payroll in Puerto Limón. But Schweppe also lobbied British Consul F. Nutter Cox in San José, assuring him that "the whole trouble arose from intimidation of the St. Kitts men by the Jamaicans who were determined to run off any labour except that from Jamaica." Convinced by this version of events, Cox downplayed West Indian unity and worker grievances in his report to London. Asserting that the Jamaicans were "caring for the St Kitts men . . . with the idea of working them up to fight the authorities," he depicted the strike as a conflict between "the forces of order and those of disorder."[71] With the company's urging and Cox's blessing, Costa Rican authorities finally cracked down on the strikers and deported their leaders. By the end of 1910, the union had collapsed.

In retrospect, the 1910 strike signified a major turning point for race and labor relations in the company's Costa Rica Division. The union's initial success had raised hope among West Indian laborers for cooperation with Hispanic migrants and the Costa Rican state. But United Fruit had torpedoed that possibility. Above all, its recruitment of Spanish-speaking strikebreakers undercut workers' tenuous attempts at interracial solidarity. By framing the November riot as a black uprising, moreover, the firm

had convinced San José to turn against the union. Still worse, the riot led
many Hispanic union members to join the strikebreakers and call for the
repression of their West Indian coworkers. As one pro-labor newspaper in
San José observed:

> What really pains us is that some Limón workers belonging to the white
> race made common cause with the authorities and . . . participated in the
> abuses committed against the blacks. . . . [T]he Company will give infinite
> thanks for the services given by the white workers who lent themselves
> voluntarily to the effort of putting the blacks down by force. . . . [T]hey
> should have understood . . . that it was an issue of *workers* and *bosses* and not
> of blacks and whites.[72]

The lessons were not lost on West Indian workers, who largely abandoned
interracial organizing.

Over the following months, racial tensions on the Caribbean coast continued to grow. Among those affected was Jamaican activist Marcus Garvey,
who had come to Costa Rica in 1909 to work as a stevedore for United
Fruit. In early 1911, after witnessing the strike, he founded a newspaper
that criticized the company, Costa Rican officials, and West Indian leaders
alike. His own troubles began that May, after a fire swept through Puerto
Limón. When Garvey accused Costa Rican firemen of ignoring black
neighborhoods, local police arrested and beat him, destroying his press in
the process. Following his release, United Fruit refused to sell him the parts
to repair it, and he soon left for Panama. But the company had not seen the
last of Garvey.[73]

Such harassment was hardly unique. Just weeks after Garvey's departure,
a British diplomat reported that a drunk Costa Rican policeman in Puerto
Limón had "without any provocation" accosted Jamaican stevedore Alfred
Sealey and shot him in the hand.[74] Despite such incidents, however, Costa
Rican and United Fruit officials generally succeeded in cultivating the good
will of British officials. This became evident during a November 1911 visit
to Costa Rica and Panama by the governor of Jamaica, Sydney Olivier. As
the author of a progressive tract on race, entitled *White Capital and Coloured
Labour* (1906), Olivier was deeply concerned with the working and living conditions of West Indian immigrants in Central America, but his U.S.
handlers carefully orchestrated his trip. In Panama, Chief Engineer George
Goethals guided him through the Canal Zone, and in Costa Rica he was
entertained by United Fruit officials and President Jiménez. Although

Olivier left convinced that West Indians faced no unfair treatment, Costa Rican hostility to black immigrants continued to mount.[75]

Dictatorship, Race, and Guatemala's Railroad

Events in Guatemala followed a similar course, but they often took more dramatic turns. This was partly due to the looming presence of President Estrada Cabrera. Like Zelaya in Nicaragua, Estrada Cabrera ruled with an iron fist at home and meddled often in neighboring states. Unlike the Nicaraguan dictator, however, he cultivated good relations with Washington, making a great show, for example, of considering (though never approving) the transfer of Guatemala's British-held debt to a U.S. bank. Even more important was his symbiotic relationship with United Fruit. In Estrada Cabrera, the company had a dictator who could offer concessions and maintain order without the democratic messiness that often arose in Costa Rica. In return, the Guatemalan president drew upon United Fruit's prestige and vast resources to strengthen his rule and pursue his development plans, the most important of which was the Northern Railway. It was these calculations that had led him to sign the 1904 contract, which granted Keith's railroad company, and hence United Fruit, control over much of Guatemala's Caribbean coast.[76]

When Keith took over construction, the railroad had sixty miles left to reach the capital. With U.S. canal construction underway in Panama, however, the problem of labor supply remained. Estrada Cabrera used *mandamientos* to supply the railroad with some workers. For his part, Keith sought to recruit experienced West Indian workers from Costa Rica. In this effort, he was assisted by the terms of the 1904 contract, which prohibited him from importing Chinese immigrants but placed no other restrictions on the entry and employment of foreign workers.[77] These West Indians joined the many African Americans still employed by the railroad. Although conditions on the Caribbean coast had improved since the 1880s and 1890s, managers still enforced strict racial hierarchy and called upon Guatemalan authorities to punish disobedient and runaway laborers. And while many local officials were already predisposed to abuse black immigrants, they also learned from the U.S. example.

As in earlier years, many African Americans sought to flee work on the railroad. During his 1908 visit to Guatemala, U.S. writer Nevin Winter encountered hundreds of Southern blacks. "A party of twenty-two had just come over on the boat that took me away and a more dejected lot of 'cullud gemmen' I never saw," he noted. "[T]hey had already heard of the life that was in store for them, and they were trying to devise ways and means for their return to 'God's Country.'"[78] Many of those unable to buy passage back to the United States moved into the Guatemalan interior. The *ladino* culture they encountered there was profoundly racialized, to be sure, but anti-black discrimination was rarely institutionalized to the same degree as in the railroad's work camps or the Southern states from which most of them hailed. In the rail hub of Zacapa, for example, blacks faced no formalized racism, and by the mid-1900s dozens of African Americans had settled in the town, several of them opening businesses and marrying *ladino* women. As their numbers grew, however, so did the hostility of local officials.

One victim of this shift was Simon Shine. Shine had come to Guatemala to work on the railroad in 1894, at the tender age of fourteen. By the summer of 1907, he had settled in Zacapa and opened a combination boardinghouse, barber shop, and saloon, which according to him catered "mostly to american coloured men from the railroad." After several months of brisk business, he came under the scrutiny of the department's presidentially appointed governor (*jefe político*), Enrique Arias, a powerful minion of Estrada Cabrera. In September 1907, on his way home from a night of heavy drinking, Arias bragged to his aides, "I am going to the house of those negroes and will give them a clubbing." Upon entering the saloon, he demanded to see Shine's license; then, without warning, he and his men brutally pistol-whipped Shine and his patrons.[79] The incident stirred tensions between Washington and Guatemala City, largely due to Shine's efforts to seek redress for his injuries. After requesting help from Edward Reed, the U.S. consul in Livingston, Shine sent a plea directly to Theodore Roosevelt, asking the president to "protect us poor niggers from being beaten to death, we have no one to look to but you."[80] When U.S. officials inquired into the case, however, their Guatemalan counterparts drew upon shared racial assumptions to justify the attack. According to William Sands, now legation secretary in Guatemala City, Arias himself asserted that "there was a certain species of American citizen who just didn't understand any other kind of treatment."[81]

Such exchanges underscored the conflict between domestic U.S. racial practices and foreign policy objectives. By the time of this incident, Washington had accepted Jim Crow at home as well as implemented aspects of it in the Canal Zone. Yet, like other imperial powers, the United States was determined to establish legal protection, if not extraterritoriality, for its citizens in weaker nations. Official attacks on African Americans in Guatemala placed U.S. diplomats in an awkward position: not only were some abuses of U.S. blacks instigated by white Americans, but U.S. officials generally shared the prejudices of their time. Sands himself later dismissed the black Americans in Guatemala as "Southern Negroes—mostly Louisiana roustabouts or 'bad niggers' from the Mississippi levees and steamboat wharves."[82] Nevertheless, he and his fellow U.S. diplomats viewed Guatemalan harassment of black Americans as a slippery slope. As Consul Reed put it, "such an exhibition of brutality . . . even though the victim be a degraded American negro, should not be passed unnoticed, lest it weaken the respect of Guatemalan officials for American citizenship, and later bear fruit in the beating of some worthy American."[83] In the end, the Guatemalan government compensated Shine, and in the coming years incidents involving U.S. blacks became rarer. Following the railroad's completion in early 1908, the number of African Americans in Guatemala declined even as the banana industry attracted growing numbers of British West Indians to the Caribbean lowlands.

Building the Enclave

As in Costa Rica, United Fruit did not introduce banana growing to Guatemala. U.S. merchant ships had purchased bananas from *ladinos* and Garífuna on the Caribbean coast for decades, and this local cultivation increased with the advent of United Fruit's regular steamship service in 1901. By March 1905, according to a report by the governor of Izabal, there were at least sixty Guatemalan-owned banana farms in the department.[84] But while United Fruit continued to purchase locally grown fruit, it was eager to develop its own plantations. Initially, it focused its effort on acquiring land for banana cultivation. Although Keith would give United Fruit access to his land concessions after completing the railway, much of the territory along the railroad's route had been scooped up by speculators with close ties to the Guatemalan government. As a result, the company was forced to purchase the most desirable lands. In June 1904, for example, its railway subsidiary bought the ranch of Quiriguá, nearly 24,000 acres in all, which would soon form the heart of United Fruit's Guatemala Division.[85] Serious efforts at development began in 1907, when the company appointed Victor Cutter as general manager. According to his

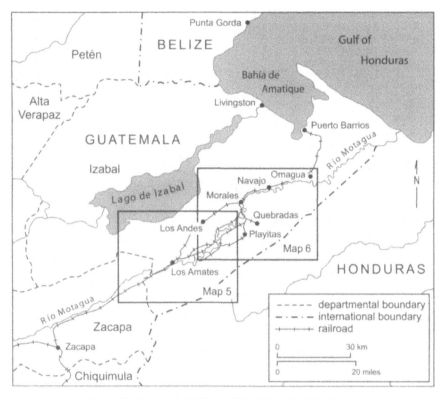

Map 4. The Guatemala Division of United Fruit. By Ole J. Heggen

friend Hugh Wilson, Cutter's three years in Costa Rica had taught him "the business of banana growing and negro management."[86] He now applied those lessons to Guatemala.

Cutter and his fellow managers sought to carve out an orderly and familiar world in the Caribbean lowlands. As in Costa Rica and the Canal Zone, this required extensive investment in sanitation, disease control, and infrastructure. Among United Fruit's top priorities was the modernization of Puerto Barrios, which was redesigned on a grid layout with a new sewage system and improved port facilities. The firm also built a medical clinic for its employees and soon after began construction of an impressive modern hospital in Quiriguá. Under the guidance of Scottish-born Dr. Neil Macphail, who headed the Guatemala Division's medical department between 1908 and his death in 1949, the Quiriguá hospital became the best medical facility in Central America.[87]

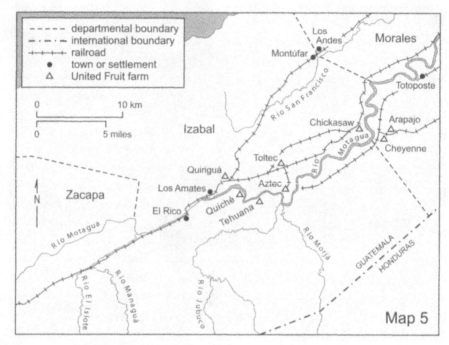

Map 5. The Southwestern Sector of the Guatemala Division, including the Quiriguá District. By Ole J. Heggen

Meanwhile, Cutter laid out farms along the Northern Railway and its feeder lines. Although some tracts in Quiriguá were already planted with bananas, cultivation spread rapidly in 1907–1908. Continuing their celebration of banana pioneering, Cutter and his fellow managers gave some farms "Western" names such as "Cheyenne" and "Arapaho" while they used others to emphasize their Northeastern roots and education, dubbing plantations "Dartmouth," "Pequot," and "Cayuga." Yet it was Cutter's headquarters of "Virginia" that perhaps bore the most appropriate title. After all, these corporate frontiersmen did not themselves clear and cultivate their banana plantations, and Cutter's most important responsibility as general manager was the recruitment and control of the company's predominantly black workforce.[88] Despite railroad construction, the labor pool in Izabal remained shallow. Although the department's population was on the rise, few *ladinos,* Garífuna, or African Americans proved eager to work on banana plantations. Building upon Keith's practices on the railroad, United Fruit turned to West Indians, especially from Jamaica and neighboring Belize, for the bulk of its labor.

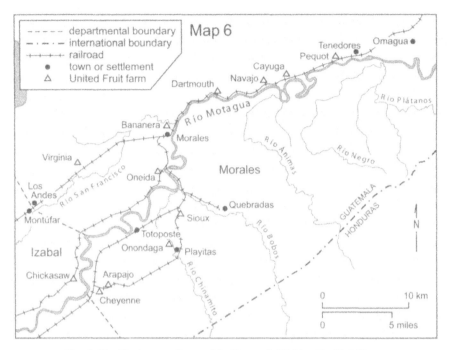

Map 6. The Northeastern Sector of the Guatemala Division. By Ole J. Heggen

The racial and labor structure that Cutter and his colleagues implemented was nearly identical to that of the Costa Rica Division. Supervisory
positions were reserved for whites, most of them Americans. In contrast,
manual labor was performed almost exclusively by black immigrants, drawn
mostly from Jamaica and neighboring British Honduras. In addition, a small
number of whites, including some Southerners, held skilled labor positions
as electricians and carpenters. From the beginning, Cutter cultivated an air
of stern but fair dealing with West Indians. Although he believed in keeping
them in their "place," he made a point of praising and promoting his most
reliable employees. But even his plaudits revealed deeper racial assumptions. Over coffee with Bishop Bury in the spring of 1909, for example, he
gushed that one Jamaican foreman was "a white man through and through,
black as he is."[89] Despite such praise, moreover, Cutter maintained strict
segregation akin to that in the Canal Zone and the company's Costa Rica
Division. Valued foremen, along with other black employees, were excluded
from white housing, dining, and entertainment facilities.

Cutter and other managers justified the company's racial policies by cit-
ing the "natural" tension between races. Like U.S. officials in Panama, they
tended to locate that tension in the presumed conflict between British West
Indians and white Southerners. As John Williams explained:

> In the relations between whites and colored, one notices at once the re-
> spect shown the whites by the negroes from the United States, and also
> by the natives of the country. . . . The big problem is the Jamaican negro.
> First of all, he is a British subject and as such he feels that he is equal to
> any other person in the world. . . . Place, then, this British subject with his
> 'cocky' attitude under the strict eye of a white boss, who let us say comes
> from the States south of the Mason and Dixon Line, and trouble forthwith
> results.

It was this animosity, he asserted, that forced the company to maintain segregation: "To avoid complications . . . a strict color line is drawn. All persons
of color must always give the right of way to whites, and remove their hats
while talking. A rule also forbids any laborer from entering the front yard
of any white man's residence." Such reasoning enabled managers, most of
whom came from the North, to adopt practices reminiscent of the Jim
Crow South while denying responsibility. Yet, as in Costa Rica, these policies ultimately undermined order in the enclave. Placed in positions of authority, white supervisors, many of whom were young and inexperienced,
often sought to cow black workers with peremptory commands and racial
epithets, which in turn stirred resentment among West Indians. Indeed,
Williams himself admitted that "as a result of this sharp color line, various
whites have been slain, and also many blacks have been ruthlessly made
away with," including the murder of one Jamaican "who had threatened to
kill one of the white supervisors."[90] And when such incidents occurred, the
racialized structure of the company's labor system ensured that black workers would see racial and class grievances as one and the same.

"Negroes Cause Trouble"

In the months preceding the December 1909 uprising, there had been
few signs of trouble. Indeed, Cutter was so confident in the social order
of his new enclave that he left for a vacation in November. In his absence,
relations between white supervisors and black laborers quickly soured. In

early December, as workers anxiously awaited their final payday before Christmas, acting general manager Warren W. Smith decided to cut pay rates. It was that decision that prompted the Cayuga timekeeper's announcement on 7 December that "$30 a month is enough for any nigger." Reports of the pay cut and racial epithets spread through the division, adding to West Indian resentment over the company's pay system, commissary prices, and racial practices. Drawing upon the predominance of Jamaicans in the workforce, several outspoken laborers called for solidarity against white managers. Within days, they announced the formation of a "Jamaica Union" and rallied their countrymen with calls of "Remember boys we are all Jamaicans."[91]

It was in this context that violence broke out at Cayuga. On 16 December, the farm's timekeeper shot Jamaican George Reid. Upon learning of Reid's death, hundreds of West Indians, facing little resistance from the nearby Guatemalan garrison, turned their anger on the farm's commissary. This led to more bloodshed, as a white store clerk named E. H. Tennison shot at least one West Indian before fleeing to Puerto Barrios. Some strikers pursued Tennison, while the rest marched toward the Dartmouth farm demanding that all workers refuse to load banana trains until the company agreed to wage increases. Occurring almost simultaneously with the U.S. removal of Zelaya in Nicaragua, the strike drew little attention in Washington, but several newspapers in the U.S. South took notice. In an article entitled "Negroes Cause Trouble," the *New Orleans Times-Picayune* lauded Tennison's actions, assuring readers that the "promptness and braveness of the lone American took the breath out of the negroes."[92] In reality, Tennison had only further enraged the strikers. Late on 17 December, Cutter, still in the United States, wired the U.S. legation that "four hundred Jamaican labourers [are] on strike and drunk raising [a] riot." Warning that the local garrisons were unable to restore order, he sent a request for 175 more Guatemalan troops to Sands, who relayed it to Estrada Cabrera.[93]

Considering the history of Guatemalan state violence toward black immigrants, Cutter's cable might well have led to brutal repression if not for the intervention of British officials. Upon learning of Cutter's request, British Consul Lionel Carden rushed to the office of Guatemala's minister of war to demand that Guatemalan troops not use force against the strikers "except as a last resort." He then instructed Vice Consul W. F. Brown in Livingston to help restore order. As a result of these efforts, Guatemalan troops peacefully occupied the troubled plantations on 18 December. Nevertheless, the situation remained tense. Six days later, U.S. Consul Reed reported that the number of strikers had grown to six hundred, most of whom were "equipped with some sort of fire-arm, and . . . not in the best of temper."[94] Despite United Fruit's continued demands for repression, however, Guatemalan troops held back, almost certainly due to the presence of British diplomats.

In the week following the uprising, another British vice consul, Godfrey Haggard, conducted an investigation into the living conditions and labor practices in United Fruit's enclave. He concluded that while the West Indian workforce included "a large proportion of bad characters," some of whom had previously been fired from the company's Costa Rica Division, the strikers had legitimate grievances. In addition to United Fruit's manipulation of its payroll, he reported, West Indians complained of "high-handed treatment and 'cursing'" and being "threatened with revolvers." All of this trouble could have been avoided, he concluded, had the firm assumed "a more sympathetic and tactful attitude" toward its black employees.[95]

United Fruit officials disagreed. Not only did they deny allegations of abuse, but they were determined to reassert their authority. Although no whites had been harmed during the clash, their flight from the banana farms had badly damaged their prestige. Initially, Cutter himself was inclined toward moderation, explaining to Sands that "it seems best simply to compel the leaders in the trouble to leave, as it affords very little satisfaction to punish ignorant and excitable negroes."[96] By February 1910, however, he was warning of "trouble in the near future." Although he continued to believe that, "in the main, our Jamaicans are a very quiet lot and are perfectly willing to work," he worried that they were being influenced by "the few bad ones whom we have here."[97] Cutter was also annoyed at the reluctance of Guatemalan officials to move against the strike's leaders, which he attributed to British interference. In one tense letter to British Consul Carden, he denied the use of "arbitrary or illegal methods for punishing laborers" and maintained that he was "anxious to employ more Jamaicans," who, if properly disciplined, "are the best workers in Central America." But he went on to complain that the British presence in the enclave had "delayed the summary punishment of the rioters."[98]

The riot also raised long-term questions of maintaining order in the enclave. Prior to the uprising, the Guatemalan state's military presence in the area was limited to two twelve-man garrisons at Morales and Los Amates and a small detachment at Virginia.[99] Although the company welcomed the stationing of additional soldiers near major farms, it balked at the Guatemalan government's demand that it pay their salaries. Eventually, however, the firm agreed to provide some housing for them. These garrisons came to occupy an anomalous place in the enclave. Although ostensibly vested with authority over those in their jurisdiction, the poorly paid soldiers were looked down upon by Americans and West Indians alike, and they often took out their frustrations on the latter. Herein lay some of the origins of the segmented labor system. To be sure, the soldiers were not direct employees of the company, and the primary division in the enclave remained that between white managers and black laborers. But the garrisons' presence helped set the tone for black-*ladino* relations, particularly after the West Indian uprising.

Prior to the 1909 strike, Cutter and his fellow white managers had relied primarily on themselves to control West Indians, often through acts of intimidation and violence. Cutter himself became legendary for his willingness to beat black workers into submission. But the rising numbers of *ladinos* in the enclave offered more indirect means of control. In addition to calling upon a growing number of garrisons to help discipline laborers, company officials sometimes hired *ladino* locals and moonlighting soldiers for extralegal coercion, which included "disappearing" troublesome West Indians. As Williams recalled:

> On my plantation was a native who would for the sum of ten dollars remove any negro from sight and no questions asked. The only stipulation he made was that the designated man be given work near the river. The deed was quietly done and the body slipped into the river where the alligators removed all evidence of the crime.[100]

Such statements hinted not only at the company's complicity in anti-black violence but also its utilization of racial tensions to divide and discipline its workers. As in the case of the 1910 strike in Costa Rica, the uprising at the Cayuga farm taught United Fruit officials the dangers of black solidarity and the value of a divided workforce.

It was no coincidence that as the company grew more confident in its ability to control its black laborers, it encouraged white family life in the enclave. Like their U.S. government counterparts in Panama, United Fruit officials understood that the presence of wives and children could reduce the turnover of white personnel, and by 1912 a growing number were joining husbands and fathers in the enclave. Among these newcomers was Charlotte Potter Sealey of Ipswich, Massachusetts. Charlotte's husband, New Jersey–born Percy Sealey, was a U.S. army veteran who had been sta-

Figure 6. West Indian laborers and domestic servants, likely employed by Cutter at Virginia, Guatemala, ca. 1914. Courtesy of Dartmouth College Library

tioned in the Canal Zone prior to accepting a position with United Fruit. Accompanied by their one-year-old son Philip, the very pregnant Charlotte joined her husband at the district headquarters of Quiriguá in September 1912 and two months later gave birth to their second son, Robert. Quiriguá must have been an isolating place for a young mother. Although it had been under cultivation since 1906 and boasted modern housing for managers, Quiriguá remained very much a man's world. Recreational facilities were largely restricted to men, and the nearest Guatemalan town, Los Amates, was known primarily as a payday destination for bars and brothels. Moreover, the growing presence of white women made managers even more determined to police the color line, and as a result white women's contact with nonwhites remained confined largely to servants, many of whom were West Indian women. Perhaps the best description of life in the settlement came from U.S. travel writer Arthur Ruhl, who visited years later:

> [W]hen you do finally get down to Quirigua, and the banana-plantations, screened overseers' headquarters and spotless hospitals of the United Fruit Company, you are, for all practical purposes, in a detached bit of the United States, with its 'colonial' ruling class as remote, psychologically, from the land it lives in, as are the Canal Zone Americans at Panama.[101]

The 1904–1912 period witnessed the critical formation of U.S. imperial culture in Central America. Even as domestic questions of race and identity roiled the nation at home, the United States extended its imperial control over much of the Hispanic Caribbean. The U.S. government's most visible effort came in the Panama Canal Zone, where the combination of West Indian immigration and U.S. racial assumptions resulted in the adaptation of domestic racial practices, including racialized labor divisions and social segregation. United Fruit's operations in Costa Rica and Guatemala shared these assumptions and followed a similar pattern. Although the company did not wield the resources and political authority the U.S. government enjoyed in Panama, it approached the challenges of commercial banana cultivation in a parallel fashion, using racial hierarchy and segregation to control its predominantly West Indian workforce.

In the relatively isolated conditions of the banana enclave, however, these practices generated labor resistance along racial lines. West Indian challenges to United Fruit's authority revealed the perils of racial and linguistic homogeneity among its workers. Indeed, the most important outcome of the labor uprisings of 1909–1910 was not the firm's success in securing state repression in both Costa Rica and Guatemala; it was, rather, its calculated turn toward recruiting Spanish-speaking laborers in order to build a divided workforce. Over the following years, United Fruit's enclaves became increasingly marked by this system of labor segmentation, but its power would not go uncontested. Although tensions between black and Hispanic workers hampered interracial labor organizing, the firm would face a variety of new challenges, including West Indian enthusiasm for Garvey's Universal Negro Improvement Association and growing calls for immigration restriction within its host nations.

Chapter 4

Divided Workers, 1912–1921

On the evening of Saturday, 9 May 1914, Nathan Gordon and Alfred Esson, two Jamaican workers in the Quiriguá District of United Fruit's Guatemala Division, were walking on the outskirts of the company's Tehuana farm when they were attacked by four Hispanic men. Gordon escaped by diving into the Motagua River. Esson wasn't so lucky: after receiving machete wounds to the hands and face, he was shot to death. The following day, an enraged group of Jamaicans marched to a Hispanic workers' camp near Tehuana to settle the score. After failing to locate the murderers, they killed two Guatemalan men unconnected to the attack and threatened to do the same to all the "Spanish," men and women alike. The rampage ended only when three African American workers convinced the Jamaicans to return to their barracks. But the violence was just beginning. Informed by the commander of the nearby Los Amates garrison that "more than 60 armed negroes" were "killing all the Guatemalan inhabitants," President Estrada Cabrera ordered the provincial governor to "take any steps you may think necessary to repress the evil." Guatemalan troops arrived at United Fruit's district headquarters of Quiriguá in the early morning of 12 May. It soon became clear that their mission was not to capture the killers but to terrorize West Indian residents. As dawn broke, the soldiers harassed, beat, and shot at black laborers who were on their way to work, and over the following two days they invaded the Tehuana, Quiché, and Mixco farms, killing several West Indians, looting black homes, and making sweeping arrests.[1]

Once most of the troops had withdrawn and order had returned, British Vice Consul Godfrey Haggard undertook an investigation. He quickly concluded that this "Quiriguá incident," unlike the 1909 uprising, did not involve United Fruit managers and had resulted from tensions between West Indian and Hispanic laborers. In fact, since no Americans had been threatened, U.S. diplomats showed little interest, and company officials seemed concerned only with the disruption to their operations. The army's attacks had caused West Indian workers to flee, virtually emptying the three plantations. As one timekeeper on the Mixco plantation complained, "There are only about ten niggers left on this farm."[2] Still, managers hoped the Guatemalan state's bloody response would assist their objective of disciplining workers. "The general sentiment . . . among the higher officials of the Fruit Company," Haggard noted, was that "these events, though deplorable, would teach the Jamaican labourer a much-needed lesson."[3]

The Quiriguá incident reflected a critical change taking place in United Fruit's enclaves. In its first decade of operations, the company's reliance on West Indian labor, along with its demands for racial separation and deference, had all but ensured that the primary division within its Costa Rica and Guatemala divisions would be between white managers and black workers. In addition to spawning racial friction, this labor structure had unwittingly fostered West Indian solidarity, which contributed to the labor upheavals of 1909–1910. As the firm stepped up recruitment of Central American migrants over the following years, however, these racial dynamics began to shift. The company's color line remained in place, but social relations within its enclaves became increasingly defined by friction between Hispanic and West Indian workers. To be sure, many factors contributed to this animosity. Anti-black racism had deep roots among Hispanic Central Americans, and it was heightened by linguistic and cultural differences. For their part, West Indians tended to look down upon Spanish-speaking migrants and distrust Central American officials. But United Fruit played a critical role in heightening these tensions. Like its corporate counterparts in the United States, the firm utilized a system of labor segmentation to foment divisions within its workforce. In addition to housing Hispanics and blacks separately, it assigned them different tasks and wages based upon race, routinely placing West Indians in charge of Spanish-speaking work gangs.

Demeaned by American managers and often subordinate to black foremen, many Hispanics responded by channeling their resentment toward West Indian coworkers. And as the Quiriguá incident illustrated, those tensions opened the door to state repression of black immigrants.

These patterns grew more pronounced during World War I. Although United Fruit managed to weather the conflict and even repair its frayed relations with Washington, the wartime reduction of shipping sharply curtailed Central American coffee and banana exports. Desperate for employment, thousands of Hispanic workers from throughout the region made their way to United Fruit's banana enclaves, particularly in Costa Rica and Guatemala. Once there, however, they found West Indians holding positions on the firm's shrinking payrolls. The resulting competition for jobs exacerbated the racial tensions already embedded in the company's labor structure. Soon, Central American migrants were demanding restrictions on black immigration and preferential hiring for Spanish-speakers. Hispanic officials in Guatemala, in particular, responded with increased harassment of West Indians, which only added to the racial divisions among laborers. By the time a wave of strikes shook Central America and the broader Caribbean between late 1918 and early 1921, Hispanic and West Indians workers in United Fruit's Costa Rica and Guatemala enclaves were profoundly divided, making it difficult for them to cooperate despite shared grievances against the company.

Empire, Migration, and the UNIA

Most scholarship on U.S.–Latin American relations between 1912 and 1921 has focused on the actions of the U.S. government, and with good reason.[4] In addition to the opening of the Panama Canal, these years brought the ratification of a protectorate treaty with Nicaragua, two military interventions in revolutionary Mexico, and the occupation of Haiti, the Dominican Republic, and eastern Cuba. But Washington's policies took shape within the broader context of U.S. corporate power, labor migration, and rising nationalism, particularly in Central America. To be sure, U.S. interventions had a profound impact on United Fruit and its host nations. But the reverse was also true. Decisions made in United Fruit's boardroom and the social relations in and around its enclaves influenced U.S. government policies, not only in Central America but in the wider Caribbean.

As in earlier years, labor migration formed a critical link between the activities of the company and the U.S. government. The early 1910s were heady years for United Fruit. The booming demand for bananas in the United States spurred the firm both to expand its operations in Costa Rica, Guatemala, and Panama, and to develop two new enclaves in Honduras. In its quest for a growing but divided workforce, it hired large numbers of Hispanic Central Americans even as it continued its aggressive recruitment of West Indians, particularly in the Panama Canal Zone. This fit well with U.S. government objectives. By 1912, with canal construction nearing completion, the Canal Commission had begun laying off and evicting thousands of black workers. Worried that jobless West Indians would threaten internal order in either the Canal Zone or their home islands, U.S. and British officials leapt at the chance to funnel them to United Fruit. In August 1913, the company announced plans to hire 10,000 former canal workers and give them free passage to its banana enclaves. Over the following months West Indians crowded the decks of the company steamers that plied Central America's Caribbean coast. These migrants included not only men but also married and single women. One example was twenty-six-year-old April Gray Campbell, who had migrated from Jamaica to Panama in 1909, at the age of twenty-one. Four years later, she responded to the cutbacks in the Canal Zone by boarding a steamer for Costa Rica. Although women such as Campbell remained excluded from work on United Fruit's banana plantations, they provided essential labor in the enclave. In her case, she later recalled, "I [made] my living as a shoemaker" for banana workers, though she hoped to acquire her own land.[5] Campbell was only one of thousands drawn to the banana lands. Like the African American Southerners making their way to Northern cities in these same years, West Indians were responding to the economic opportunities generated by U.S. industry. And as in the U.S. North, black newcomers faced racial animosity in their new surroundings. By mid-1914, calls for restrictions on West Indian immigration were growing throughout Central America.[6]

World War I brought another shift in migration patterns. In response to the banana industry's wartime contraction and rising hostility from Hispanic officials and coworkers, thousands of West Indians left Central America. Some entered the British army, but many others made their way to Cuba and even back to Panama, where the U.S. government was planning to build fortifications for the canal. In Cuba, one of their largest employers was none other than United Fruit, whose sugar enclaves in the Oriente province enjoyed a wartime boom. Here, too, the company maintained a divided workforce, in this case consisting mostly of Spanish-speaking Cubans, English-speaking West Indians, and French-speaking migrants from U.S.-occupied Haiti. As in Central America, black immigrants in Cuba faced nativist hostility, which became evident during a sugar strike in February 1917. Although British West Indians played little role in the work stoppage, Cuban officials targeted them for repression and carried out at least one massacre of Jamaican workers.[7] This upheaval, which threatened the property of United Fruit and other sugar interests, in turn prompted the U.S. military occupation of eastern Cuba. West Indians faced similar animosity in Panama. Although their numbers had declined since the height of the construction, they still accounted for the bulk of the Canal Zone's 17,000 workers. By the late 1910s, they confronted not only the resentment of Hispanic Panamanians but also the rising influence of the Ku Klux Klan among white American canal employees.[8]

It was in this transnational context of labor migration and racial tension that Marcus Garvey's UNIA appeared. Although founded in Harlem in 1917 and usually associated with the racial politics of the United States, the UNIA had its roots in the West Indian diaspora. Indeed, Garvey's critiques of U.S. race relations drew upon not only his upbringing in Jamaica, as many scholars have noted, but also his time in the U.S. empire. Years before his famous 1916 tour of the United States, Garvey had his first encounters with U.S. racial culture in Costa Rica and Panama; and although documentary evidence is scarce, it seems likely that these earlier experiences, particularly the 1910 strike in Costa Rica, contributed to his skepticism toward interracial labor organizing. Indeed, although Garvey was often critical of United Fruit and other corporate interests, he reserved a special disdain for labor activists who called on black workers to embrace class solidarity.[9] The only path to progress, he maintained, was racial unity and uplift. This message resonated with West Indian migrants in U.S. enclaves in Central America and other parts of the Hispanic Caribbean, who daily confronted both white American domination and Hispanic hostility, and the UNIA quickly gained a large following among them. Over the following years, Cuba came to boast the greatest number of branches with 52, followed by Panama (47), Costa Rica (23), Honduras (8), and Guatemala (3). It was hardly a coincidence that the UNIA's growth closely mapped U.S. business and government expansion in the region. After all, American enterprises had drawn West Indians to these nations and provided the infrastructure for the UNIA to spread. By mid-1919, United Fruit's steamers and railcars

were unwittingly carrying Garvey's publication *The Negro World* throughout Central American and the broader Caribbean.[10]

Garvey's goal was not merely to piggyback upon white corporate power
but to challenge it. Even as he expanded the UNIA's membership, he
pushed to develop a black business network, the centerpiece of which was
a new steamship line. Announced in May 1919 and christened the Black
Star Steamship Company, the ambitious venture aimed to compete with
U.S. and British shipping firms. Indeed, Black Star's very name was a racial
retort to Garvey's corporate adversaries, which included the Cunard-
owned White Star Steamship Company as well as United Fruit's steam line,
which shared with the U.S. Navy the title "the Great White Fleet." But
although UNIA supporters invested large sums in the project, Black Star
faced significant obstacles. In addition to the difficulty of finding service-
able ships and competent crews, the company was unable to secure sufficient cargo, partly because United Fruit and other firms refused to allow it
to carry their products.[11]

Nevertheless, West Indian enthusiasm for the UNIA and the Black
Star Line alarmed U.S. government and corporate officials. One reason
for their anxiety was timing. The UNIA began its rapid spread in 1919,
just as a wave of radicalism and labor upheaval swept the United States
and its empire. U.S. diplomats in Central America worried in particular
about the influence of the Mexican Revolution, which they believed
had taken a turn toward "Bolshevism" during the war. Within the U.S.
enclaves on the Caribbean coast, moreover, these concerns were combined with United Fruit's fears that the UNIA would promote militancy
among West Indians and perhaps drive them to race war. In September
1919, the company's general counsel warned Secretary of State Robert
Lansing that if Garvey was not stopped, he "might repeat the French
experience in Haiti."[12] These anxieties only grew when a massive strike
paralyzed the Canal Zone in February 1920. Initially, the predominantly
West Indian strikers looked to the UNIA for help, and many U.S. officials assumed the organization was behind the work stoppage. In reality,
Garvey refused to support the strike, which was soon crushed by U.S. and
Panamanian authorities. Although many West Indians resented Garvey's
stance, the strike's failure, along with rising Hispanic hostility, lent appeal to his message of racial unity. Indeed, by the time Garvey undertook
a fundraising tour of the greater Caribbean in the spring of 1921, the
UNIA's limitations as a vehicle for labor organizing in Central America
were already apparent.[13]

The New Banana Republic

That trend toward divided labor was evident in Honduras, which was rapidly becoming a major exporter of bananas. As in other Central American nations, United Fruit played a central role. In contrast to its monopolies in Costa Rica and Guatemala, however, the firm faced competition in Honduras, particularly from the Vaccaro Brothers (later Standard Fruit) and Samuel Zemurray's Cuyamel Fruit Company—both based in New Orleans. Throughout the 1910s, jockeying among the three firms contributed to the political destabilization of Honduras. In 1917, a land dispute between Cuyamel and United Fruit along the border of Honduras and Guatemala nearly drove the two nations to war, and by the end of the decade the companies were practicing their own form of Dollar Diplomacy in the impoverished country. In August 1919, for example, the Honduran state was forced to ask United Fruit for funds to put down a rebellion. As British Consul Joseph Walter observed, "the Government can have no other source of supply, as they already owe over 600,000 pesos to the Banco Atlántida and the Banco de Comercio, both of which are owned by the Vaccaro Company."[14] This financial leverage enabled the companies to carve up Honduras's Caribbean coast with little state inference. Cuyamel took the western region near Omoa and Puerto Cortes, Vaccaro Brothers the port of La Ceiba and its environs, and United Fruit the lands surrounding the ports of Tela and Puerto Castilla.

United Fruit's new enclaves quickly assumed a familiar form. In 1913, the company brought Victor Cutter from Guatemala to build the new division around Tela, which would be run through a subsidiary, the Tela Railroad Company. As in Guatemala, Cutter ordered improvements to the port, the building of new rail lines, and the clearing of plantations—which he again gave names with frontier resonance, such as "Dakota" and "Montana." He and his colleagues also focused on the recruitment and discipline of labor. Having learned their lesson in Costa Rica and Guatemala, they immediately established a segmented workforce, hiring local Hispanics and Garífuna as well as recruiting British West Indians.[15] In addition to utilizing ethnic and racial divisions, United Fruit depended on Honduran authorities to intimidate and discipline workers, particularly Garífuna and West Indians. The company's practices and power posed problems for British officials. In October 1913, for example, British Consul Jack Armstrong objected to the appointment of a Tela resident named George Mee as British vice consul on the grounds that Mee was employed by the Tela Railroad

Company. Because "many of the abuses of British subjects are committed at the instigation of the Company's employees," Armstrong explained, "Mr. Mee might find it highly embarrassing to protect them against abuse, which would be the main object of his appointment to the post."[16] But West Indians were not the only recipients of abuse. Spanish-speaking laborers who came to the enclave found themselves treated as inferiors in their own country. According to the wife of one United Fruit engineer, Americans routinely "bossed and humiliated" Hispanic "natives," especially in the enclave's early years.[17]

The subordinate position of Spanish-speaking laborers complicated United Fruit officials' relations with Hispanic locals, as the experience of Edward Thornton shows. Like many Americans hired by the firm, the Virginia-born Thornton had previous experience in the U.S. empire. His first job came in 1907 in Cuba, where he helped build railroads for the U.S. sugar industry; and he next worked in the Panama Canal Zone. After brief service in World War I, Thornton accepted a job in Tela and was impressed by what he found there. "Tela is practically a company town," he wrote his mother in October 1919. "The native village which consists of little more [than] a main street with a few stores, lies across a small creek. The American part of the town has everything a man needs except a barber." But despite this familiarity, Thornton found interaction with Hispanics confusing. In a January 1920 letter, he reported:

> Saturday night, Mr. Goodell, the manager, gave a big dance in the Club to General [Ernesto] Alvarado, his staff, and a party of native girls from La Ceiba. . . . Two of the girls were rather good looking, and seemed to be entirely white. However, I have my doubts as the 'tar-brush' has been used quite extensively. If a Honduranian [*sic*] has not kinky hair, and is not darker than a pair of tan shoes he claims to be white. This makes social life rather interesting down here. It is rather pitiful to see the girls put layer after layer of powder on in an effort to seem to have white skin.[18]

Immersed in U.S. imperial culture, he found the racial pretensions of even elite Hispanics absurd.

By the time Thornton wrote, Honduran resentment of the banana firms was already pronounced. Despite the shared experience of corporate racism and domination, however, Spanish-speaking laborers did not make common cause with their black coworkers. This owed much to Hispanic Hondurans' longstanding distrust of Garífuna, which transferred easily to

British West Indians. But it also reflected a labor structure that accentuated racial differences in order to prevent class solidarity. This became apparent during the postwar labor upheavals. By the fall of 1919, amid a heated presidential campaign, Honduran workers were denouncing the banana companies and demanding higher wages; but they were also calling for restrictions on the employment of West Indians. In the short term, their efforts proved successful. In addition to winning wage increases from United Fruit and its competitors, Hispanic workers helped convince the new Honduran president to ban Jamaican immigration in June 1920. In the long run, however, xenophobic rhetoric only deepened the divide among banana workers. As Hispanics came to define black immigration as the main obstacle to their own economic security, West Indians turned away from interracial labor organizing and toward the UNIA and other race-based institutions. By the early 1920s, black and Hispanic workers in Honduras's Caribbean lowlands saw their interests as mutually exclusive.[19]

Monopoly and Labor Segmentation in Costa Rica

United Fruit's policies had a similar impact in Costa Rica. The early 1910s were the golden age of the nation's banana industry. By 1913, United Fruit had made Costa Rica the leading banana exporter in the world, shipping some 11 million stems annually. In contrast to its position in Honduras, moreover, the firm held a monopoly on the Costa Rican banana trade, which it guarded fiercely. This was evident in its treatment of non-company farmers. Despite the expansion of its own farms, United Fruit continued to purchase the bulk of its fruit from independent growers, many of whom were West Indians who had long cultivated small plots. Drawing upon practices from their home islands, these farmers grew a mixture of subsistence crops such as yams and plantains, as well as commercial bananas for sale. With the international banana market booming, however, they increasingly resented the company's control over prices and transportation. As a result, when agents from the upstart Atlantic Fruit Company appeared in the summer of 1912 offering higher prices, many banana farmers embraced it as a welcome alternative. United Fruit's response underscored its power in Costa Rica. Asserting that the farmers were under exclusive contract, the firm obtained a court order to stop them from harvesting and commanded local police to arrest Atlantic Fruit's representatives for "stealing" fruit. This repression in turn brought out festering racial resentments among West Indian farmers, many of whom were former employees of the firm. On 5 July, United Fruit mandador L. W. Merrill reported that Jamaican farmers had recently "walked the streets of Estrada threatening to shoot all the U.F.C. white men" and declaring that "embargoed or not they will cut their fruit and deliver to the Atlantic."[20]

Despite this resistance, United Fruit soon drove Atlantic Fruit from the country and reasserted its authority over non-company farmers. This included aggressive efforts to either evict or force rental contracts on West Indians who lacked title to their lands, whom the firm referred to as "squatters." Although many had farmed their plots for years, even decades, their lack of citizenship and Spanish language skills had prevented them from establishing legal ownership, making them vulnerable to United Fruit. Just one day after the protests in Estrada, for example, General Manager W. E. Mullins ordered Superintendent George P. Chittenden to make a survey of all squatters in his district; soon after, the firm began buying up non-company lands. Mullins summed up this policy in his discussion of a West Indian family that had worked its land for a generation: "D. Kelly and his daughter Dora Kelly claim to have supplementary title, but such can easily be demolished when necessary proceedings are started." A similar fate befell the renters and squatters on land the company acquired from a Costa Rican planter named Joaquín Figula. Because "Mr. Figula is in control of the squatters and negro growers in his locality," Mullins explained, the company now had authority over them. If these farmers wished to stay on their plots, they would not only have to pay rent to United Fruit, but also agree to grow only bananas and sell them only to the company.[21]

Such policies went hand in hand with United Fruit's efforts to strengthen its hold on Costa Rican commerce in general. Although the nation's Pacific railroad remained outside of company control, the importance of Atlantic markets ensured that the vast majority of coffee exports continued to rely on Keith's railroad. In fact, United Fruit's power in Limón province was so complete that even some U.S. officials grew uneasy. In May 1914, the American consul in Puerto Limón, Chester Donaldson, sent a report to the State Department entitled "The Strangulation of Competition and Elimination of Private Planters, by the United Fruit Company." After reviewing the firm's expulsion of Atlantic Fruit, Donaldson warned that United Fruit officials were not only "driving from . . . this Port all other lines of steamers competing for the trade," but "they also mean to dominate all other interests and are using their powerful influence and great wealth to prevent other legitimate enterprises from entering the field."[22] By late

1914, the Wilson administration was considering an anti-trust suit against the company.

In this same period, United Fruit continued to refine its labor control strategies. In response to the Jamaican-led strike of 1910, managers had stepped up recruitment of Central American as well as West Indian workers to meet rising labor needs. The success of this approach became apparent in early 1914, when the company's decision to switch from hourly to task pay for banana loading prompted a work stoppage by West Indians. In response, the company hired Hispanic laborers to take their place. As one U.S. official later explained, "the strike was broken and the task system established on loading by using natives from the interior."[23] Indeed, United Fruit's turn toward labor segmentation was a driving force behind the rising Hispanic migration to Limón province, which would continue into the 1920s and 1930s. With economic prospects declining in many parts of Central America, the relatively high wages of the banana enclave proved attractive to Hispanic workers, particularly those from the Costa Rica's Guanacaste province and neighboring Nicaragua. Equally important, United Fruit's efforts to publicize its sanitation and disease control efforts made employment on the Caribbean coast seem more appealing.

As Hispanic migration to the enclave grew, West Indians began to assume a privileged place in the company's labor hierarchy. In addition to those who served as foremen over Spanish-speaking workers, West Indians held most skilled positions among laborers and routinely earned higher pay. In 1914, pro-company writer Frederick Adams described the structure of this system among the stevedores of Puerto Limón. "On each [platform] are a couple of darkies," he explained, "who pass the bunches [of bananas] down to the team below. At the bottom are Spaniards [Hispanics] who carry the heavy bunches . . . to other Jamaicans, who pack them for the voyage."[24] There were several reasons for black laborers' elevated status. First, nearly all West Indian laborers spoke English, which facilitated communication with American managers. Second, black immigrants tended to be older and more experienced in the banana industry than their Hispanic coworkers. But most important of all was United Fruit's goal of cultivating divisions within its workforce. By placing Hispanic laborers in a position of inferiority to West Indians, the company encouraged Hispanics to direct their daily resentments toward black immigrants. For this same reason, the firm maintained separate housing for Hispanic and West Indian employees, while keeping both groups segregated from white managers and their families.[25]

As in Honduras, the subordinate status of Spanish-speaking workers influenced white Americans' views of Hispanics in general. Prior to the 1910s, United Fruit officials' interactions with Costa Ricans had been confined primarily to light-skinned elites: government officials, coffee planters, and the small number of Costa Rican mandadors and timekeepers. While some company employees had disparaged Costa Ricans in these early years, most seemed to accept their claims to whiteness. With the growing Hispanic migration to the enclave, however, U.S. attitudes became more demeaning. This change stemmed partly from the class and physical appearance of the migrants themselves, who tended to have darker skin than Costa Rican elites. More important, however, were power relations. As white Americans grew accustomed to commanding Hispanic laborers, they became less respectful of Costa Rica itself. By the mid-1910s, company officials routinely informed journalists and travel writers that the firm ruled the country, and such statements invariably influenced written accounts of the country. After his 1912 visit to United Fruit's Costa Rica Division, for example, newspaper editor George Putnam went so far as to claim that in the late nineteenth century Costa Rican leaders had "opposed the construction of railroads" and that United Fruit had "done more for Costa Rica than it ever could or would have done for itself." In a similar vein, Adams insisted that Costa Rica had no seaport or commerce until Keith had arrived to rescue the nation.[26] With this imperial narrative circulating amid Washington's wave of interventions, it is hardly surprising that Costa Rican leaders grew increasingly defensive of their nation's sovereignty and racial identity.

War and Labor Trouble

Although elites in Costa Rica had worried about black immigration for decades, popular xenophobia had previously focused on Asians. By the mid-1910s, however, as Spanish-speakers moved to the banana enclave and noted the presence and apparent privileges of West Indians, many began calling for immigration restrictions on blacks; and a growing number of elite and middle-class nationalists agreed. United Fruit's policies during World War I contributed to these tensions. In response to reduced shipping and the spread of banana disease on its plantations, the firm imposed pay cuts and workforce reductions. Despite the claims of Hispanic workers that only Central Americans were being fired, black workers suffered the largest number of layoffs. By mid-August 1914, British officials estimated there were 1,500 unemployed British West Indians in Puerto Limón. Many hoped to leave, either to enlist in the British army or to seek employment elsewhere, and Costa Rican officials encouraged them. When the Costa Rican minister of agriculture learned that a large number of Jamaicans could not pay the required departure tax, for example, he recommended that the fee be waived.[27] For their part, British officials remained optimistic about the future prospects for West Indians in Costa Rica. In September, Consul F. Nutter Cox observed that they "are well behaved and are treated with consideration by their employers, and by the Costa Rican authorities."[28] Indeed, West Indians did enjoy better treatment from local officials than in Guatemala or Honduras. As the war dragged on, however, anti-black sentiment in Costa Rica continued to grow.

Initially, United Fruit's wartime treatment of independent farmers seemed to open space for common grievances against the company. Shortly after the fighting in Europe broke out, the company halted purchases from non-company growers and raised freight rates on the railroad. Costa Rican and West Indian farmers alike condemned these moves, and nationalists in San José supported them. Newspapers in the capital accused Mullins of using the crisis to bilk Costa Rica, and President Alfredo González Flores soon joined in, calling on United Fruit to either resume its purchases and restore its former rates or face new taxes from the government. Unlike many of his successors, González also seemed sympathetic to black immigrants, a stance that stemmed partly from personal experience. In early 1915, the president was returning to Puerto Limón after inspecting the desperate conditions of the West Indian workers in the company's Sixaola district, near Panama, when heavy seas drove his ship aground near the small settlement of Cahuita. After the mostly West Indian residents rescued and sheltered the president and his party, González granted public land to the community. The episode likely contributed to his reluctance to support the eviction of squatters in Limón province, to the annoyance of United Fruit.[29]

In August 1915, the company brought Victor Cutter from Honduras to replace Mullins, in part to repair its strained relations with San José. Most Costa Rican newspapers welcomed the change, particularly after Cutter announced the resumption of banana purchases. But editorials in Costa Rican newspapers retained their nationalist tone. In October 1915, San José's *El Imparcial* asserted that it was pressure from the González government, not corporate benevolence, that had led United Fruit to change its policies. In doing so, it reminded Cutter and his colleagues that Costa Rica had played a key role in their company's rise. United Fruit had earned millions from the "virgin lands" of the Limón province, the paper noted. "Now that the region has fallen on hard times, this company—which owes its riches, splendid steamships, railroads, hospitals, wireless stations, its very influence to the Atlantic Zone—needs to find a way to lift it up again."[30] While usually couched in appeals for cooperation, such rhetoric hinted at continued resentment toward the company.

Tensions mounted over the next year and a half as González continued to demand changes from United Fruit. The company's relations with the independently minded president worsened with the transfer of Cutter to Jamaica in June 1916.[31] Meanwhile, friction between San José and Washington was also growing, due largely to the U.S. Senate ratification of a revised protectorate treaty with Nicaragua. Claiming that the treaty threatened regional sovereignty, Costa Rica and El Salvador contested it in the Central American Court, which the U.S. government had helped found a decade earlier. When the court ruled against Washington, however, the Wilson administration ignored it, effectively destroying the court. In this context, United Fruit may well have calculated that it could undermine González with little interference from Washington. Over the following months, the company encouraged politicians and military leaders who were plotting the president's overthrow. The coup came in late January 1917 and was led by Minister of War and Navy Federico Tinoco. A longtime politician, Tinoco and his family held large banana estates in Limón province and were heavily in debt to United Fruit. Company officials hoped this financial leverage would give them influence over the new dictator; for his part, Tinoco likely assumed United Fruit could help him gain recognition from Washington. But despite the dogged efforts of company lobbyists and lawyers, among them John Foster Dulles, the Wilson administration stuck with its nonrecognition policy toward unconstitutional regimes and privately scolded United Fruit for its role in the coup.[32]

The company soon worked its way back into Washington's good graces. Following the U.S. entry into the war in April 1917, the firm leased most of its steamships to the U.S. Navy. As a public relations move, it was a masterstroke. At a time when it had reduced need of its fleet, the firm managed to boost its standing with Washington and the American public. Meanwhile, Tinoco tried to bolster his position through other means, including some attempts to harness growing anti-black sentiment. In January 1918, he signed a law requiring immigrants to register with the Costa Rican government. In theory it applied to all foreigners; in practice, it was enforced almost exclusively against West Indians. Although United Fruit officials objected to the law, they were loath to undermine Tinoco, particularly as unrest was growing among its laborers.[33]

The first strike came in Sixaola just a month after the armistice in Europe. Although United Fruit officials blamed the trouble on "Bolshevik" influence, the real issue was wages. Workers in Sixaola had assumed that the firm would restore their previous wage rates once the war had ended, but the company hoped to retain the cuts. Laborers were furious. As one British official explained to a United Fruit manager, the combination of wage reductions and high prices "means that your colored employees had to live half as well . . . as they could afford to live in 1914."[34] When the strike erupted in December 1918, the company responded in its usual fashion, importing Hispanic strikebreakers and calling on local officials to repress the workers. But it also took matter into its own hands. By early 1919, United Fruit officials were engaging in widespread violence against black workers and burning West Indian homes and farm plots. Throughout the bitter strike, Tinoco backed the company, which in turn continued to press Washington to recognize his regime. But while the firm succeeded in breaking the strike, Tinoco fell from power in August 1919.[35]

Contending with the UNIA

Meanwhile, United Fruit attempted to contain labor tensions in the Costa Rica Division itself. In early 1919, as racial violence broke out in Sixaola, talk of a possible strike spread to Limón. But West Indian and Hispanic workers had difficulty finding common ground. While many black laborers were receptive to labor organizing, Hispanic workers tended to view the presence and position of West Indians as one of their grievances against the company, and the prospects for labor solidarity quickly collapsed. It was at this same moment that the UNIA appeared in Costa Rica. In the wake of the Sixaola strike, United Fruit officials worried the new organization would stir up more bitterness between West Indians and white managers. Like U.S. and British officials, they usually framed their concerns in paternalist terms. As General Manager H. S. Blair explained to one British diplomat in June 1919:

> With few notable exceptions, the negro labourer has little initiative,—he
> is an imitator—and must have leadership and guidance. . . . This direction

should be furnished him by his employers or by a responsible government. This responsibility should not be shirked. When it is shirked the negro turns to follow whatever other sort of leadership may offer and here is where he is exposed to all sorts of exploitation which is usually presented to him as some sort of uplift.[36]

At first, company concerns about the UNIA seemed justified, for West Indians did not always interpret Garvey's message as he intended. Frustrated by the collapse of the postwar strikes, many black workers welcomed the organization as a vehicle for labor organizing apart from Hispanic coworkers. As a result, United Fruit managers initially viewed Garvey as an extremist who might bring racial or class conflict. Their anxieties rose in the late summer of 1919, when copies of *Negro World* began circulating in Puerto Limón. Although the firm cooperated with U.S., British, and Costa Rican officials to confiscate the publication, the UNIA continued to spread.[37] In December, George Chittenden, now general manager of the division, reported that "Henrietta Vinton Davis, the international organizer of the Negro Improvement Association, had just landed in Colon [Panama] . . . [and] intended shortly to visit Bocas and Limon." Noting that "the Jamaicans here state openly that her arrival will start a strike," Chittenden wondered if the company should try to keep her out of its enclaves altogether. "We are taking a chance to allow her to land," he observed:

> There is a great difference between our Government allowing such a woman aloose [*sic*] on the Canal Zone, where the presence of 20,000 troops in itself is sufficient to brake any uprising, and our Government allowing such a woman to enter a Central American country inadequately policed, and where the respect for the British Government on the part of the Jamaicans is the only real control that exists over them.

In the event of trouble, the Costa Rican authorities would attempt to restore order, he conceded, but only after "many of both races, African and White, have been killed." In this context, he hoped the U.S. government could be persuaded to "stop her progress through these countries."[38]

In the end, United Fruit had little to fear from the UNIA. To be sure, racial tensions between white managers and West Indians remained, and episodes of black resistance continued to occur.[39] But the company soon realized that the UNIA could serve as a stabilizing rather than radicalizing force. This became apparent when Garvey undertook his 1921

Caribbean tour. The trip had two main purposes: to collect money for the UNIA and Black Star and to reassure local government and corporate officials. Between speaking engagements, he met privately with U.S., British, and Central American officials in order to emphasize his peaceful intent. Coming just two months after a strike by West Indian stevedores in Puerto Limón, Garvey's arrival in Costa Rica in April 1921 raised concerns among company officials. When he offered to meet with them, however, the Northern Railway extended a rare honor, providing the UNIA leader a complimentary ride to San José aboard a car usually reserved for whites. After a conference with President Jiménez, he met with Chittenden, who reported that Garvey expressed his support for the company and emphasized that "he too is an employer of labor, understands our position, is against labor unions, and [is] using his best behavior to get the negro race to work and better themselves through work." For his part, Chittenden was inclined to view Garvey not as a fellow capitalist but as the black employee that he once was. As Chittenden explained to the division manager in Almirante, Panama, where Garvey would travel next, "[I]f you play up to his vanity a little, and talk to him the way you would talk to one of your own laborers with whom you were on extra good terms, you will have no trouble with him."[40]

To the relief of United Fruit officials, Garvey proved true to his word. In Puerto Limón and on various stops along the railroad, he counseled West Indians to avoid labor militancy and invest their money in the UNIA. As Chittenden observed in a cable to Cutter:

> Garvey was the most conservative man of any attending the meetings. He told them they should not fight the United Fruit Company, that the work given them by the [company] meant their bread and butter and that they would not only deserve but receive the same respect as the United Fruit Company, once they had farms, railways, and steamships of their own and showed that they could operate them. He said that in order to operate such an enterprise they must have money and that in order to get money they had to work.[41]

It was the same message Garvey offered black workers in the United States: eschew labor organizing, curry favor with white capitalists, and focus on upward mobility. Although it disappointed many black workers, it was well suited to trends in Limón province. Not only did West Indians enjoy an increasingly privileged position in the company's labor hierarchy, but many were finding success as small business owners in and around Puerto Limón. Alienated by rising Costa Rican hostility, this upwardly mobile West Indian community would form the core of one of the largest and longest lived UNIA divisions in the Hispanic Caribbean. Members remained loyal to Garvey even after the U.S. government convicted him of fraud in 1923 following the collapse of the Black Star line. In November 1925, for example, the UNIA chapter in Estrada, Costa Rica, petitioned President Calvin Coolidge to pardon Garvey, declaring that "we are anxious to have him with us to carry on the great work of negro uplift, and African redemption."[42] As in other Central American nations, however, the organization's growth reflected not only black unity but also the effectiveness of United Fruit's labor control strategies.

Labor Segmentation and Corporate Power in Guatemala

In these same years, similar trends appeared in Guatemala's Caribbean lowlands. Despite the December 1909 uprising, United Fruit continued to view British West Indians as its most reliable workers, and in 1912– 1913 hundreds, perhaps thousands, of them recruited in the Canal Zone arrived at Puerto Barrios aboard company steamers.[43] But they were joined by a growing number of Spanish-speaking workers. Eager to construct a divided workforce and confident in the improving health of its enclave, the company stepped up recruitment of Guatemalan workers in the early 1910s. These efforts caused concern among many Guatemalan elites, who worried the company's high wages would raise labor costs and lure away indebted workers from coffee farms. Not coincidentally, these years brought the first sustained criticism of the company in Guatemalan newspapers. In addition to warnings about the dangerous living and working conditions on United Fruit's plantations, this included the first denunciations of West Indians' supposedly privileged position in the enclave. One revealing editorial appeared in July 1913 in the Guatemala City newspaper *La Campaña*. The writer began by deploring "the appearance of recruiting parties (*pandillas de enganchadores*), hired and paid by the banana men, that roam the Republic recruiting and seducing ignorant people with gold payrolls." But he quickly focused his ire on the growing presence of the "Negro race, true scourge of the nation," which, along with the "blond-haired" managers of United Fruit, was gaining control of the "immense and rich territories of the North [Coast]."[44] Such rhetoric contributed to

ladino distrust of white Americans and black immigrants alike, but it failed
to discourage migration to the Caribbean coast. Indeed, throughout the
early 1910s, *ladino* labor proved critical to United Fruit's efforts to both
expand and divide the workforce of its Guatemala Division, which by the
spring of 1914 boasted thirty banana farms and employed between 4,000
and 5,000 laborers.[45]

As in Costa Rica, World War I forced the company to reduce its operations in Guatemala. Despite its declining payroll, however, the company
continued to refine its system of labor segmentation, above all by recruiting
Spanish-speaking workers. As one Guatemalan official observed in April
1916, although United Fruit had previously hired Jamaicans almost exclusively, it now "accepts and prefers to hire Guatemalans of any reputation,
Salvadorans, Hondurans, from whatever part of Central America."[46] From
the beginning, these Hispanic migrants saw West Indians as their primary
adversaries. Some friction was inevitable regardless of the company's labor
policies, and it bears repeating that white Americans were not the only
practitioners of racial discrimination and social segregation in Guatemala.
Yet, as in Costa Rica, United Fruit was hardly a passive beneficiary of the
divisions that developed in its enclave. The company consciously implemented task and pay differentials, as well as residential segregation, to foment divisions among its laborers; and as in Costa Rica, it placed blacks
above Hispanics in the labor hierarchy. White managers usually justified this
by emphasizing racial differences among the laborers. As Frederick Adams
put it, while Garífuna and West Indians were strong and maintained good
personal hygiene, Hispanics tended to be "dirty in their habits" and had
"very little disease-resisting power."[47]

The subordinate position of Spanish-speaking workers clashed sharply
with the racial assumptions of Hispanic Central Americans, and particularly
Guatemalan *ladinos.* Since the colonial period, blacks and indigenous Maya
had occupied the bottom rungs of Guatemala's social hierarchy, and over
the previous forty years political rhetoric had consistently identified *ladinos*
as the nation's superior racial group. Yet *ladinos* in the banana lands, like
most other Hispanic workers, found themselves positioned below blacks in
the labor hierarchy and expected to show the same sort of social deference
to white managers that *ladinos* themselves demanded of the Maya. By the
1910s, mandadors and timekeepers on company farms were increasingly
open in their disparagement of Hispanics, referring to them as "spigs" and
sometimes "niggers." According of John Williams, "the attitude of the average white employee of the fruit company is one of sneering contempt for

the native of the country. 'Spig' is the epithet applied to all Latin Americans irrespective of their official or social position." The tensions that such attitudes might generate with elite Guatemalans were kept muted, he observed, because "the banana districts are not frequented by any of the upper class people of the country." But like their counterparts in Honduras and Costa Rica, Hispanic laborers in Guatemala regularly encountered discrimination from white managers.[48]

Meanwhile, United Fruit continued to tighten its economic hold on Guatemala itself. As in Costa Rica, the company's power hinged upon control of steamship trade and railroad transportation. In Guatemala, however, this monopoly became far more complete in 1912, when Keith acquired the nation's Pacific rail lines. Shortly after, he merged them with the Northern Railroad to form the new International Railway of Central America (IRCA). In Guatemala, as in Costa Rica, Keith maintained the fiction that his railroad interests were separate from United Fruit, but in reality they cooperated closely. Soon after its formation, the IRCA established preferential shipping rates that channeled Guatemalan coffee exports toward Puerto Barrios. This shift drove the Pacific Mail Steamship Company out of business and gave United Fruit a virtual monopoly over the coffee as well as the banana trade. This consolidation of corporate power worried many Guatemalan officials, including President Estrada Cabrera. Despite the dictator's longstanding cooperation with United Fruit, he ordered Guatemalan officials to step up their monitoring and regulation of the firm's operations. Annoyed by this interference, United Fruit turned to the U.S. government in early 1914. Despite its misgivings toward the company, the Wilson administration dispatched General George W. Davis—the former colonial governor of the Philippines, Puerto Rico, and the Canal Zone—to remind Estrada Cabrera of his "obligations" to United Fruit.[49]

It was in this context of growing tensions with the company that the May 1914 Quiriguá incident occurred. On the surface, Esson's murder and the Jamaicans' retaliation might seem an isolated affair. During his investigation, British Vice Consul Haggard heard rumors that the attack had resulted from a simple gambling dispute. In the end, however, he attributed the violence to the bitter tensions between West Indians and the "natives," and while he acknowledged the prevalence of anti-black sentiment in Guatemala, he placed the blame primarily on Jamaican immigrants, who tended to be "quarrelsome by temperament and overbearing in their attitude toward their Guatemalan fellow-workman."[50] Missing from Haggard's analysis was the corporate labor structure that encouraged West Indians to be "overbearing." Black employees in the enclave almost invariably held positions above Hispanic coworkers, often serving as their foremen. In addition to subverting the established racial hierarchy in Guatemala, this labor system afforded West Indians higher pay, and hence greater resources, which enhanced their appeal to *ladino* women. Haggard's superior, British Consul Albon Young, noted this trend in his report on the Quiriguá incident. Although Guatemalan authorities had justified their sweeping arrests of black workers in part by claiming West Indians frequently raped *ladino* women, Young observed that "it is not the violation of women that rankles but the readiness with which the native women leave their kin and go to live with the negroes." Like Haggard, Young did not blame United Fruit for these racial tensions. But he did add, suggestively, that the company was "prone in cases of this sort to wash its hands of its negro employees in order to avoid giving displeasure to the Government."[51]

Immigration Restrictions and Official Repression

By mid-1914, that displeasure was evident. Although anti-black xenophobia had a long history in Guatemala, the Quiriguá incident marked a watershed in the state's treatment of West Indians. News of the Jamaicans' retaliation against Hispanic residents galvanized many *ladinos* against black immigrants. Estrada Cabrera seized upon the issue to bolster his nationalist credibility. On 14 May, the semi-official Guatemala City newspaper *La República* warned that "dark bands of insolent negroes" in United Fruit's enclave had been able to "plunder, assassinate, and violate with impunity." In contrast to British officials in Guatemala, moreover, the newspaper attributed the violence directly to the company's labor structure. Although "thousands of natives work in the plantations giving full satisfaction to overseers and contractors," it observed, the firm claimed Guatemalans were "incapable of carrying out the work" in order to justify hiring West Indians, who were paid higher wages and encouraged to consider themselves superior to *ladinos*. The only solution, it implied, was to restrict black immigration.[52]

Over the following months, the Guatemalan government made moves to do just that. In August, it announced that foreigners arriving in Guatemala would be required to deposit $500 with customs officials. United Fruit protested vigorously, noting that the law would cripple its operations. In response, Guatemalan officials reduced the requirement to $100 and privately assured company officials that it would be enforced only against black immigrants. Nevertheless, it remained a serious threat to the firm's labor segmentation system, for the $100 deposit was beyond the means of most West Indian workers. After tense discussions with United Fruit and U.S. officials, Estrada Cabrera issued a new decree in November 1914 that reduced the deposit to $50 and made it applicable only to "colored" immigrants. Although the new amount was less prohibitive, the law's passage underscored the growing determination of the Guatemalan state to regulate immigration.[53] By this time, the economic downturn caused by World War I, along with United Fruit's layoffs and pay cuts, had heightened racial tensions in United Fruit's enclave. With the number of banana jobs shrinking, Hispanic workers demanded that "men of the homeland" receive preference from the company.[54]

Meanwhile, Guatemalan authorities stepped up their harassment of West Indians, particularly those who lived with Hispanic women. Within weeks of the Quiriguá incident, local *comandantes* began fining *ladino* women who cohabited with United Fruit's black workers. Those who could not pay often found themselves grinding corn for the garrisons. It was a deeply symbolic punishment. The daily grinding of corn for *tortillas* was one of the most onerous, time-consuming, and gendered tasks in Guatemalan society. Although garrison soldiers in the banana enclave were often paid too little to buy adequate food, they shunned the "women's work" of making their own *tortillas*. Like other *ladino* men, moreover, they resented the sight of Guatemalan women performing such labor in the homes of United Fruit's better paid West Indian workers. By fining and extracting such labor from *ladinas* who had relations with blacks, Guatemalan authorities aimed to restore the proper racial and gendered order. In their correspondence, they described all such women, whether common-law wives of West Indians or openly practicing prostitutes, as "women of bad conduct."[55]

The most notorious enforcer of this policy was Cornelio Ortega. As the *comandante* at Quiriguá, Ortega had the responsibility of keeping order among United Fruit's divided workers in the wake of the Quiriguá incident. Like many *ladino* men, he resented the privileged position of West Indians on the company's farms, and particularly their access to Hispanic women. The most chilling example of his practices came in the case of James White, a thirty-six-year-old Jamaican employee at United Fruit's Maya farm. According to his later deposition, White had brought a *ladina* named María Exaltación Rivera to live with him in March 1915. When the couple arrived in Quiriguá, however, Guatemalan soldiers marched them to the local garrison, where Ortega explained that "by the order of the President every black that has a *ladina* must pay ten pesos gold." White convinced the *comandante* to take nine, paid him, and assumed the matter closed. The following May, however, while White was away from home, Ortega again detained Rivera. He and two soldiers loaded her onto a small rail engine and headed for the garrison. When White learned of the abduction, he went to Quiriguá to await their arrival. As the rail car came into sight, however, he realized it was on a collision course with a train. Amid White's frantic warnings, Ortega and his men leapt from the car, leaving Rivera to be "torn to pieces" in the collision.[56]

White's troubles were not over. When he confronted Ortega, the *comandante* threw the grief-stricken man in jail. Three days later he made White an offer. Acknowledging that Rivera's death "went against me," Ortega declared, "I'm going to give you one of these women I have milling corn here and we'll leave it at that." White apparently agreed. The following November, however, when Ortega fined him yet again for living with a *ladina,* White sought help. At first, he went to United Fruit officials, who showed little sympathy. Finally, in desperation, he appealed directly to Estrada Cabrera himself, who ordered an investigation of Ortega. Initially, the *comandante* denied charging West Indians who had *ladina* wives or domestic partners—whom he referred to not only as "women of bad conduct" but also as *"negreras"* ("women who group with blacks"). But he then reversed himself, claiming "Jamaicans did not like him because he employed prostituted women, who sold themselves, in the fields or farms of the United Fruit Company's Quirigua Division." While admitting he lacked authorization for this policy, Ortega maintained that it was necessary to "keep order"—by which he likely meant keeping blacks cowed. Although Ortega was removed from his post and jailed for several months, many *ladino* men sympathized with his objectives, and other *comandantes* continued their efforts to separate West Indians from Guatemalan women.[57]

At times, harassment by local officials intersected directly with United Fruit's labor hierarchy. This was evident in the case of Jamaican James Dempster, a foreman on the Dartmouth farm. In February 1917, Juan Fajardo, the *comandante* at Dartmouth, accused Dempster of "disobedience and offenses to the authorities." According to Fajardo, the trouble began when he had tried to arrest another Jamaican, Samuel Cooper, on the Dartmouth farm. Fearing resistance, he asked three *ladino* laborers to assist him. Although the men were willing to help, Dempster, their foreman, forbade them; and when three went anyway, he fired them. In response, Fajardo arrested Dempster along with Cooper.[58] In the investigation that followed, however, a more complex picture emerged. Days before, Fajardo had stolen wooden planks that Cooper had been making as part of his duties for the company. After Cooper recovered them from Fajardo's home, the enraged *comandante* set out to arrest him. It was at that point that he encountered resistance from Dempster, who knew about the stolen planks. For assistance, Fajardo had then turned to the farm's *ladino* laborers. Confronted with his misdeeds, Fajardo, like Ortega, turned to racially charged language sure to resonate with higher officials. Claiming that Dempster's defiance "showed that the blacks do not want to be governed by the authorities," he called on the investigators to "impress respect [for] justice upon the black race, which views with such indifference, and even makes a joke of, our laws." After the full story came to light, both Dempster and Cooper were freed.[59]

In other instances, United Fruit itself instigated the actions of Guatemalan officials. This was especially common in cases of eviction. Because most workers lived in company housing, the firm called upon local officials to remove employees who had quit or been fired. This combination of corporate power and *ladino* enforcement could have a devastating impact on West Indians' lives. One example was that of Jamaican Hubert Parkes and his wife, who in September 1918 were planning to return to Jamaica with over $1,300 in cash, including their own savings and those of friends. After Parkes quit his job with United Fruit, however, company officials ordered him evicted from his home. As Vice Consul Edward Reed reported, because Parkes had "all of his personal property in the house, and some fowls to dispose of," he "was not in a position to leave the house in a moment[']s notice." The next morning, while Parkes and his wife were away from home on errands, Guatemala soldiers under company orders threw their possessions out of their house, and in the process made off with their $1,300.[60]

Although United Fruit bore some responsibility for such abuses, company managers understood that the increasingly anti-black stance of Guatemalan officials presented a long-term threat to their labor system. While the firm welcomed the assistance of local authorities in maintaining order, it worried that state harassment, along with tightening immigration restrictions, would limit its access to West Indian workers. In June 1919, for example, Cutter's successor, G. M. Shaw, complained to Governor Monzón that unless the *comandante* of Morales halted his abuses, West Indian workers "will abandon the locale to look for work in some other place where they can enjoy their rights."[61] That may very well have been what local officials had in mind.

Labor Upheaval and the 1920 Revolution

Despite these tensions, glimpses of solidarity between West Indian and Hispanic workers did appear during the labor upheaval that followed World War I. Regardless of their diverse origins, all of United Fruit's laborers resented the wartime pay cuts, and this shared grievance allowed for some interracial solidarity. In January 1915, West Indian and Hispanic stevedores briefly cooperated in a work stoppage in Puerto Barrios, and such unity appeared on a larger scale after the war.[62] In December 1918, the same month the strike in Sixaola began, United Fruit's dock workers in Guatemala declared another stoppage. According to Reed, because "all previous strikes at Puerto Barrios and on the [railroad] had been made by Jamaicans," Governor Luis Monzón assumed West Indians were to blame and asked the British vice consul to accompany him on a boat from Livingston. When the two men arrived at Puerto Barrios, however, they discovered that while black workers were cooperating with the stoppage, it had been "brought about by the natives and was being managed by them." Several West Indians assured Reed that the *ladinos* had coerced them, but he concluded that "the Jamaicans and Caribs sympathized with the strikers."[63]

Even as United Fruit's laborers grew more restive, Estrada Cabrera was losing his grip on power. In late 1917, a major earthquake had struck Guatemala City, followed by the arrival of the worldwide influenza epidemic in 1918–1919. The dictator's inept handling of these crises provoked popular outrage. By late 1919, a coalition of middle-class professionals, religious reformers, and labor leaders had formed the Unionist Party, which called for Estrada Cabrera's overthrow and the formation of a new Central American federation. For their part, both United Fruit and the U.S. government generally opposed the Unionists. Although some American officials sympathized with the rebels, the Wilson administration remained opposed to political change outside of the electoral process, which presented problems for the Unionists, because Estrada Cabrera did not allow elections. The dictator also attempted to use the anxiety surrounding the Red Scare to delegitimize his opponents. Urged on by United Fruit, he denounced those opposing him as Bolsheviks and proposed legislation that would outlaw the Unionist Party. In the face of massive popular demonstrations in March 1920, however, Guatemala's National Assembly refused to approve the measure.[64]

Meanwhile, most of United Fruit's workers threw their support behind the Unionists. Estrada Cabrera's close relationship with the company made

it a natural alliance. In early April 1920, as Unionists clashed with government forces in Livingston, members of the Railroad Workers' League
initiated a strike that shut down the railroad in Izabal province. Supported
by United Fruit's dock workers and many of its farm laborers, the work
stoppage disrupted Guatemala's international commerce, further weakening Estrada Cabrera. Under the pretext of protecting American property
and lives, Washington dispatched the USS *Niagara* from Panama to Puerto
Barrios. But this limited intervention failed to deter the Unionists, who
took power on 15 April.[65]

Bereft of its friendly dictator, United Fruit struggled to end the strike.
As it had so often before, it turned to racial division, pressuring West Indian
workers to return to work. But most black employees opted for solidarity
with their *ladino* coworkers. For many, this was likely a matter of expedi-
ency. With Unionists and their supporters voicing longstanding grievances
against the company and its support of Estrada Cabrera, the political and
personal dangers of breaking the strike were clear. But many black employees likely sympathized with the demands of their Hispanic coworkers,
and the strike enjoyed broad support within the West Indian community.
This included the local division of the UNIA, which had been formed in
February 1920 by Barbadian lawyer Clifford Bourne and other prominent
West Indians in Puerto Barrios.[66] As in Costa Rica, United Fruit asked its
host state for help repressing the UNIA, but Estrada Cabrera was too consumed with his own political survival. By the time of the April 1920 strike,
the UNIA's division in Puerto Barrios had grown to 250 members and
inspired the formation of new chapters in Morales and Los Amates. And
while Garvey himself discouraged interracial labor organizing, the local
chapters helped fund the strikers. By May, United Fruit had given in to
most of the workers' wage demands.

Although several factors had contributed to Estrada Cabrera's overthrow
and the strike's success, West Indians in Puerto Barrios were justifiably
proud of their role in these events. When Bourne attended the UNIA convention in New York City the following August, he could hardly contain
his enthusiasm. Addressing his colleagues in Madison Square Garden, he
declared:

> When we started our association, the United Fruit Company, a company
> that has tried to down everything done by the Negro, and especially the
> Black Star Line, tried to get the President of the Republic, Manuel Estrada
> Cabrera, to forbid us from having our meetings. But [I] told him he could

not stop us. I told him: "you may stop us temporarily, but we are going to be conquerors in the end."

At first, the firm had refused to bow to laborers' demands, he recalled. But "when the white man saw that we were determined not to be led by him, the manager of the company gave the men a 100 per cent raise."[67]

Indeed, on the surface, the events of 1920 seem to indicate a failure of United Fruit's labor control strategies. Throughout the 1910s, the company had carefully cultivated a system of labor segmentation that hinged primarily on the elevation and isolation of West Indian employees within the larger workforce. During the strike, however, black employees had sided with Hispanic coworkers against United Fruit and in the process helped topple its most pliant ally. Yet, the 1920 revolution represented only a temporary pause on the path to racial division. Because Estrada Cabrera had so completely alienated Guatemalans and black immigrants alike, and because the company was so closely associated with his rule, most West Indians willingly cooperated with *ladino* strikers whose objectives they shared. But this broad opposition to dictatorship and wartime wage cuts only briefly submerged the racial tensions that had come to define life in United Fruit's enclave. Black leaders such as Bourne may have hoped that the strike's success would secure the acceptance of West Indians in Guatemala, but it would soon become apparent that the Unionist triumph had opened the door to anti-black hostility on a national level.

Between 1912 and 1921, the American empire in the broader Caribbean experienced profound transformations. Even as the U.S. government completed the Panama Canal and undertook a series of military interventions and occupations, United Fruit rapidly expanded its operations in Central America while developing strategies to prevent the labor resistance that had shaken its enclaves in 1909–1910. In both Costa Rica and Guatemala, as well as in its new enclaves in Honduras, this resulted in the increased hiring of Hispanic workers as well as the continued recruitment of West Indians. In order to prevent class solidarity, the company implemented a system of labor segmentation that aimed to accentuate racial and cultural tensions between Spanish-speaking laborers and English-speaking blacks. But although this strategy succeeded in dividing the company's workforce, the elevated position of West Indians in the labor hierarchy brought Hispanic calls for immigration restriction.

These tensions only grew during World War I, as the company laid off workers and slashed wages. By the late 1910s, hostility toward West Indians was on the rise throughout the Hispanic Caribbean, and Central American leaders sought to shore up their nationalist credibility by adopting anti-black policies. Confronted with surging xenophobia, many West Indians shunned interracial labor organizing in favor of racial unity, particularly through membership in Garvey's UNIA. The postwar strikes of 1919–1920 brought some cooperation between black and Hispanic workers in efforts to reverse United Fruit's wartime pay reductions, but the underlying divisions remained. The firm's labor policies encouraged Central American elites and workers alike to associate West Indian immigration with the threat of U.S. domination. In the following years, amid rising anti-imperialist sentiment throughout the region, these labor divisions and xenophobic currents would generate a powerful wave of racial nationalism.

Part III

IMPERIAL TRANSITIONS

Chapter 5

The Rise of Hispanic Nationalism, 1921–1929

On 13 July 1924, a local doctor and politician named Girón Aguilar rose before a gathering of Central American workers in Trujillo, Honduras, to denounce the presence of black immigrants in the surrounding banana enclave. Trouble had been brewing for some time. Beginning in 1923, the Truxillo Railroad Company, United Fruit's local subsidiary, had offered West Indians free passage to the nearby company town of Puerto Castilla, and over the following months hundreds had arrived, many of them fleeing state harassment in neighboring Guatemala. According to U.S. Vice Consul Willard Beaulac, several weeks before Girón Aguilar's speech, a Jamaican watchman had shot and killed a Hispanic local seen "prowling" around a warehouse, and, soon after, a rash of plantation fires prompted the firm to lay off hundreds of workers. "With several thousand negroes still employed by the company and a large number of natives without work," Beaulac explained, "the feeling against the negroes was raised to a high pitch." Girón Aguilar sought to exploit that hostility. Positioning himself as both an "anti-American agitator" and spokesman of an "anti-negro movement," he called upon "all loyal Hondurans to unite to expel the negroes from the country." Nor should they be squeamish about acts of racial violence in a U.S. enclave; after all, he announced, "in one state in the United States thirty-five negroes had been lynched in one year." Reminding them that there were forty-eight states in all, he asked his listeners to "draw [their] own inference."[1]

They did. The following morning, fliers appeared around Puerto Castilla. One, signed by the North Coast National Labor Party, warned "all negroes residing at the North coast of Honduras to lea[v]e the co[u]ntry i[m]mediately under the penalty of death." Another, depicting a graveyard, announced, "Negroes, you can receive free passage to this field—simply get in touch with any Latin American."[2] As the early shift began, angry Hispanic workers confronted Barney Ness, the company's superintendent of construction. "The mob spirit was not one of a strike," Ness reported, "as there was no demand from the men to me for either betterment of working conditions or increase of pay." Rather, their sole demand was that the company "discharge the negro from service, [and] deport him out of the country"; if the company refused, they threatened to "eliminate the negro population." The exchange was punctuated, he recalled, by exclamations of "Let's kill the negroes" and "Chop their heads off" as well as references to an anti-black strike the previous year in Puerto Barrios, Guatemala.[3] Tensions mounted that night, when the strikers stole a company train and drove through the banana plantations recruiting Hispanic workers and terrorizing West Indians. As Jamaican James Soule recalled, at about 1 a.m. "a train carrying several hundred natives descended and notified the negroes living at Lerida farm, numbering about thirty, that if they had not left the farm by the time the train returned on its way to Puerto Castilla they . . . would kill the negroes." Soule and his pregnant wife managed to hide in the bushes until the train departed, but their troubles were not over. At dawn, twelve soldiers from a nearby garrison stormed into their home warning Soule to leave or "they would kill [me]."[4]

By this time, news of the danger had reached Puerto Castilla. At 7 a.m. on 15 July, Beaulac cabled Washington that "three hundred strikers are on their way to Puerto Castilla with the avowed purpose of expelling all foreign negroes from the city" and observed that the Honduran government "is taking no action and apparently sympathizes with the strikers." Fearing a racial massacre, United Fruit loaded nearly 1,000 West Indian men, women, and children onto a ship in the harbor. In response to pressure from both Beaulac and the company, local troops prevented the train from entering the city, but assaults against black workers continued. For their part, many West Indians accused the company of "false promises" about their role in Honduras and demanded passage out of the country.[5] Beaulac sympathized with them. Emphasizing that "British negroes employed by the fruit companies are traditionally steady dependable workers, while natives can not, as a rule, be depended upon to stay at work," he warned that "an exodus of negroes would compel [the] company practically to cease operations."[6] Over the following days, the turmoil died down, but Hispanic workers and nationalists continued their calls for the expulsion of West Indians.

The events at Puerto Castilla reflected a critical development in United Fruit's enclaves. Labor upheaval was, of course, nothing new for the firm. In contrast to the strikes that shook its Central American divisions in earlier years, however, worker militancy in the 1920s was confined largely to Spanish-speaking workers, who increasingly framed their demands in terms of Hispanic nationalism. This trend was closely tied to broader regional changes. The 1920s brought a surge of nationalist sentiment throughout Latin America, which eventually spurred the U.S. government to end most of its military occupations in the Hispanic Caribbean. But in Central America, criticism of U.S. "imperialism" also extended to United Fruit. Hispanic workers resented their high-handed treatment by white American managers and denounced the firm's apparent favoritism toward British West Indians. For their part, Central American leaders and middle-class nationalists increasingly viewed black immigration as inseparable from the problem of U.S. domination. By the mid-1920s, amid the wave of immigration restrictions in the United States and throughout the hemisphere, the Central American states made their push to safeguard national identity and sovereignty by restricting West Indian immigration.

This was certainly true of Costa Rica and Guatemala. During the 1920s, anti-imperialist sentiment mounted in both countries. Inspired by nationalists elsewhere in Latin America, including Nicaraguan rebel Augusto Sandino, Costa Rican and Guatemalan nationalists aimed much of their criticism at Washington. But they also targeted United Fruit, calling for an end to the company's control over their nations' commerce and infrastructure. Meanwhile, anger was building among the United Fruit's Hispanic workers, who found themselves subordinated to West Indian immigrants and denigrated as "natives" and "spigs" by American managers. Despite hailing from a number of countries, Spanish-speaking laborers found common ground in their resentment of the company and West Indian coworkers. For their part, many elite and middle-class nationalists in Costa Rica and Guatemala sympathized with the grievances of Hispanic banana workers but hoped to limit labor militancy. In this context, black immigrants became tempting targets for politicians who sought to burnish their nationalist credentials while avoiding radical labor reform or direct confrontation with

United Fruit. Paradoxically, then, although the number of black immigrants employed in the Costa Rican and Guatemalan banana industries declined markedly in the 1920s, West Indians came under increased attack as symbols of "Yankee imperialism" and racial degradation. United Fruit had not created this anti-black sentiment, to be sure; but the firm's labor strategies had helped draw out the most virulent strands of racial nativism. And just as the U.S. government was forced to alter its policies in response to anti-imperialist sentiment, United Fruit found it impossible to ignore the Hispanic nationalism that now threatened the order and autonomy of its enclaves.

Currents of Nationalism

The nationalism that swept Central America in the 1920s was a complex phenomenon. On the surface, much of it focused on Washington's policies. As residents of the region grew ever more resentful of the U.S. government's interventions, particularly in Nicaragua, many looked to a renewed Central American union as a safeguard for regional sovereignty. By 1921, Unionists had come to power in Costa Rica, Guatemala, El Salvador, and Honduras, and the latter three briefly formed a federation in 1921. Although these efforts soon faltered, anti-imperialist sentiment remained strong. During the 1923 inter-American conference in Santiago, Chile, for example, Central American delegates figured prominently in efforts to pass several nonintervention resolutions. Although the U.S. government managed to defuse some of this anger by ending its occupations of eastern Cuba, the Dominican Republic, and Nicaragua by 1925, anti-American sentiment was not limited to Washington's actions. By the 1920s, the Latin American definition of Yankee imperialism had expanded to include financial and corporate domination. In eyes of many Central Americans, United Fruit and other U.S. businesses were an integral part of an American empire that aimed to subordinate Hispanic peoples; and their demands included calls for economic and racial, as well as political, self-determination.[7]

Central American nationalists drew inspiration and support from the Mexican Revolution. In 1917, following two U.S. military incursions, Mexico had adopted a radical constitution that called for the nationalization of all subsoil resources, including the vast petroleum and mining deposits owned by U.S. firms. Over the following years, even as Washington pressed Mexican leaders to reverse the law, Mexico extended its influence into Central America. This came in the form of subsidies for anti-imperialist and pro-labor activists and newspapers as well as a new racial ideology that promoted Hispanic nationalism. At the forefront of this effort was Mexico's minister of education, José Vasconcelos. Inverting a Western racial hierarchy that had long denigrated Latin Americans as mongrel, Vasconcelos argued that the historical mixture of Spanish conquerors and indigenous peoples had produced superior peoples and societies. Although it left little space for "pure" Indians or people of African descent in Hispanic identity, this celebration of *mestizos* appealed to nationalists throughout Latin America, many of whom coupled their newfound racial pride with denunciations of Washington. These included Peruvian dissident Víctor Raúl Haya de la Torre, who called on Latin Americans to embrace their "Indo-American" background and became a vocal critic of U.S. imperialism. Such rhetoric powerfully influenced Central American nationalists, among them Nicaraguan rebel Augusto Sandino.[8]

Sandino's life illustrated the transnational currents that shaped Hispanic nationalism in Central America. Born an illegitimate son of an elite landowner in 1895, Sandino had come of age during the first American occupation of Nicaragua, and like Marcus Garvey he had extensive encounters with the U.S. empire, initially in the form of private enterprise. In the early 1920s, he worked as a mechanic for a number of U.S. firms, including the Vaccaro Brothers in Honduras, United Fruit in Guatemala, and a subsidiary of Standard Oil in the Mexican oil port of Tampico. Over the course of his travels, Sandino met workers and nationalists from throughout Central America and Mexico. He also witnessed the close ties between corporate and government power that defined what he called the "Yankee empire." He was in Tampico in early 1924, for example, when a strike by local workers prompted the landing of U.S. warships, and he was there in December 1925, when the Mexican government began the process of nationalizing its oil resources. Immersed in these revolutionary tides, Sandino imbibed both the radical critiques of American power and the racial ideology of Mexican nationalism.[9]

He drew upon both in his subsequent struggle against the United States. In late 1926, U.S. Marines reoccupied Nicaragua, igniting a firestorm of criticism throughout Latin America. At the time, Sandino was working for an American mining company near the Honduran border, but he soon joined the Liberal Party's war against the occupation. Following the surrender of other Liberal commanders, he assumed leadership of the struggle. Making astute use of interviews and propaganda, he portrayed the conflict not simply as Nicaragua's fight but as the front line of the "Indo-Hispanic" race's struggle against U.S. aggression. Latin American nationalists responded enthusiastically, and by late 1927 Sandino's war had become a cause célèbre throughout the hemisphere. The breadth of anti-American sentiment became apparent in January 1928 at an inter-American conference in Havana, where U.S. delegates barely managed to scuttle an embarrassing resolution condemning intervention in other nations' affairs.[10]

It was no coincidence that these same years brought an aggressive push by nationalists in the Hispanic Caribbean to restrict U.S. employment of black immigrants. Perhaps the most striking example was the very country that hosted the 1928 conference. By the early 1920s, some 150,000 black immigrants resided in Cuba, the vast majority of them either British West Indians or Haitians. With the postwar slump in sugar prices, Cuban workers accused these immigrants of undercutting local labor, and many elites joined the chorus. In late 1922, the Havana-based *Heraldo de Cuba* denounced Jamaicans for living "in a perpetual holiday" in which they "reduce their necessities to a minimum" and "neither work, nor produce, nor consume."[11] As nativist sentiment grew, black immigrants found themselves trapped between the hostility of Cuban coworkers and the demands of American employers. During a strike in late 1924, for example, Jamaican Lucas Samuel Lugg recalled that when he reported to work for the Warner Sugar Company, he was "threaten[ed] by the Cubans that if I should . . . break the strike I would lose my life." But when the frightened man left his post, Warner Sugar fired him.[12] Indeed, U.S. firms in Cuba seemed little concerned with hostility toward their black immigrant employees. According to British Consul T. J. Morris, Americans thought only of "the effect the prohibition of labour from Jamaica would have on American sugar estates in Cuba" and the possibilities of acquiring workers from other colonies. For their part, Cuban politicians sought to exploit this racial xenophobia. Faced with growing domestic opposition and criticism of his close ties to U.S. interests, dictator Gerardo Machado used anti-black rhetoric to shore up his regime, and in the months after the January 1928 conference he deported thousands of Jamaicans and Haitians.[13]

Similar tensions lay behind nationalist sentiment in Honduras. As in other nations throughout the region, denunciations of West Indians preceded the 1920s. In July 1916, for example, newspaper owner Froylan Turcios, a future ally of Sandino, had published several editorials attacking West Indians as "unnecessary immigrants" who threatened to dilute the country's racial character. But in the 1920s, these rhetorical attacks took on an increasingly nationalist tone. In 1921, the government passed new labor legislation designed to deter black immigration. As one Honduran official explained, the law aimed to protect local workers from "the competition of the colored population that comes to offer itself for inferior salaries and in depressive conditions."[14] With the influx of West Indians into Puerto Castilla, hostility on the ground only grew, especially among Hispanic workers who found themselves working under black immigrants. In October 1922, for example, a Hispanic laborer named Trinidad Lira beheaded and mutilated his Jamaican foreman, Herbert Forbes, on United Fruit's Cayo farm. Although Lira's identity was common knowledge, Honduran officials in Trujillo waited nearly a year to arrest him, and they did so only in response to pressure from the British government.[15]

That official reluctance reflected broader trends. By the early 1920s, Honduran elites had realized they could tap into anti-black xenophobia for political purposes. In August 1923, the newspaper *El Precursor,* based in Trujillo, printed an editorial entitled "The Negro Problem." Claiming that "The negro in this region . . . is nothing less than the immediate superior of the native," it complained that "[if] a Honduran and a negro request employment together, the negro is attended to first, and if there is room for the compatriot he is made to labor under the orders of the negro." Declaring that black privilege and "insolence" had "provoked the indignation of the people and aroused national sentiment," it called on West Indians to leave the country. During the contentious presidential election that followed, General Tiburcio Carías ran an openly anti-black campaign, and following his electoral defeat he launched a rebellion that quickly spread to the Caribbean lowlands. Fearing racial violence and damage to American property, Washington sent marines to occupy La Ceiba in early 1924 and brokered a deal to keep Carías out of power. But anger against West Indians continued to grow over the following months, contributing to the Puerto Castilla uprising. Over the following years, rhetorical attacks on West Indians continued to play a key role in Honduran politics, and in 1929 the Liberal government banned black immigration altogether.[16]

West Indians faced similar hostility in Panama. Following a wave of layoffs in the Canal Zone in the early 1920s, thousands of black laborers made their way to Colón and Panama City, where they faced frequent harassment from local officials.[17] By the mid-1920s, many had found work with United Fruit, both in Bocas del Toro and in its new division in Chiriquí province. But they faced bitter denunciations from Panamanian workers and nationalists, who called for such jobs to be reserved to Panamanian citizens. In late 1926, Panama's national assembly responded by banning the immigration of non-Spanish-speaking blacks and requiring that at least 75 percent of the employees of all businesses be Panamanian. Likely modeled on similar legislation passed earlier that year in Guatemala, the 75 percent rule threatened the operations of American firms in Panama. As U.S. diplomat John G. South warned, laws to restrict West Indian immigration would "seriously hinder such new development work as the establishment of banana plantations by the United Fruit Company in the Chiriqui region and other agricultural and mining enterprises." Echoing Beaulac's earlier observations in Honduras, South observed that "it would be extremely difficult for them to find enough native laborers to make up the required proportion" as the "native Panaman[ian] is considered a less efficient and less steady worker than the West Indian." In the end, the legislation had little effect on U.S. interests: the Panamanian government lacked jurisdiction over labor policy in the Canal Zone, and U.S. officials convinced reluctant Panamanian negotiators to exempt United Fruit from the law's requirements. Nevertheless, hostility toward black immigrants increasingly threatened the firm's system of labor segmentation.[18]

Fordism, United Fruit Style

Hispanic nationalism was only one of several challenges that United Fruit confronted in the 1920s. At first glance, the decade seemed to bring the company unprecedented success. As it recovered from the wartime downturn, it expanded its plantations, merchant fleet, and market control. Utilizing new technologies, it also pushed to mechanize and streamline its operations, reducing labor costs while delivering bananas ever more cheaply to American consumers. But the firm also faced a range of threats. By the 1920s, a soil-borne plant pathogen known as "Panama disease" had already forced the company to shift much of its operations in Panama from Bocas del Toro to the nation's Pacific coast, and it was spreading to other enclaves.[19] At the same time, rising nativism in Central America increasingly threatened the company's access to West Indian workers. More broadly, Latin American nationalists, and a small but growing number of Americans, were denouncing the company as an "imperialistic" monopoly that exploited its host nations.

United Fruit's response to this criticism revealed its immersion in U.S. corporate and imperial culture. Like many American businesses in the 1920s, the firm followed Henry Ford's lead in adopting and publicizing "corporate welfare" policies, which aimed to cultivate worker loyalty and discourage labor organizing. United Fruit's version of Fordism included improved housing and medical care for laborers, better stocked company commissaries, and an increase in the civic and leisure activities available in its tropical divisions.[20] It was in these same years, ironically, that Ford himself tried to replicate United Fruit's success by establishing a rubber enclave in Brazil, dubbed "Fordlandia." Despite promising to "uplift" Brazilian laborers in the same way he believed he had workers in Detroit, Ford faced the unfamiliar challenges of tropical agriculture and foreign labor control, and by the early 1930s disease in his rubber trees and worker resistance had torpedoed his plans.[21]

Even as Ford tried to build an overseas empire, United Fruit set out to convince its detractors that it wasn't one. Indeed, the 1920s brought a key shift in the company's approach to public relations. Rather than portray itself as a corporate expression of white colonial rule, as it had so often in its earlier years, United Fruit increasingly presented itself as a "progressive" force that fostered stability and raised living standards throughout the Hispanic Caribbean. As one of the company's rising stars, Victor Cutter played a key role in this effort. Working out of the Boston headquarters in the early 1920s, Cutter courted the good will of U.S. officials and journalists, often by facilitating their travel to company enclaves. Such efforts helped shape public perceptions of the firm. After visiting his son in Honduras, for example, Federal Appellate Judge George W. Anderson could scarcely contain his enthusiasm. In a September 1922 letter to Cutter, he observed that he had never seen a group of "so generally thoroughbreds as the men I met with your Company," and he went on to commend United Fruit for "doing a great work of civilization, and without [the] faults of exploitation and disregard of local and native rights incident to so much of the advance of big business into new regions, and in dealing with weaker, so-called inferior races." Although "bitterly opposed" to formal imperialism such as U.S. rule in the Philippines, Anderson agreed that "Central America and the islands of the Caribbean . . . must be brought into use at least as effectively as the Mississippi Valley."[22]

Cutter continued this public relations effort after ascending to the presidency of United Fruit in the fall of 1924, following the death of Andrew Preston. Newspapers throughout the country hailed Cutter's Horatio Alger–worthy climb up the corporate ladder, and United Fruit's own newsletter predicted a bright future for this new head of "the largest and most progressive agricultural company in the world."[23] As president, Cutter proved determined to shield his company from accusations of imperialism. "I hold no brief for imperialism and deprecate any slightest imperialistic tendency on the part of the United States towards Latin America," Cutter declared in an August 1925 speech. What Americans needed, he emphasized, was a "clear cut understanding that we are dealing with sovereign governments . . . and I firmly believe that we must avoid even the appearance of attempting to dominate them." In doing so, he acknowledged that the interventions associated with Dollar Diplomacy had stirred bitterness. The Monroe Doctrine was a fine idea, he noted, provided it "does not carry as a corollary control or domination" and that it "be completely separated from any trace of economic imperialism." Ignoring his company's own practices, he even suggested that Hispanics be referred to not as "natives" but rather as fellow "Americans."[24]

This Pan-American rhetoric partly reflected a brief window of good feelings in the mid-1920s. At the time of Cutter's speech, the United States had ended most of its military interventions, and Washington's relations with Mexico seemed to be improving.[25] In Cutter's eyes, these developments, combined with the positive influence of American capital, disproved charges of imperialism. The notion that the United States "imposed itself imperialistically" on Latin America was "sheer bosh," he declared in October 1925. "The people of Latin-America are now fairly well convinced that the United States has no imperialistic aims."[26] By the end of 1926, however, the marines had returned to Nicaragua, bringing a resurgence of anti-imperialist rhetoric in Latin America, some of which targeted United Fruit. It was poor timing for the firm, which was negotiating new banana contracts with both Costa Rica and Guatemala. Over the following months, it faced fierce criticism in its host countries, as well unprecedented efforts to restrict its ability to hire West Indian workers.

In this heated atmosphere, Cutter struggled to distinguish United Fruit's activities from American imperialism. In April 1927, he again acknowledged Latin American fears of U.S. domination but denounced "narrow-minded propagandists" who equated large-scale capitalism with imperialism. Far from exploitation, he declared, vast corporations such as United Fruit brought stability and progress. "Undeveloped countries should welcome large developments backed by large capital, for this means responsibility and permanency," he explained. In sum, corporate giants were not the problem; they were the solution. "It must be remembered," he asserted, "that all past troubles . . . have been caused by small, irresponsible companies and individuals, and by unjust concessions, sometimes improperly obtained."

In contrast, large corporations brought "development without exploitation."[27] Cutter also stressed the company's modernizing influence on host nations, particularly as measured in local consumer spending. "Fifteen years ago we did a general merchandise business of $3,000,000 in the undeveloped coastal regions which surround the Caribbean," he observed in October 1927. "Today we are doing a business of $10,000,000." Ignoring the impact of population growth, he argued that the increase stemmed from "educational methods, by learning what these people wanted and giving it to them, and by . . . increasing their purchasing capacity."[28]

Cutter's arguments had merit. United Fruit's material contribution to the development of Central America was undeniable. In addition to constructing railroads and ports, it offered relatively high wages and quality health care to its employees. In this sense, it was indeed "a product of the Progressive Era," as one recent admirer has written.[29] Like other overseas firms of its age, however, United Fruit's "progressive" policies were inextricably linked to the economic, racial, and imperial assumptions of its time. In the end, the issue is not whether the firm saw itself as an agent of benevolent uplift, as it maintained publicly, or operated as the cynical *pulpo* (octopus) that critics increasingly depicted. In all likelihood, Cutter meant every word he uttered in celebrating United Fruit's efforts in Central America, and his narrative echoed that of Ford and scores of other capitalists and colonialists throughout the world in the 1920s. The issue, rather, is the impact of the company's power and policies on the region. By the end of the decade, United Fruit enjoyed unrivaled control of the infrastructure and trade of Central America and held massive investments in Cuba and Colombia. And despite growing efforts by host states to regulate the company's employment of black immigrants, United Fruit's divisions continued to operate largely beyond the purview of local sovereignty while demanding the assistance of host states in repressing labor militancy. The perils of this situation became apparent in December 1928, when Colombian troops massacred striking workers in the company's Santa Marta enclave.[30] Such events convinced many Latin Americans that, despite Cutter's assurances, United Fruit had much in common with other forms of imperialism.

Nationalism and Labor Division in Costa Rica

Many Costa Ricans agreed. Fears of U.S. domination had been building in Costa Rica for decades. Commercially dependent on United Fruit and bordered by two nations held under U.S. protectorates, Costa Rica could not help but worry about the dangers of American control. With the rise of Unionist President Julio Acosta in 1920, moreover, the nation became a center for both Central American unionism and anti-imperialist agitation. In late 1920 and early 1921, San José hosted a regional conference to discuss a revived federation. Costa Rican Foreign Minister Alejandro Alvarado urged all of the Central American states to ratify the resulting "Pact of San José," which provided for the formation of a new union. But this effort quickly stumbled. Under U.S. pressure, Nicaragua refused to join, claiming the pact would violate its treaty with the United States. Meanwhile, the political and racial currents of Costa Rican exceptionalism undermined Alvarado's call for Central American solidarity. Led by former president Ricardo Jiménez, many prominent Costa Ricans warned that a federation would threaten the nation's stability and racial homogeneity. After nearly a century of separation, they asked, what did Costa Rica have in common with its neighbors? A brief border war with Panama in March 1921 further weakened pro-union sentiment.[31] Despite this failure to join the federation, anti-imperialist sentiment in Costa Rica continued to grow. Throughout the early 1920s, the nation's newspapers and journals printed a steady stream of articles and editorials criticizing the United States, and at the 1923 Santiago conference the Costa Rican delegation, led by Alvarado, called on all Latin Americans to resist U.S. domination.[32]

In this charged atmosphere, United Fruit's power and labor policies increasingly clashed with Costa Rican calls for self-determination. By the mid-1920s, the company's hold on the country was stronger than ever. Not only did it monopolize banana exports, but it retained near-total control over national trade and transportation. As U.S. Consul John J. Meily reported in his 1925 survey of labor practices in Limón province, the firm "has complete charge of the wharfage facilities at Port Limon including the receiving of ships and the handling of both ships and cargo; and . . . the Northern Railway effectively controls transportation of freight and passengers from and to the interior."[33] He also emphasized the continued predominance of West Indians in the company's workforce. Although the number of Hispanic migrants to Limón province was growing, Meily found that blacks still accounted for nearly two-thirds of the 6,200 employees of United Fruit and the Northern Railway, and they continued to hold the positions of greatest responsibility and prestige among laborers. This was partly the result of United Fruit officials' perceptions of the racial characteristics of their laborers. According to Meily, managers regarded "colored" men as stronger, "more reliable and more efficient" than Costa Ricans and other Central Americans, whom they lumped together as "natives." But the company's elevation of West Indians within the workforce also reflected an ongoing strategy of separating them from Hispanic migrants. This effort entailed not only better positions and pay for black workers but also subsidies to West Indian churches, English-language schools, and even the UNIA. In the long term, these forms of corporate welfare cultivated West Indian loyalty to the company. Conflicts between black laborers and white managers still occurred, to be sure; but by the mid-1920s West Indians were steadily backing away from labor militancy, particularly as tension with Hispanic coworkers grew.[34]

Of course, that tension was an integral part of United Fruit's labor control system. Although the company publicly maintained that it deplored conflict between West Indian and Central American workers, its strategy of fomenting such tensions was an open secret. Meily observed that it used "mixed gangs" to prevent worker resistance and that "dissension" between West Indian and Hispanic workers was "favored if not more or less openly encouraged by the labor policy of the United Fruit Company in order to render effective organization . . . less likely." As part of this strategy, he explained, the firm also ran its own "secret service" that employed West Indians to gather information among workers and disrupt labor organizing.[35] In this context, it is hardly surprising that Spanish-speaking workers came to associate black immigrants with American domination.

This growing anti-American and anti-black sentiment contributed to a shared sense of grievance and regional identity among Hispanic workers, who came from throughout Central America. Although many in Limón were Costa Rican, a large number came from Nicaragua and Panama. Regardless of origin, however, in United Fruit's enclave they found themselves labeled as "natives" and often subordinated to West Indians. This labor structure proved especially disorienting for Costa Ricans, who were accustomed to claiming the privileges of whiteness and citizenship elsewhere in the nation. For their part, Nicaraguans and Panamanians had other reasons for resentment. Hailing from homelands under U.S. occupation, they often harbored fierce anti-American sentiments even before they arrived, and Nicaraguans in particular gained a reputation for talking back to U.S. bosses. But despite these distinct backgrounds, Central American workers found common ground in their anger toward the company and their black coworkers. And as anti-imperialist sentiment surged in Central America, they drew upon the language of Hispanic nationalism to demand restrictions on black immigration and employment.[36]

Fear of the Black Belt

Costa Rican leaders had their own reasons for pushing such measures. With the rising influence of scientific racism and eugenics in the 1910s and 1920s, nations throughout the world had tightened their immigration policies. In 1921 and 1924, for example, the U.S. Congress passed racialized immigration restrictions that essentially halted immigration from regions other than the Western Hemisphere and northern Europe. In this context, the Costa Rican elite, like their counterparts throughout Latin America, increasingly viewed immigration policy as a means of asserting their nation's racial identity. If Costa Rica accepted the "undesirables" that other nations excluded, they asked, how could it remain a white nation? Although much of the anxiety focused on the small number of Asian and Middle Eastern residents in the country, the sheer numbers of Limón's West Indian population guaranteed that it would be the primary target of racial nativism. With United Fruit's Hispanic workers calling for restrictions on black immigration, moreover, Costa Rican leaders realized the political appeal of anti-black rhetoric. In April 1926, for example, the U.S. legation reported that Costa Rican politicians and newspapers were attempting to "crystalize public opinion sufficiently to bring about government action to check the steady influx of negroes, particularly from Jamaica." The alarm was based "not only on economic considerations," it added, but the fear that "Costa Ricans, who claim to be of pure white blood, will eventually become intermixed with negro blood."[37]

It was in this atmosphere of rising racial anxiety that the Costa Rican government released the national census of 1927. In the document's preface, the census director, José Guerrero, sought to assure Costa Ricans of their enduring whiteness:

> As can be judged by these figures, the population of Costa Rica includes a high percentage of [the] white race. With good reason the conditions of social and political order which have prevailed in our country, and which have endowed us with those habits of peace and work so traditional among our people, have been attributed to the racial homogeneity of the Costa Ricans.

But Guerrero could not hide the presence of West Indians in Costa Rica. The first census since 1892, the document revealed the transformation that the activities of Minor Keith and United Fruit had brought to Limón. According to census data, although the numbers of blacks in the Central Valley remained small, some 20,000 resided in Limón province, where they constituted 55 percent of the population. Partly for this reason, census officials made every effort to maximize the number of residents counted as white. In contrast to their more complex categorization of the rest of the country, they imposed a strict racial binary on Limón's population, drawn along linguistic lines. While West Indians were defined as "black," the province's diverse Spanish-speakers were labeled "white." This formulation is particularly striking in light of the fact that many Hispanic workers in the enclave hailed from Guanacaste and neighboring Nicaragua, whose residents were usually described as *mestizo*. By moving to United Fruit's enclave, they had become white in the eyes of a Costa Rican state eager to buttress national claims of homogeneity. Nevertheless, the total number of West Indians in Limón province startled residents of the Central Valley, most of whom had never visited United Fruit's enclave. Despite Guerrero's assurances, the black population on the Caribbean coast struck many as a serious threat to Costa Rica's image as the white nation of Central America.[38]

The writings of American journalists and travelers in these years only added to Costa Rican anxieties. Since the mid-nineteenth century, the nation's elite had depicted the light-skinned, coffee-growing Central Valley as the "real" Costa Rica, and the vast majority of foreign observers had agreed. By the 1920s, however, Americans visitors showed increased interest in Limón province. And while most acknowledged the racial and cultural distinction between the banana lands and the Central Valley, their accounts underscored the size and vibrancy of the West Indian community in Costa Rica. In 1927, for example, writer Wallace Thompson described residents of San José and the rest of the Central Valley as "a people of almost pure European blood, as free from the Indian problem as the United States or Canada." But the rail trip from Puerto Limón to San José brought different sights: "banana lands and negroes; negroes individually, in gangs, in huts on stilts, in villages on stilts—everywhere." "The black belt and the banana belt climb together," he noted, and "the black belt never breaks; not once, all the long day's ride, till we reach Cartago." A year later, Arthur Ruhl conveyed a similar impression. While the Central Valley remained populated by Spanish-speaking whites, he observed, "the banana-lands of the East Coast, with their Jamaica negro laborers and American superintendents, make almost a separate English-speaking country."[39] That was precisely what worried many Costa Rican nationalists.

Contract Negotiations and the Immigration Debate

These rising racial concerns formed the backdrop for a new round of negotiations between the company and the Costa Rican government. The impetus for the talks was Panama disease. Carried from farm to farm by drainage water and workers' boots, the soil-borne fungus had begun to threaten all of Costa Rica's banana industry by the mid-1920s. Hoping to acquire uninfected lands, United Fruit initiated negotiations with San José for a new banana contract in late 1925. In return for vast new land concessions in Limón province, the firm promised to accept a modest tax increase. Ricardo Jiménez, once again president, seemed inclined to agree, but the deal ran headlong into nationalist opposition. Independent banana planters pressed the government to secure better terms for the sale of their fruit, Hispanic workers called for preferential hiring over West Indians, and nationalists throughout the country demanded the company submit to higher taxes and more regulation before it received further concessions. And hovering behind it all was simmering resentment of United Fruit's role in stimulating black immigration.[40]

Among the most outspoken critics of both the company and its West Indian employees was Marco Aurelio Zumbado. A cofounder of the nationalist Economic Society of Friends of the Nation, whose membership included census chief José Guerrero, Zumbado publicly denounced United Fruit as an imperialist force that threatened to undermine Costa Rica's sovereignty and racial integrity. In a November 1926 petition to the Costa Rican Congress, he warned that "foreign capitalism tends to convert people into colonies wherever it goes." In the case of United Fruit, he asserted, "banana money remains in the Company's commissaries and returns to Boston, or the negroes carry it directly to Jamaica," and he went on to warn that "the negro benefits only the Company [and] . . . mixes our race, which is already blackening." As such, he called on Costa Rican officials not only to end United Fruit's domination but to adopt tight immigration restrictions. He also suggested they study the eugenic campaigns in the U.S. South, which aimed to sterilize blacks in order to "avoid the propagation of the race."[41] In an announcement printed in the official *La Gaceta* the following February, Zumbado's association again condemned United Fruit's impact on the nation. Not only had the company asserted its "dominion and control" over a "vast extension of the Atlantic Zone," the letter declared, but it had sponsored the growth of a black immigrant community, "which, as is known, is predisposed to infirmities such as tuberculosis, leprosy, syphilis, and insanity."[42]

The U.S. Marines' reoccupation of Nicaragua only heightened this hostility. As newspapers throughout Costa Rica denounced Washington's intervention in the neighboring country, nationalists grew ever more determined to resist United Fruit's demands. One of the leading voices was former foreign minister Alejandro Alvarado, now head of the Costa Rican Congress and a political ally of Zumbado. Warning that the proposed concessions to United Fruit would encourage "Yankee political imperialism," Alvarado called on President Jiménez to join with other banana-producing nations to negotiate a better deal with the company. Soon after, in February 1927, he pushed an anti-imperialist resolution through the Congress over Jiménez's opposition.[43]

By this time, United Fruit had suspended negotiations with San José, but anti-imperialist sentiment continued to mount. Over the next two years, Costa Rican students and nationalist politicians lambasted the U.S. war in Nicaragua as well as the threats posed by "economic imperialism." The atmosphere grew tenser in September 1928, when Peruvian nationalist and labor leader Víctor Raúl Haya de la Torre delivered a series of anti-imperialist lectures in San José. Recently expelled from Guatemala and El Salvador, Haya took advantage of Costa Rica's political openness to voice his criticism of U.S. military and corporate domination in Central America. As U.S. officials noted to their chagrin, the crowds attending Haya's lectures included not only students and laborers but also many well-to-do Costa Ricans. Furious that a Sandino supporter with Mexican connections would be allowed to criticize the United States, U.S. Minister Roy Davis demanded the Costa Rican government expel him, but it refused.[44]

Meanwhile, popular demands for immigration restriction grew louder. As in other Central American nations, these focused on West Indians rather than Spanish-speaking immigrants. Amid calls for Hispanic unity, few Costa Ricans advocated the exclusion or expulsion of fellow Central Americans. Indeed, several prominent champions of Central American unionism became leading advocates of immigrant restriction. This was certainly true of Alvarado. Having previously led regional opposition to U.S. imperialism, the former foreign minister made a natural transition to anti-black agitation by the late 1920s. In June 1928, he joined with other prominent nationalists to found the Civic League. Tied closely to Costa Rican banana planters, the organization explicitly linked United Fruit's domination to the racial threat posed by black immigrants. According to one U.S. diplomat, it amounted to a "Costa Rican Ku Klux Klan."[45]

United Fruit did its best to wait out this nationalist fervor. In response to criticism of the company's hiring practices and economic power, managers in the Costa Rica Division followed Cutter's lead, emphasizing their increased employment of Hispanic laborers as well as the firm's contribution to Costa Rican development. And although calls for immigration restriction worried company managers, their operations continued to benefit from tensions between Central American and West Indian workers. Nevertheless, as Panama disease cut into the firm's Costa Rican production, United Fruit officials grew more determined to secure new lands from San José. By the end of the 1920s, moreover, they were beginning to realize that if they wanted to neutralize Costa Rican nationalism and gain the desired concessions, they would have to compromise on the issue of black immigration and employment.

Unionists and United Fruit in Guatemala

Nationalist currents proved even more unpredictable in Guatemala. The Unionists who overthrew Estrada Cabrera in 1920 had drawn support from a range of political reformers, labor leaders, and conservative elites. While their more radical plans were never realized, the Unionists initiated a decade-long political opening in which the National Assembly and press remained relatively free from executive domination. At first, Washington seemed to accept this new order of things. In June 1920, the Wilson administration recognized the new government, and in September it welcomed the victory of Provisional President Carlos Herrera in the first free election in Guatemalan history. But the Unionists' rhetoric and policies soon rankled U.S. officials. Not only did nationalists in the assembly denounce Washington's longstanding support of Estrada Cabrera, but they also called for closer relations with Mexico and moved forward with plans to form a Central American federation. In October 1921, just weeks after hosting a celebration of the centennial anniversary of Central American independence, Herrera announced a union with El Salvador and Honduras—the two other nations that had ratified the Pact of San José.

This democratic opening also allowed for the first public debates over United Fruit's role in the country. Having initiated its operations in Guatemala during Estrada Cabrera's rule, the firm had benefited tremendously from its ties to his regime. With the dictator gone, nationalists now called for a reining in of both United Fruit and Keith's rail monopoly, the IRCA. Pressure came especially from planters and commercial interests who demanded the IRCA end its distorted rate system, which continued to channel most of the nation's commerce through Puerto Barrios. In the waning days of the Wilson administration, some U.S. officials sympathized with these grievances. Noting that the IRCA's monopoly would never be tolerated in the United States, one American diplomat declared, "the one reason which prevents the government from taking steps to better the situation is the fear of the influence of the United Fruit Company in Washington."[46]

Despite his reluctance to confront United Fruit, Herrera could not ignore the rising currents of nationalism and labor militancy. One of his principal challenges was the Railroad Workers' League, a union that was growing in strength despite the IRCA's refusal to recognize it. By early 1921, the league had purged its few remaining African American and West Indian members and allied itself with its counterpart in Mexico, a connection made easier by the fact that many of its members were Mexican. Soon after, the union began calling on the Guatemalan government to curb the IRCA's power and force the company to place Guatemalans in managerial positions.[47] With the rail workers making effective use of nationalist rhetoric, Herrera felt increasingly compelled to confront the IRCA. In May 1921, following a brief strike by the Railroad Workers' League, he canceled a 1908 concession that would have allowed the IRCA to extend a rail line to El Salvador. In response, Keith turned to Washington, where the pro-corporate Harding administration took up his cause. Although some American diplomats protested that Herrera remained friendly to U.S. business and adhered to "democratic principles," Washington was adamant that he restore the contract. The Guatemalan president refused to back down, however, and as Estrada Cabrera had done in 1914, he followed up his challenge to the IRCA by squeezing United Fruit's labor supply. In October 1921, with anti-American resentment building throughout the country, Herrera quadrupled the deposit required of black immigrants from $50 to $200 and made it retroactive to 1914. Fearing, quite rightly, that the new measure would chase West Indians from the country and thereby undercut its labor system, United Fruit once again requested support from the U.S.

government. In this case, however, American diplomats proved reluctant to pressure Guatemala City, for the U.S. Congress itself had passed immigration restrictions the previous month. Nevertheless, the weakened Herrera fell to a military coup in December 1921.[48]

Both the U.S. government and United Fruit initially welcomed the new government headed by General José María Orellana. Despite noting with concern that the new president was "certainly more than half Indian," a special U.S. envoy declared him "stronger, more pro-American, and more honest" than his predecessor.[49] Over the following year, Washington helped Orellana shore up his regime, including offering assistance in the formation of a new Guatemalan constabulary. Part of a larger U.S. strategy beginning to take hold in the Hispanic Caribbean, this training of local security forces aimed to secure order and project U.S. influence without the economic and political costs of overt intervention. As in other nations in the region, the form this policy took hinged to a great extent on American perceptions of the local population, which were in turn rooted in U.S. imperial culture. Security forces "would require a different type of trained man in some of the Republics from that which would be acceptable in some of the others," explained Major Fred T. Cruse, the U.S. military attaché:

> I consider that officers of our Philippine Scouts or Philippine Constabu-
> lary would be most suitable to organize the force in Guatemala, because
> these officers have had experience in the Philippines dealing with divers[e]
> native tribes, and that is what they would have to deal with in Guatemala.[50]

For their part, United Fruit managers hoped Orellana, a close associate of former president Manuel Estrada Cabrera, would prove friendlier to their interests and labor needs. But they were quickly disappointed. Although the new president annulled the Unionist constitution and withdrew from the federation with El Salvador and Honduras, he made no attempt to coerce the legislature or curb what one U.S. official described as Guatemala's "excessive" freedom of the press.[51] And while Orellana hoped to repair relations with United Fruit, he understood that his political survival hinged to a great extent on his willingness to address nationalist concerns. Despite fierce pressure from Washington and United Fruit, he refused to restore the IRCA's contract, and he maintained strict enforcement of the deposit requirement on black immigrants. Such policies set the stage for another bitter strike in Puerto Barrios.

The 1923 Strike and Racial Nationalism

For months, labor organizers with ties throughout Central America had been working to form a union among the banana and port workers of Guatemala's Caribbean coast. With the workforce starkly divided along racial lines, however, labor solidarity proved elusive, and Central American organizers quickly abandoned efforts to include West Indians. The pitfalls of this approach became apparent when the organized laborers attempted a strike. On the morning of 3 February 1923, 200 Hispanic stevedores suddenly refused to load some 36,000 stems of bananas onto the waiting steamer *Suriname*. Although white United Fruit supervisors initially cajoled some of the men into ignoring the stoppage, labor leaders soon succeeded in halting all work on the pier. From the beginning, the strikers framed their grievances in the language of Hispanic nationalism. In addition to higher pay rates and recognition of their union, they demanded restrictions on the hiring of immigrants. As in Costa Rica, however, they did not advocate the exclusion of all noncitizens; in fact, Salvadorans and Hondurans were among the strike's principal leaders. Rather, they called on United Fruit to improve its treatment of Spanish-speaking workers and end its employment of West Indians. The fact that the strike's organizers were able to voice these demands publicly, in full view of local authorities, suggests that Guatemalan officials sympathized with Hispanic workers' anger toward both the company and black immigrants.[52]

United Fruit turned to those same immigrants to break the strike. Desperate to load its bananas, the company transported 300 West Indian farm laborers by train to Puerto Barrios to serve as temporary stevedores. But the strikers and their supporters met the train and attacked the black workers and white managers aboard. As the violence spread, United Fruit requested assistance from Izabal's governor; but he refused to intervene. As a result, the *Suriname* sailed away nearly empty, leaving 30,000 stems to rot on the dock. Over the following days, strike leaders seized company rail engines, using them to recruit more workers on the banana farms, just as strikers in Puerto Castilla, Honduras, would do the following year. Soon Hispanic laborers were occupying farms and facilities throughout the enclave in what amounted to a sit-down strike.[53]

At first, the strikers enjoyed strong support in Guatemala City. On 5 February, the newspaper *El Excelsior* laid bare the racial and national significance of the work stoppage. In addition to its history of abusing Guatemalan employees, the editor asserted, United Fruit had long "given preeminence to people of color, whose work is as and sometimes less efficient than that of natives." The time had come for the Guatemalan government to "protect our workers, giving them ample guarantees and the preference to which their status as Guatemalan citizens entitles them."[54] Other newspapers supported the strikers' calls for increased taxation of United Fruit and an end to its control over Guatemalan commerce. Orellana and his advisers shared many of these views. Although the president replaced Izabal's pro-labor governor, he held private talks with the strike leaders, convincing them to return to work in return for his promise to press United Fruit for concessions. Over the following weeks, he and his top aides urged United Fruit to consider the workers' demands for pay raises and preferential hiring for Hispanics. The government's stance flummoxed company officials. According to R. K. Thomas, the division's general manager, Orellana's minister of development seemed "openly antagonistic to the Company . . . and more than sympathetic with labor unions," at one point warning United Fruit that "a Government must always be on the side of its own citizens, and . . . that in case of a strike even the soldiers could not be relied upon not to act on the side of the strikers"—a position Thomas dismissed as "nothing short of Bolshevism."[55] Soon, however, pressure from United Fruit and Washington, along with rumors of a possible political uprising, convinced Orellana to turn against the strikers, and in March 1923 he deported the union's non-Guatemalan leaders. Along with the arrival of a U.S. warship, this repression scotched any plans to revive the strike. It also raised racial tensions to new heights. Many Hispanic workers blamed their defeat on the refusal of West Indians to join the strike, ignoring the fact that their anti-black demands had precluded such solidarity.[56]

In the wake of the strike, Orellana attempted to bolster his nationalist credentials by asserting himself with United Fruit. This effort became apparent in the new banana contract completed in 1924. In addition to providing for an annual rent (eventually set at $14,000) on the company's operations in Izabal, the agreement imposed a one cent tax on each bunch of bananas exported.[57] In doing so, it removed the exemption that Keith had received for banana exports in the 1904 contract, bringing policy in Guatemala in line with that of Costa Rica. At the same time, Orellana stepped up harassment of West Indians. In late 1924, his government ordered the registration of all black residents in Izabal and tightened efforts to prevent illegal entry from Honduras. In this atmosphere of racial nationalism, Spanish-speaking laborers discovered they could tap into anti-black sentiment in order to gain advantage over West Indian coworkers. Indeed, by the mid-1920s, a growing number of complaints and legal proceedings were initiated against black foremen by *ladinos* and other Hispanic laborers, who almost invariably referred to themselves as "*hijos de la patria*" ("sons of the fatherland").[58]

The following years brought further government efforts to influence United Fruit's labor policies. In April 1926, Orellana issued decree 1367, which required the workforces of all businesses operating in the nation to be at least 75 percent Guatemalan—which likely helped inspire similar legislation in Panama later that year.[59] Although in theory the decree would apply to all noncitizens, in practice it aimed to limit West Indian employment. On its face, it seemed to pose little threat to United Fruit. Hispanics already constituted over 75 percent of its workforce in Guatemala, and government officials assured the company that the law "would not be enforced rigorously" against Hispanic Central Americans. Over the following months, however, government officials faced mounting pressure from nationalists and labor organizations to use the legislation to exclude black immigrants. This was especially true of Orellana's successor, Lázaro Chacón, who in the words of one U.S. diplomat found it "politically advisable" to "force foreign firms to employ Guatemalans."[60] For its part, United Fruit offered surprisingly little resistance to the law, perhaps because the immigration debate took public focus off the firm's efforts to gain new concessions on the Pacific Coast.

Toward the Pacific Coast

United Fruit was not the first company to attempt development of Guatemala's Pacific slope. A number of small enterprises had been active in the region for several years.[61] By the mid-1920s, a company calling itself Guatemalan Plantations, based in Britain, had acquired a large concession and begun efforts to establish an enclave around its headquarters in Tiquisate. Over the following years, it attempted to grow bananas and other tropical fruit for the California market, but it faced several obstacles. The first was labor supply. Like the Caribbean lowlands prior to the banana boom, the Pacific Coast was sparsely populated, and few *ladinos* or highland Maya were willing to work in the humid region. Nor could Guatemalan Plantations import the laborers who had built United Fruit's operations in the Caribbean lowlands. As U.S. Minister Arthur Geissler observed in April 1926, because public opinion in Guatemala was "strongly opposed to permitting further importation of negroes," one of the conditions of the government concession to Guatemalan Plantations was "under no circumstances will [it] bring negroes, mongolians or natives of the ports."[62] The second major obstacle was United Fruit itself. Because labor and transportation costs were so high on the Pacific, the massive corporation could simply undersell Guatemalan Plantations. Indeed, one U.S. consul believed that development of a banana industry on Guatemala's Pacific Coast would prove impossible "unless [United Fruit] were itself interested."[63]

At first, such interest seemed unlikely. In a meeting with the owners of Guatemalan Plantations in late 1925, Cutter declined suggestions of a co-operative venture. But developments on Guatemala's Caribbean coast soon altered United Fruit's stance. By 1926, the company had already begun to shift its operations in Izabal from declining lands around Virginia to a new headquarters dubbed Bananera. With the continued spread of Panama disease, however, United Fruit and its subsidiaries became increasingly eager to expand to the Pacific Coast. In 1926, the IRCA purchased the decaying wharf facilities at Puerto San José, and two years later United Fruit founded a new subsidiary, the Compañía Agrícola de Guatemala, which entered negotiations with the Guatemalan government over the new Pacific division. As in Izabal, United Fruit's main objective was not land acquisition: it proved relatively easy to buy up cheap lands on the coast. Rather, in the guise of the Compañía Agrícola, the firm pressed for a commercial monopoly similar to that in Puerto Barrios.[64]

The proposal came at a volatile moment in the region. In early 1928, the Cuyamel Fruit Company had begun building a railroad near the Guatemalan border. Backed by the Honduran government, the project caused a war scare in Guatemala. With banana divisions in both nations, United Fruit remained officially neutral in the clash. In the context of the Havana conference and anger over the Sandino War, however, many Latin Americans depicted United Fruit and Cuyamel as puppet masters pitting Guatemala and Honduras against each other.[65] Tensions mounted with the arrival of Haya de la Torre to Guatemala. In July 1928, the Peruvian activist delivered the same anti-imperialist lectures that he would soon give in Costa Rica. In response to U.S. pressure, Chacón deported Haya and cracked down on the press.[66]

But this repression did not extend to the critics of United Fruit. Chacón's approval of new rail and port concessions on the Pacific Coast had brought fierce resistance from nationalists, who resented the rates charged by the IRCA and denounced the extension of its monopoly. Despite United

Fruit's widespread bribery of Guatemalan newspapers, the firm proved unable to muzzle this opposition, and the National Assembly refused to approve the concession.[67] For his part, Chacón realized the political necessity of presenting himself as the defender of the nation and its workers. Like many of his counterparts elsewhere in the Hispanic Caribbean, however, he focused his demands in large part on West Indian immigration. Rather than attempt to break the IRCA's rail monopoly or secure better terms for Guatemalan banana planters, he pushed for the exclusion of black immigrants from any new developments on the Pacific Coast. By 1929, the negotiations had stalled, but Chacón's demands pointed the way to a future accommodation between United Fruit's desire for concessions on the Pacific and Guatemalan nationalists' demands for black exclusion.[68]

The tense negotiations between Guatemalan and United Fruit officials underscored the contested nature of the U.S. empire in Central America. The United States emerged from World War I with unrivaled political and economic dominance in the region. But the 1920s brought an unprecedented wave of Hispanic nationalism throughout Latin America. In Central America, this came in the form of anger toward United Fruit and its labor policies as well as resentment of U.S. military interventions. By the mid-1920s, both the U.S. government and United Fruit had taken steps to defuse anti-American sentiment. In Washington's case, this effort faltered with the reoccupation of Nicaragua, which galvanized nationalists throughout the hemisphere. United Fruit, too, suffered setbacks. Amid record profits, the firm faced growing charges of exploitation and economic imperialism from U.S. and Latin American critics alike. And even as Victor Cutter and other company officials sought to burnish the company's progressive image, they faced rising opposition from Central American nationalists and laborers, who condemned its employment of West Indians as well as its commercial power.

Leaders in Costa Rica and Guatemala could ill afford to ignore this nationalist tide, and most shared the anxiety toward United Fruit and black immigration that was growing throughout the region. But while they made some moves to limit the company's power, they shied away from direct confrontation, which might open the door to intervention from Washington or social upheaval at home. Instead, they sought to channel nationalist sentiment away from radical reform or labor mobilization and toward anti-black agitation. This strategy framed the approach of the Costa Rican and Guatemalan governments to negotiations with United Fruit. Although officials in both nations were eager for renewed contracts with the company and willing to extend new concessions, they pushed for restrictions on its employment of West Indians. Determined to maintain control over its labor policies, the company resisted these demands in the late 1920s, contributing to the collapse of negotiations in both countries. In the following years, however, the appearance of a more virulent banana disease, along with the global economic crisis and the U.S. government's turn toward Good Neighbor diplomacy, would spur United Fruit to compromise with Hispanic nationalism at the expense of its black workers.

Chapter 6

Reframing the Empire, 1929–1940

Long before she departed for Guatemala, Frances Emery-Waterhouse
thought she knew what to expect. When the 35-year-old Maine journalist
met and married United Fruit engineer Russell Waterhouse in 1937, she
already had well-formed notions of life in colonial enclaves. "A hearty diet
of tropical literature taught me that gringos live in low, rambling houses . . .
where a white-robed servant is always gliding in with gin fizzes," she
recalled. Her first glimpse of Puerto Barrios offered little promise of such
leisure, but it did arouse her sense of the exotic, and the erotic. Observing
stevedores loading bananas on the wharf, she marveled at the "burly
Negroes . . . stripped down to 'drudgin' clo's' . . . their magnificent torsos
gleaming like polished satin," and once ashore she spied an "overblown
Negress wink[ing] knowingly at a pair of American sailors" and displaying
"a great dark, rubber-nippled breast, as shiny and as substantial as a purple
breadfruit."[1] In addition to confirming stereotypes of tropical sensuality,
such sights made it impossible to ignore the black presence on Guatemala's
Caribbean coast. But while local *ladinos* seemed to accept the Garífuna as
partial members of the nation, she noted that British West Indians were
"exceedingly unpopular." She attributed this hostility to a single incident
years earlier when a West Indian man descending from a train had collided

with a Guatemalan woman, causing her baby to fall and die. "All up and down the line there was a 'thinning out' of Negroes," Emery-Waterhouse explained. "Several hundreds of them, mostly Jamaicans, were killed."[2] Conveyed to her by either United Fruit officials or a Guatemalan acquaintance, this explanation neatly elided the role of corporate labor policies and Hispanic nationalism in shaping race relations on Central America's Caribbean coast.

Emery-Waterhouse had little reason to ponder such matters, for she was not headed to a banana farm in Izabal. Instead, she boarded an IRCA train for Tiquisate, the hub of United Fruit's new Pacific subsidiary, the Compañía Agrícola de Guatemala. The journey itself stirred imperial comparisons. "Riding through a Stanley and Livingstone jungle," she recalled, "you suddenly come out into the homey sunshine of a train settlement which has all the conveniences and luxuries one would find in an exclusive suburb in the States." Upon settling into her residence at the company farm of Siguacán, eighteen miles from the Pacific Ocean, she found many of her colonial fantasies fulfilled. Although she encountered only one black employee, a Jamaican who staffed the company commissary, she benefited from the close attention of several highland Maya, whom the firm hired as servants for white managers. "We ladies of Siguacán were pampered and spoiled by the quiet, lovable, and . . . efficient Mayan Indian servants," Emery-Waterhouse admitted. "From the moment they brought . . . coffee to our bedside, until they turned down our sheets at night, they were our constant shadows."[3]

Nevertheless, she found much to dislike on the Pacific Coast. Although she taught herself Spanish and tried to interact with Hispanic residents, she discovered that racial and labor divisions in the enclave were "governed by a caste system both rigid and inflexible" and that social distinctions were "as sharply observed as machete blades." Despite the absence of black laborers, company officials and their wives maintained a strict color line, separating themselves from not only Hispanic wage laborers but also the many "fine and cultured" Guatemalan supervisors, whom Americans "treated with ill-disguised contempt." In doing so, United Fruit managers and their wives enforced strict conformity among themselves. "Because I made no secret of my liking for these Latin-American friends," Emery-Waterhouse recalled, "I was sharply criticized":

> If I invited them to my home in company with gringos, they met slight
> courtesy. After a few uncomfortable evenings, and one wretched afternoon

when a party of norteamericanos refused to shake hands with a charming little Guatemalteca who was having tea with me, I entertained Northerners and Southerners at different times. This incited a new landslide of recrimination: if I wished to hold my 'social position,' I would have to stop inviting Latinos to my home.

Emery-Waterhouse stirred another scandal by declaring she would not stop her daughter from marrying a "Latino." She eventually learned not to argue, concluding that such practices simply "mirrored the attitude of Siguacán, as well as any spot in the American Tropics where Americans and Englishmen foregather." Nevertheless, she remained a believer in Pan-Americanism and continued to espouse the values associated with Washington's Good Neighbor Policy. "We are Americans, all," she later wrote, "each country a vital and essential part of the greatness which goes to make up our America."[4]

Emery-Waterhouse's journey provides a glimpse of the U.S. empire in a critical period of transition. By the 1930s, Latin American resistance had nudged Washington away from military intervention and toward a new posture of mutual respect that would become known as the Good Neighbor Policy. To be sure, discrimination toward Hispanics continued within the United States and throughout its empire. But the Good Neighbor Policy initiated a favorable tilt in U.S. rhetoric and attitudes toward Latin America that would continue through World War II. This shift came at a price, however. In Central America, in particular, it went hand in hand with the rise of authoritarian regimes and the cresting of anti-black xenophobia. Although both of these trends owed much to the economic desperation stirred by the Great Depression, they also stemmed from U.S. imperial culture. Just as Washington's military interventions helped lay the foundation for pro-American dictatorships in the region, U.S. labor policies drew out virulent strands of racial nationalism, which in turn shaped the demands that host states made on both United Fruit and the U.S. government. In countries held under protectorates such as Cuba and Panama, nationalists espoused Good Neighbor rhetoric not only to end U.S. imperial control but to press American officials and employers to acknowledge local racial hierarchies and accept immigration restrictions. By the late 1930s, Washington had made key moves to accommodate this nationalism, agreeing to end its protectorates over Cuba and Panama and accepting some regulation of American businesses in host nations. But the U.S. government refused to relinquish control over racial and labor policies in the Panama Canal Zone, and Panamanian officials had few means to force a change.

United Fruit found itself in a weaker position in relation to its host nations. Struggling with falling stock prices at home and banana disease and labor militancy along Central America's Caribbean coast, the firm grew increasingly desperate to develop new divisions on the Pacific slopes of Costa Rica and Guatemala. Leaders in both countries were eager to prevent the company from withdrawing, but they were also reluctant to grant new concessions in the face of nationalist sentiment. United Fruit attempted to ease this hostility by muting its imperial rhetoric and forming subsidiaries to mask its power, but the Costa Rican and Guatemalan governments demanded more. By the mid-1930s, the firm had arrived at similar agreements with both states: in return for concessions on their Pacific lowlands, it would exclude blacks from its new enclaves, thereby abandoning the system of labor segmentation that had characterized its operations on the Caribbean coast. United Fruit's version of the Good Neighbor Policy, it seemed, meant coming to terms with the racial antagonism it had helped generate.

Race and the Good Neighbor Policy

Although scholars disagree over the objectives and outcomes of the Good Neighbor Policy, its basic outlines are well known. Beginning with the administration of Herbert Hoover (1929–1933), Washington made a concerted effort to reduce anti-American sentiment in Latin America through a shift in rhetoric and policies. By the mid-1930s, the succeeding Roosevelt administration had ended most U.S. protectorates and military interventions in the Hispanic Caribbean and undertaken an aggressive effort to revive hemispheric trade. At the same time, it threw its support behind pro-American dictators who seemed capable of maintaining political and economic order in volatile times.[5] What is often left unacknowledged in accounts of the Good Neighbor Policy, however, is the context of racial and labor tension in which it took shape. To be sure, much of that tension was linked only indirectly to the United States. The collapse of global trade in the 1930s heightened racial friction in Central America and the rest of the Hispanic Caribbean, as Hispanic and West Indian workers competed for a shrinking number of jobs. In addition, economic contraction in Great Britain and political turmoil in its Caribbean colonies made British officials more reluctant to protect the rights of black subjects in Cuba and Central America. In March 1930, for example, one British official informed Charles

Eberhardt, the U.S. minister to Costa Rica, that "it is practically understood
by British consular representatives that they are to do nothing by way of
protecting the rights and interests of West Indian negroes."[6] More broadly,
the charged tone of international discourse, emanating especially from
Fascist Italy and Nazi Germany, raised racial tensions throughout the world,
particularly after Italy's 1935 invasion of Ethiopia. Nevertheless, racial and
labor clashes in the Hispanic Caribbean took place in a social landscape
that had been profoundly influenced by the U.S. empire over the previous
three decades, and the upheavals that empire faced in the 1930s were in
large part the consequences of its own power and policies.[7]

The bloodiest example took place in the Dominican Republic. Despite
ending its occupation of the small country in 1924, Washington had retained
its financial protectorate, and by the early 1930s American officials were
grooming Rafael Trujillo as a reliable pro-American strongman. Following
the withdrawal of U.S. Marines from neighboring Haiti in August 1934,
however, Trujillo began to stir tensions on the island. The conflict had deep
historical roots, for the Dominican Republic had long defined its racial
identity against its darker, more populous neighbor. Confronting spiraling
unemployment, Dominicans now focused their anger on the thousands of
Haitian immigrants in their nation, many of whom worked for American
companies. The Trujillo regime passed employment quotas in order to
force out Haitian workers, but the resistance of U.S. diplomats and employers limited their effectiveness. As a result, Dominican authorities turned to
a more vulnerable target: Haitian farmers living along the border of the two
nations. In October 1937, following Trujillo's denunciation of the black
"invasion" of his country, the Dominican army massacred some 12,000 of
these squatters. While U.S. officials interceded to prevent a war between the
two nations, Dominican officials sought to justify themselves in terms they
believed Washington would understand. As Trujillo's foreign minister put it,
the Dominican government had to expel the Haitians in order to "defend
the clean, traditional customs of our citizens" and to "preserve our racial
superiority over them."[8] Although appalled by the violence, the Roosevelt
administration proved reluctant to discard a useful ally.

Racial tensions also played a key role in Cuba. By the early 1930s, black
immigration and U.S. labor policies had become key issues of contention,
but the presence of a large Afro-Cuban minority ensured that calls for immigration restrictions often took the form of nativism rather than sweeping anti-black rhetoric. In fact, many Afro-Cubans joined lighter skinned
coworkers in condemning Jamaican and Haitian immigrants. The Cuban

government had attempted to exclude black foreigners in the 1920s, but United Fruit and other U.S. firms resisted such efforts, with the support of the U.S. government. Consequently, as in Central America, nationalists and workers increasingly conflated black immigration with U.S. domination. Their bitterness emerged in the summer of 1933, when a series of strikes brought the nationalist government of Ramón Grau to power. In addition to adopting labor reforms and unilaterally abrogating the Platt Amendment, it banned Jamaican and Haitian immigration and passed employment quotas designed to expel black foreigners. Concerned with the new government's radicalism, if not its racial policies, Washington orchestrated Grau's overthrow in January 1934. But because the Roosevelt administration hoped to maintain its Good Neighbor image, it allowed the succeeding government to retain many of his policies. In addition to agreeing to abandon the Platt Amendment, U.S. officials accepted Cuban immigration restrictions, despite protests from United Fruit and other American businesses.[9]

Washington took a harder line in Panama, where it had more direct interests at stake. Like their Cuban counterparts, Panamanian nationalists seized upon the Good Neighbor Policy to push for changes in their country's relations with the United States. Their main demands focused on the 1903 canal treaty, which gave Washington the right to intervene in Panama as well as to expropriate national territory. But other grievances centered on issues of race and labor. Although West Indian immigration had slowed to a trickle by the 1930s, Panamanian hostility toward foreign blacks had continued to grow. In the eyes of the Panamanian elite, the large West Indian communities in Colón and Panama City threatened the nation's Hispanic culture and aspirations to whiteness. For Panamanian workers, English-speaking blacks represented unfair competition for jobs in both the Canal Zone and United Fruit's enclaves. Such concerns influenced Panama's approach to negotiations with Washington. By demanding authority over its ports as well as control over movement between the Canal Zone and national territory, for example, the Panamanian government hoped to enforce its anti-black immigration restrictions on the U.S. government's enclave and reduce the West Indian presence in Panama itself. Panamanian negotiators also pressed for changes in the Canal Zone's labor structure that would grant Hispanic Panamanian applicants preference over West Indians on the silver roll and equal access to positions on the gold roll. The latter demand went beyond economic opportunity: it meant extending to Hispanics the privileges and prestige of whiteness in the Canal Zone.[10]

American negotiators proved more flexible on issues of sovereignty than on questions of race and labor. Fearful that anti-American resentment might open the door to Axis influence in Panama, Washington agreed to discard the protectorate and renounced the right to appropriate Panamanian territory. But it rejected demands to alter employment practices in the Canal Zone. U.S. canal officials were reluctant to accept the exclusion of West Indians, which would limit their access to valued workers and undermine their system of labor segmentation on the silver roll. For their part, white American "Zonians" fiercely opposed the notion of placing Panamanians on the gold roll. When U.S. officials floated the idea of opening the gold roll to qualified applicants of all nationalities, however, it was Panama's negotiator who balked, explaining that such an arrangement left a "hint of an equality of a Panamanian with a Jamaican and a Negro and that is the actual problem."[11] But U.S. officials would go no further. Within the context of the Good Neighbor Policy and impending war in Europe, Washington was eager to eliminate sources of inter-American resentment, including the glaringly colonial features of the 1903 treaty. But it had no intention of allowing Panama to dictate labor policies in the Canal Zone. For its part, the Panamanian government had little leverage with American officials other than the threat of popular disorder, for the U.S. government needed no new concessions from Panama. As a result, although the treaty signed in March 1936 made gestures toward Panamanian dignity, it offered no compromise with the anti-black current of Hispanic nationalism.[12]

United Fruit's Depression

United Fruit found itself in a more vulnerable position than the U.S. government. Like many American businesses, the firm entered 1929 with high expectations and continued to expand its operations aggressively. Despite mourning the death of cofounder Minor Keith in June, it weathered the October stock market crash and soon after reached an agreement with Samuel Zemurray to acquire full control over Cuyamel Fruit. With access to new lands in Honduras and its impressive new Guatemalan headquarters of Bananera nearing completion, the company seemed poised for uninterrupted success. But the early 1930s brought a rude awakening. The fall in global trade cut deeply into United Fruit's railroad and steamship revenue even as the spread of Panama disease made it more difficult for the firm to meet the reduced market for bananas in the United

States. In order to revive its fortunes, it needed access to uninfected lands. But nationalist sentiment and the growing strength of labor movements made host states reluctant to extend new concessions.[13] Like other U.S. businesses in Latin America, moreover, United Fruit could no longer count on Washington's support in its confrontations with nationalists. As the Roosevelt administration's acceptance of Mexican oil nationalization made clear, hemispheric solidarity had taken precedence over the unstinting protection of U.S. investments.

United Fruit responded to these challenges with its own Good Neighbor Policy, adopting a more respectful tone toward host nations and publicly acknowledging the racial equality of Hispanic peoples. In a sense, this was a natural extension of the rhetorical shift Cutter had initiated in the 1920s, and United Fruit's president would repeatedly claim that his company had in fact invented the concept of the Good Neighbor. In truth, however, the firm's public relations efforts in the 1930s represented a significant break from earlier years. Since its founding in 1899, the company had openly celebrated its power and influence in Central America. To be sure, its tone during the 1920s had shifted from an imperialist identification with white global rule to a Fordist emphasis on "uplifting" the region and its workers, but the company's public celebration of its own power remained. By the early 1930s, however, it had become clear that the firm's visible power was part of the problem. Like the U.S. protectorates over Cuba and Panama, United Fruit's ubiquitous presence constantly reminded Central Americans of their own attenuated sovereignty. The company's solution was to obscure its power, particularly through the formation of subsidiaries to develop new enclaves on the Pacific Coast. Like Washington, it also sought to cultivate closer ties with local strongmen. But it discovered that its continued employment of black immigrants formed a serious obstacle to both of these strategies.

On the surface, this might seem a trivial matter. By the 1930s, West Indians accounted for a relatively small proportion of United Fruit's workforce. Moreover, company executives shared many of the racist impulses of Hispanic nationalists. According to his friend Hugh Wilson, Cutter himself had, in his transition from plantation timekeeper to company president, "kept the grin, the abrupt manner and, I suppose, the willingness to bash a buck negro should the latter become drunk and obstreperous."[14] But such an interpretation ignores the importance that black immigrant workers had played in United Fruit's success. As Cutter well knew from years of personal experience, English-speaking West Indians had been critical to

the company's early growth as well as its later strategy of labor segmentation. Although their numbers on the payroll had declined sharply by the
1930s, they still provided an essential source of foremen, skilled laborers,
and strikebreakers who were generally loyal to the company and distrustful
of Hispanic workers and officials. Shorn of access to British West Indians,
the company's labor system would function very differently. Rather than
managing divided laborers in enclaves largely isolated from the host country, United Fruit would face entirely Hispanic workforces unified by ties of
language and Central American identity and far more likely to gain sympathy from local and national officials.

Cutter did not remain at the helm to confront these challenges, for he
too proved a victim of the depression. His downfall emerged from what had
initially appeared his greatest triumph: the acquisition of Cuyamel Fruit.
The deal left the retired Samuel Zemurray as the single largest holder of
United Fruit stock. With Zemurray apparently pleased to retire to his estate
near New Orleans, the granting of this influence to a former rival was only
a minor concern for Cutter. In January 1933, however, with United Fruit's
stock price plummeting, Zemurray emerged from retirement to become
"managing director" of the company, thereby undercutting most of Cutter's
power. The conflict between the two men was revealing. Even more than
Cutter's, Zemurray's was a rags-to-riches story. A Jewish Bessarabian immigrant, he had scraped his way up from fruit hawker on the wharves of
New Orleans to major player in the banana industry. During his rise, he
had arranged the overthrow of at least one president of Honduras, and he
now orchestrated a similar removal of Cutter as head of United Fruit. It
was a bitter pill for Cutter. Although he remained on United Fruit's board
until his death in 1952, he retired to his New Hampshire estate, named
"Musa"—the scientific term for banana. For United Fruit, Zemurray's
takeover underscored the fading New England identity of the multinational corporation.[15]

Despite his triumph over Cutter, Zemurray faced the same problems as
his predecessor, and he continued Cutter's policy of compromising with
nationalist demands in return for new concessions. This pattern was evident in his old stomping grounds of Honduras, where anti-American and
anti-black sentiment reached a crescendo in the early 1930s. Despite the
1929 ban on black immigration, nationalists had continued to target West
Indians in the country, and by the early 1930s Honduran chapters of the
Ku Klux Klan appeared in San Pedro Sula, near the Caribbean coast. Then,
in 1933, the rabidly anti-black Tiburcio Carías came to power. As in other

Central American nations, United Fruit moved to accommodate this surge of racial xenophobia. With Panama disease spreading through its hold-ings, Zemurray's firm could not afford to quibble over immigration policy. Instead, it cultivated a close relationship with Carías and acceded to the deportation of West Indian immigrants from Tela and Trujillo in the mid-1930s. By the end of the decade, it was moving toward an entirely Hispanic workforce, a shift that was taking place at the same time in Costa Rica and Guatemala.[16]

"What Do We Want Costa Rica to Be—Black or White?"

Like most agrarian nations, Costa Rica was hit hard by the Great Depression. In addition to slumping coffee exports, Panama disease threatened to throttle the banana industry. By the late 1920s, United Fruit had already abandoned several of its banana plantations, laying off hundreds of workers, and the blight was also spreading to non-company farms. These developments exacerbated the racial tensions that had been simmering throughout the 1920s. As the competition for the shrinking number of banana jobs grew fiercer, Costa Ricans demanded that citizens be given hiring preferences, while Hispanic workers called for the exclusion of black immigrants from United Fruit's payroll. Meanwhile, a small but growing number of West Indians made their way into the Costa Rican interior searching for jobs. Against this backdrop, the company resumed its negotiations with San José for a new banana contract. Costa Rican officials were eager to prevent United Fruit's withdrawal from the nation and encouraged it to expand its operations. But they recognized the need to address nationalist concerns by pressing reforms on the firm. The completed contract, presented to the Costa Rican Congress in the summer of 1930, seemed to meet many of these conditions. In return for the right to initiate operations on the Pacific Coast, the company accepted a tax increase from one to two cents per stem and promised to improve the living and working conditions of its employees. In addition, the contract required the company to extend hiring preferences to Costa Ricans and to grant some of its infected lands in Limón province to Hispanic settlers.[17]

These compromises were not enough for many nationalists. By giving the company new concessions, they warned, the government was open-ing the door not only to greater corporate domination but also to fur-ther threats to Costa Rica's racial exceptionalism. As U.S. minister Charles

Eberhardt explained in March 1930, "The Costa Rican is very proud of the fact that he has remained white while his Central American brother is, for the most part, a mixed product." And although the government had historically accepted black immigrants as essential to United Fruit's operations, it hoped to confine them to Limón province. "For many years the tunnel on the Limón–San José railway was considered to be the point beyond which blacks could not penetrate into the interior of the country," he noted, "but recently they have been coming up onto the Central Plains in great numbers, all of which is causing uneasiness here."[18]

The tone of public discourse was set by census chief José Guerrero, who in August 1930 published a widely read public letter entitled: "What Do We Want Costa Rica to Be—Black or White? The Black Racial Problem and the Current Banana Negotiations." In it, he linked United Fruit's expansion to the threat black immigration posed to the nation. "The Negro is the shadow of the banana," he warned. "Although today this shadow is confined to the Atlantic Zone, it will move toward other sectors of the republic, which remain unknown because the banana negotiations of 1930 deliberately silence the issue." "Those who manage nigger workforces [*negradas*] in foreign lands, indifferent to the fate of other races already settled there, can dedicate themselves solely to the extraction of wealth," he observed. "[B]ut how can we Costa Ricans who live permanently on this soil be indifferent to the Negro invasion of other sections of our nation?" While maintaining that he had "nothing against anyone, white, Chinese, or Negro," he declared that immigration restriction was simply "a biological matter or more specifically, a eugenic one."[19]

Guerrero's letter received a stirring reply from the *Searchlight,* a West Indian newspaper published in Puerto Limón, which had previously offered sharp critiques of the anti-black rhetoric emanating from San José. Rejecting the notion that blacks threatened Costa Rica's identity and progress, W. A. Petgrave, a resident of Siquerres, asserted that the nation owed its prosperity to West Indians. Echoing the rhetoric that United Fruit had largely discarded, he declared that "were there no Minor Keith, and as a consequence no United Fruit Company, and no Negro, who was able to stand the hardships," Costa Rica would have remained undeveloped and in debt. Therefore, he declared, "the Negroes can with as much reason claim Costa Rica as the land of their adoption as the Spaniard can and they have every right of being proud of their achievement, of making the Atlantic [Zone] what it is." Petgrave went on to dismiss Costa Rican pretensions to whiteness and civilization: "What Costa Rica needs [are] more Negroes becoming Citizens, what Costa Rica needs [are] men who are broad-minded, who have travelled to civilized centres abroad." If blacks were only treated fairly in Costa Rica and neighboring countries, he concluded:

> Latins would be forced to admit after all, that the Negroes, notwithstand-ing what the Yankees would like to say of them[,] are as a matter of fact, as pure [and progressive] . . . as any other race groups, and we would all alike win their respect and appreciation, not as [shadows] for banana trees, but as real he men, and she women.[20]

Despite Petgrave's letter, public denunciations of West Indians and United Fruit continued. Days later, a group of congressional deputies released a statement warning of the "Africanization" of Costa Rica and demand-ing that at least 60 percent of United Fruit's workforce be Costa Rican. Increasingly, anti-black rhetoric was becoming shorthand for hostility toward the company.[21]

It was no coincidence that as debate over the contract and black im-migration raged, United Fruit took several steps to reduce its imperial pro-file. One striking example was the formation of a new subsidiary to take control of the Costa Rica Division. As General Manager M. M. Marsh announced in a September 1930 circular to all United Fruit employees, the new Compañia Bananera de Costa Rica "has acquired all the properties of the Costa Rica Division of the United Fruit Company and . . . will take over all operations of the latter Company." Over the following months, the ubiquitous "United Fruit" signs throughout the enclave gave way to this new title, which aimed to give the company a patina of local identity. Likewise, United Fruit eschewed its practice of giving its banana farms American names. In contrast to titles such as "Buffalo" and "New York" in Limón, farms in its new Pacific division would carry the names of Costa Rican cities, such as "Heredia," "Alajuela," and "Cartago."[22]

Race, Radicalism, and the 1934 Strike

Despite such efforts, resentment of the company and black immigrants continued to grow. In the summer of 1933, the Costa Rican Congress formed a commission to investigate United Fruit's compliance with the 1930 contract. Its members traveled through Limón province interviewing Hispanic farmers and workers. Although the commission's mandate encompassed the entire contract, its final report focused on the supposed predominance of West Indians in United Fruit's workforce. In addition to the commission's own observations, the report included a petition signed by 500 Hispanic residents. "We wish to refer especially to the black problem, which is of transcendental importance," the petition declared:

in the province of Limón it constitutes a situation of privilege for this race and of manifest inferiority for the white race to which we belong. It is not possible to live among them, because their bad morals do not permit it: for them the family does not exist, nor does female honor, and for this reason they live in an overcrowding and promiscuity that is dangerous for our homes, founded in accordance with the religion and good morals of Costa Ricans.

The petitioners went on to warn that Limón "has been transformed, thanks to the passivity and complicity of the authorities and the machinations of the UFCO, into a black colony or fief, which needs only its own authorities and an independent administration to be able to put up a sign saying, 'This was Costa Rica.'" Calling on San José to "remedy this humiliating situation in our homeland by a race inferior to our own, which has no right to invade our lands, our cities and our homes," they declared that "the sovereignty of the nation is at stake."[23]

Racial tensions were raised even higher by a new round of negotiations between United Fruit and the government. By late 1933, the company had concluded that Limón province was beyond recovery and hoped to shift its operations entirely to the Pacific Coast. To do so, however, it needed to secure not only more land concessions but the extension of its commercial monopolies to ports on the Pacific. Its negotiating partner was President Ricardo Jiménez, in his third and final administration (1932–1936). Although Jiménez remained sympathetic to the company's needs, he faced fierce political opposition from both economic nationalists and the rapidly growing Communist Party. In this context, anti-black xenophobia offered him an opportunity to shore up public support while directing nationalist anger away from the terms of the contract. As negotiations proceeded in late 1933 and early 1934, Jiménez and his supporters sought to focus attention on black immigration. In March 1934, the president signed a law banning visas and visa extensions for "the negro race," and some congressional deputies suggested legislation prohibiting blacks from residing in any province other than Limón.[24]

These attempts to contain and exclude West Indians coincided with similar efforts throughout the Hispanic Caribbean. It was in these same months, for example, that the Grau government in Cuba was banning black immigration and Panamanian negotiators were pushing for control over immigration to the Canal Zone. These parallels were not lost on Costa Rican elites. As one British diplomat observed, Costa Ricans seemed terrified of following the example of Panama, "which is already on the way to becoming a black republic."[25] American officials agreed, though they shied away from acknowledging the U.S. role in fomenting these racial anxieties. As one U.S. diplomat observed, because "Costa Ricans in general are of the Aryan race and quite proud of this fact and are making an endeavor to keep their race pure, . . . the fact that large numbers of negroes had been entering the country has been giving the Government some cause for alarm."[26] In reality, few West Indians were entering Costa Rica or any other nation in the Hispanic Caribbean in the 1930s, but anti-black rhetoric kept nationalists and workers focused on immigration.

In the midst of such attacks, it is hardly surprising that West Indians proved reluctant to cooperate with Hispanic labor organizers, including those of the Communist Party. By 1933, party activists had expanded their activities in Limón province. Although they made some initial attempts to overcome the racial divisions among banana workers, they faced a frosty reception from the black community. West Indians in the region were generally better off than their Hispanic counterparts and less resentful of United Fruit. In addition to having access to higher-paid positions in the company's labor hierarchy, they made up a significant proportion of the independent farmers and shopkeepers in and around Puerto Limón. Equally important, decades of Hispanic hostility had made most West Indians skeptical of interracial cooperation. As a result, Communist organizers quickly abandoned efforts to organize black workers.[27]

The ramifications of this decision became apparent when the party launched a banana strike in August 1934. Although the union's initial demands focused on bread-and-butter issues such as hours, wages, and treatment, few black workers supported the strike. This response stemmed not from a lack of sympathy with strikers' grievances but rather from West Indians' painful awareness of their tenuous position in Costa Rica. With the Jiménez government chipping away at the rights of black immigrants and the British government offering less protection than in previous years, many West Indians viewed United Fruit as their only ally in Costa Rica.

Moreover, West Indian laborers understood that the strikers' calls for class solidarity were opportunistic at best, as Hispanic workers continued to demand preferential hiring for Spanish-speakers and even the exclusion of blacks from company jobs. Local UNIA leaders contributed to this anti-strike stance, calling on West Indian workers and community members to stand by United Fruit.[28]

West Indian loyalty to the company in turn drew out the barely concealed anti-black sentiment among Hispanic workers. As the strike dragged on, Hispanic laborers complained that West Indians were enabling United Fruit to resist their demands. As a result, the strikers' focus on economic issues soon gave way to calls for black deportation and exclusion. For its part, the Costa Rican government played up these divisions. Despite the virtual absence of West Indians among the strikers, government officials and newspapers in the capital attributed the strike to "foreign" agitation. The accusation contained a grain of truth, as a large number of the strikers were from other Central American nations. But many Costa Ricans read "foreign" as "black." Consequently, West Indians found themselves accused of both inciting and undermining the strike.[29]

Negotiating Exclusion

Nor did West Indians' loyalty to United Fruit help their cause. Even before the strike ended in September 1934, the firm had agreed to a new contract with San José. In return for receiving a virtual monopoly over the banana industry on the Pacific Coast, United Fruit pledged itself to better treatment of private planters, hiring preferences for Costa Rican citizens, and the complete exclusion of "Jamaicans and other Negroes" from its new Pacific enclave. Such language betrayed the racial nationalism driving Costa Rican demands.[30] Rather than applying to all noncitizens, the contract singled out black immigrants. For its part, United Fruit was hardly pleased with this compromise. Company officials remained convinced that West Indians were more reliable and efficient than Hispanics, and they were loath to abandon the labor segmentation system that had proven so successful. United Fruit also feared that an entirely Hispanic workforce would be more difficult to control. Nevertheless, most company officials accepted black exclusion as the price they had to pay for concessions on the Pacific Coast. Fewer recognized that the firm itself had helped generate the anti-black sentiment that now constricted its labor system.

From the perspective of West Indians in Costa Rica, the 1934 contract was a devastating betrayal. Since its founding, United Fruit had relied on black immigrant laborers to build and maintain its enclave. Although it had consciously used them to foster divisions within its workforce, it also provided some protection from Costa Rican calls for immigration restriction and deportation. Equally important, United Fruit had served as a vehicle for social mobility, providing West Indians with opportunities to rise to positions as foremen and skilled laborers and to gain the capital needed to establish their own farms and businesses. Now, as the company shifted its operations to Pacific Coast, West Indians found themselves excluded from those opportunities.[31]

At the same time, the atmosphere in Limón province grew ever more hostile to black residents. Following the defeat of the strike and signing of the 1934 contract, Costa Rican officials and Hispanic employees of United Fruit proved eager to assert their authority over West Indians, and in the process buttress their claims to whiteness. These efforts emerged in the exchanges between the American managers and Costa Rican employees of the Northern Railway. In October 1934, for example, Northern Railway supervisor Justino Vallejo reported to his American supervisor that he had seen "38 darkies [*negritos*]" stealing rides on a work train. The train coalmen did little to stop them, he complained, because "they are darkies too, who let their Countrymen travel on the trains for free."[32] The violent potential of such attitudes became apparent a month later when railroad conductor Juan Montero shoved West Indian Isaac Robinson to the floor of a train car after Robinson asked to pass him in the aisle. In his complaint to railroad manager Frank Sheehy, Robinson declared that he had lived in Costa Rica since 1902 and had "never [been] push[ed] by no man" and demanded that the conductor be punished. For his part, Montero at first denied pushing Robinson, then attributed the incident to black insolence. In response to a letter from Sheehy emphasizing the need to treat passengers with respect, Montero explained, "I understand well my responsibilities with respect to the public, but some Passengers of Color abuse their rights, walking from one car to another while the train is moving." When conductors force them to take their seats, he noted, "they protest, and this they call mistreatment."[33]

Government policies reflected this determination to put West Indians in their place. In addition to strengthening San José's authority in Limón, the 1934 contract provided for the transfer of much of United Fruit's property in the province to the Costa Rican government, including nearly the entire Zent district.[34] Costa Rican officials planned to use these lands to promote crop diversification by sponsoring new agrarian settlements, which they viewed as a means of securing Hispanic predominance in the region. By excluding blacks from its benefits, the resulting land grant program accelerated the Hispanic migration that had been building since the 1910s.[35] And as the number of Spanish-speaking residents increased, so did popular pressure to subordinate the West Indian community. By 1935, the municipal government of Puerto Limón had begun to exclude blacks from public parks, and soon segregated cinemas and bathing facilities appeared. Such practices had much in common with those in United Fruit's enclave, and indeed many Costa Ricans attributed segregation to the influence of the company and the expectations of American tourists. More broadly, however, these trends were symptomatic of a rising racial nationalism that aimed to assert the racial supremacy and whiteness of Hispanic Costa Ricans.[36]

The bitter irony of these trends was not lost on the West Indian community. In the late nineteenth century, when Costa Ricans had shunned the Caribbean lowlands, it was black immigrants who had built the railroad, cleared the lands, and poisoned the mosquito-breeding swamps. Now that their labor had raised the living conditions of the province, Hispanic migrants were calling for their subordination and even expulsion. The situation only grew worse after 1935, when Sigatoka disease appeared in Limón. Unlike Panama disease, which spread via the soil, the airborne Sigatoka could spread over long distances.[37] The disease threatened to cripple corporate and independent banana farming throughout Central America and hastened United Fruit's shift away from the Caribbean coast. As banana jobs moved from Limón to the Pacific lowlands, however, West Indians remained locked out of the new enclave. The result was rising unemployment and desperation, particularly among young blacks in Costa Rica. Even those born in the country were barred from jobs on the Pacific Coast. Limón-born Martin Luther, for example, recalled traveling with a friend in 1937 to Puntarenas province, where they met an American employee of United Fruit who had previously been a supervisor in one of the company's machine shops in Limón. According to Luther, the American was "glad to see" the two English-speaking West Indians and tried to find them positions. In the end, however, "he [was] not able to employ us" because of the "law that the colored people should not go on the Pacific side."[38] Over the following decades, this exclusion from employment in the Pacific enclave proved so complete that Costa Ricans and West Indians alike would misremember it as legally confining blacks to Limón province.

Nationalism and a New Contract in Guatemala

Regional trends and the global economic crisis had a similar impact on
Guatemala. Despite growing pressure from reactionary forces, the nation's
political opening remained largely intact through 1929 and most of 1930.
The National Assembly retained its autonomy, and newspapers in Guatemala
City continued to criticize the policies of both the U.S. government and
United Fruit. In September 1929, for example, the newspaper *Nuestro
Diario* condemned Washington for supporting "dictatorial" and "tyrannical"
regimes that served U.S. business interests.[39] The onset of the Great
Depression only heightened these tensions. The global decline in trade and
prices brought massive wage cuts and layoffs, particularly in the coffee sector.
In an effort to boost his faltering public support, President Lázaro Chacón
again turned to racial xenophobia. Despite the fact that immigration had
nearly ground to a halt by early 1930, government officials and nationalist
newspapers stoked fears of an "invasion" by foreign undesirables, including
not only West Indians but Jewish and Gypsy "peddlers." Indeed, in February
1930, Chacón added most Middle Easterners and Eastern Europeans to
Chinese on the list of banned immigrants.[40]

Amid this heightened economic and racial anxiety, Guatemalan and
United Fruit officials resumed their contract negotiations. As in Costa Rica,
the company's primary objective was to gain concessions in the Pacific lowlands. With Panama disease continuing its spread in Izabal, the firm needed
access to new lands. For his part, Chacón remained willing to cooperate, but
he sought to prevent a public backlash by inserting several nationalist demands in the agreement. The contract, announced shortly after Chacón's new
immigration restrictions, granted United Fruit land and commercial rights
in the department of Escuintla on the Pacific slope and exemption from
Guatemalan labor laws. In return, United Fruit agreed to build a new port,
hospital, and school in the region. As in the 1880s, Guatemalan leaders hoped
to use foreign capital to develop an impoverished region of the nation. At the
same time, however, they planned to prevent a full replication of the company's Caribbean enclave. Under the new contract, United Fruit and its employees were now obligated to obey all immigration laws, including the $200
deposit for black immigrants, and the company was to ensure that 75 percent
of its employees were indeed Guatemalan citizens. Although less explicit than
the terms of Costa Rica's contract four years later, these conditions aimed to
prevent the company from importing West Indians to its new enclave.[41]

Despite these requirements, nationalists denounced the agreement, warning that it would tighten the company's stranglehold on the country. In the spring and summer of 1930, the National Assembly repeatedly rejected the contract, to the applause of students and independent banana planters. Meanwhile, as the economic crisis worsened and unemployed workers and *campesinos* grew restive, the Guatemalan elite worried increasingly about social disorder. In late 1930, the ailing Chacón resigned, giving way to Jorge Ubico, a Liberal military officer who had distinguished himself during Estrada Cabrera's reign. In a hastily organized election in February 1931, Ubico ran as the only name on the ballot, and won by the decisive margin of 305,841 to 0. Over the next thirteen years, he would rule Guatemala as a dictator.[42]

Dictatorship and Depression

Ubico's regime reflected the broader wave of authoritarianism that swept Central America in response to the social unrest of the early 1930s. In addition to Carías in Honduras, this included the rise of Salvadoran strongman Maximiliano Hernández Martínez, who ordered the massacre of some 30,000 rebelling *campesinos* in January 1932. Nicaragua moved in the same direction. Following the U.S. Marines' withdrawal in early 1933, Washington vested political power in the U.S.-trained national guard led by Anastasio Somoza, who over the following three years assassinated Sandino and established a personal dictatorship. By the mid-1930s, Costa Rica was the only nation in Central America that retained a constitutional government. Although U.S. officials generally regretted this trend toward authoritarianism, they accepted right-wing dictators as the best means of maintaining order and American influence, particularly within the confines of the Good Neighbor Policy.[43]

United Fruit agreed. Over the previous decade, the firm had grown weary of negotiating with democratic governments. From the company's perspective, dictators such as Ubico could provide a friendlier and more predictable business environment. In addition to keeping laborers in check, they could grant generous concessions without the public debates or nationalist opposition that often marked democratic rule. Cutter certainly saw it that way. In a speech delivered just two months before his own ouster, the United Fruit president observed, "I don't know about spiritual values in countries that are ruled by dictators, but I do know that they are always run efficiently. In fact, I wouldn't mind seeing dictators in Massachusetts right now—and in Washington as well. At least things would be run on an efficient basis."[44]

Ubico indeed ran Guatemala efficiently, at least in the eyes of company officials. As an heir to Liberal dictators such as Barrios and Estrada Cabrera, he placed top priority on good relations with foreign capital, and particularly United Fruit. With the decline of coffee prices to one-third of their 1920s levels by 1931, moreover, the banana industry assumed unprecedented importance in the Guatemalan economy, and Ubico was determined to keep the firm happy. In May 1931, he pushed the stalled Pacific contract through the National Assembly and then cracked down fiercely on all opposition to the agreement. It was a sign of things to come. By early 1932, as the neighboring Salvadoran regime was carrying out its massacre, Ubico moved against his own political opponents, rounding up labor leaders and political dissidents. Such repression ensured that United Fruit would confront none of the labor militancy and Communist agitation in its Guatemala Division that it faced in Costa Rica.[45]

Nevertheless, labor issues loomed large in the rest of Guatemala. With the fall of coffee prices, Guatemalan planters had slashed their wages, which were already among the lowest in the hemisphere. Now, with even less hope of paying off their debts, an unprecedented number of seasonal Mayan laborers failed to appear at coffee estates during the harvest season. By the mid-1930s, the labor system that had supported Guatemala's main industry since the 1870s was approaching collapse. In May 1934, Ubico attempted to resolve this labor crisis with a decree outlawing debt peonage, eliminating with a stroke of a pen the debts of Mayan laborers. Just days later, however, he announced a new vagrancy law. Henceforth, all Guatemalans below a set income level would be required to sell up to half of their workdays to employers, and they could also be forced to labor on national roads without wages. Under the guise of progressive reform, in other words, Ubico had expanded the nation's coercive labor system and placed labor procurement in the hands of the state. Americans in Guatemala generally welcomed these measures. U.S. diplomats had long viewed the nation's system of debt peonage as a holdover of the colonial period, and they largely ignored the troubling implications of the vagrancy law. For its part, United Fruit hoped the reforms would free up more laborers for its new Pacific division.[46]

The Pacific Enclave

Although the company had been contemplating development of a Pacific enclave since the 1920s and had secured extensive rights in the region under the 1930 contract, it was the appearance of Sigatoka disease in 1935 that lent urgency to the project. As in Costa Rica, with farm after farm being abandoned on the Caribbean coast, the company increasingly looked to the Pacific slope to replace rather than supplement the production of its older enclave. But by this time, United Fruit was reevaluating the wisdom of building a new Pacific port. Not only would it be an expensive investment in a time of shrinking revenue, but a new port would open the firm to competition from Pacific shipping lines such as W. R. Grace. By exporting the new division's bananas through Puerto Barrios, in contrast, the company would provide badly needed freight to both the IRCA and United Fruit's steamship line. To accomplish this, however, the company would have to convince Ubico to free it from its obligation under the 1930 contract to construct the Pacific port. In a new round of negotiations in 1935–1936, Zemurray and his negotiators adamantly maintained that the combination of slumping markets and Sigatoka disease left the firm with insufficient funds to build the port.[47]

Ubico was sympathetic to such arguments. Determined to maintain export revenue and eager to avoid offending Washington as he continued to consolidate his power, the dictator agreed to amend the 1930 contract. In the context of Sigatoka's rapid spread, however, Guatemalan negotiators found themselves in a stronger position than their Costa Rican counterparts two years earlier. Although United Fruit could still threaten to withdraw from Guatemala, company officials desperately wanted to retain their concessions on the Pacific slope. The contract of 1936 reflected these competing objectives. In return for the suspension of its obligation to build the Pacific port, United Fruit accepted a hike in the annual rent of its operations in Izabal and an increase of the banana export tax to 1.5 cents per stem—still less than Costa Rica's. In addition, it agreed to provide Guatemala with a low-interest $1 million loan and to transfer 35,000 acres of its land in Izabal to the Guatemalan state, which Ubico planned to offer to Hispanic settlers. Finally, the company strengthened its commitment to exclude black workers from its new enclave. As in Costa Rica, United Fruit's desire to expand to the Pacific had provided its host state with the opportunity both to exclude black immigrants from jobs in the new division and to accelerate the Hispanicization of the Caribbean coast.

Faced with shrinking economic opportunities and *ladino* hostility, the West Indian population of Izabal continued to decline in the late 1930s.[48]

Meanwhile, United Fruit's Pacific enclave was booming. By the time Frances Emery-Waterhouse arrived in 1937, some 150 American personnel lived in the headquarters of Tiquisate, which boasted a school, church, clubhouse, golf course, swimming pool, tennis courts, baseball fields, a bowling alley, and a modern hospital modeled on that of Quiriguá.[49] Indeed, on the surface, it seemed to replicate the structures and practices of the firm's Caribbean enclave. But there were also striking differences that mirrored those of the new Pacific division in Costa Rica. First, in an attempt to obscure its power and minimize nationalist resentment, the company ran the entire division through its subsidiary, the Compañía Agrícola, and used Guatemalan rather than American names to map its territory. In contrast to "Virginia" in Izabal, for example, the company retained the title "Tiquisate" for its new headquarters on the Pacific; likewise, farm names such as "Cayuga" and "Dartmouth" gave way to indigenous titles such as "Zuñil" and "Siguacán." At the same time, the Compañía Agrícola hired a small but growing number of educated, light-skinned Guatemalans for supervisory positions. Although such employees often faced discrimination from American coworkers, they found some common ground in their views of the Maya. Unlike Guatemalan coffee planters, United Fruit managers considered the highland Maya, along with all women, too frail for plantation work, but they did embrace elite *ladino* claims that indigenous peoples made natural servants. Indeed, in contrast to United Fruit's Caribbean enclave, where labor in managers' homes tended to be performed by West Indians, nearly all of the domestic servants in the Pacific enclave were Mayan.[50]

Second, and far more consequential, the workforce on the new enclave's banana farms was entirely Hispanic. While United Fruit continued to view West Indians as its most loyal and reliable employees, it remained limited by the anti-black sentiment that it had helped foment over the previous three decades. Although a few West Indians worked in the pharmacy and commissary of Tiquisate, the company excluded them from positions on the enclave's banana farms and rail cars. As in Costa Rica, it would be unable to replicate the labor segmentation system that had served it so well in the Caribbean lowlands. The Spanish-speaking workforce in its new enclave was not homogenous, to be sure. Along with Guatemalan *ladinos*, many of whom had followed the banana jobs from the Caribbean coast to the Pacific, a significant number of laborers came from other Central American nations, as well as Mexico. But despite differences of nationality, these workers would prove far more difficult to divide and dominate, particularly during the democratic awakening of the 1940s.

The 1930s had brought striking transformations to the U.S. empire in Central America and the rest of the Hispanic Caribbean. The most visible change was Washington's Good Neighbor Policy, which put an end to the imperial protectorates and military interventions that had long marked U.S. government policy in the Hispanic Caribbean. But the same nationalist resentment that pushed Washington to alter its policies led United Fruit to its own version of the Good Neighbor. In the company's case, this meant not only espousing Pan-American rhetoric and forming subsidiaries to hide its sprawling power but also ending a labor system that had played a critical role in U.S. expansion. Since the 1850s, American businesses, as well as the U.S. government, had employed British West Indian laborers to build the infrastructure and commercial enclaves that formed the foundation of the U.S. empire in Central America. Even after their proportion in the workforces of U.S. enclaves began to decline in the mid-1910s, black immigrants remained critical to the labor control strategies of United Fruit and other American employers. But those same labor policies all but ensured that anti-black sentiment would form a central component of the nationalism and labor radicalism that swept the region in the 1920s and 1930s. The result, by 1940, was the banning of West Indians from nearly all U.S. employment in Central America.

At the time, the full implications of this change for United Fruit were not immediately apparent. Although host nations had long pressed the company to limit black employment and obey immigration restrictions, the exclusion of West Indians hardly seemed a major victory for Hispanic nationalism. True, black workers were locked out of banana jobs on Central America's Pacific Coast, but Spanish-speaking "natives" still occupied a racially subordinate position in the new enclaves. Despite appearances, however, the compromise on black employment marked a sea change in the company's relationship to its host nations. By acquiescing to racial nationalism in Costa Rica and Guatemala, United Fruit had deprived itself of the labor system that had been the foundation of its operations since the 1910s. Unable to impose a similar degree of segmentation on its Hispanic workers, the firm found itself ever more vulnerable to nationalist agitation and democratic reform. Although the company would continue to wield tremendous power in Central America, the racial exclusions of the 1930s augured the end of United Fruit's era of corporate colonialism.

Epilogue

On 17 May 1954, the U.S. Supreme Court handed down its unanimous decision in the case of *Brown v. Board of Education* declaring segregated schools "inherently unequal." The result of a long legal battle waged by the NAACP, the ruling opened the door for the modern Civil Rights Movement and the eventual defeat of white supremacy in the U.S. South. On its face, the Court's decision had little to do with the U.S. empire in Central America, except for the role played by Dr. Kenneth Clark. A psychologist active in racial issues, Clark had conducted the famous research known as the "doll test," which was cited by the Court as evidence of the psychological damage that segregation inflicted on black children. He was also a product of the intersection between U.S. imperial expansion and West Indian migration. Clark had been born in the Panama Canal Zone in July 1914, just weeks before the canal's opening. His Jamaican parents, Arthur and Miriam Clark, were among the thousands of British West Indians who had migrated to Panama during the construction years, and by the time of Kenneth's birth Arthur held a well-paying position as a cargo supervisor and passenger agent for United Fruit. In 1919, Miriam decided to move her children to New York City, joining the wave of West Indian immigrants to Harlem in the late 1910s and early 1920s, among them Marcus Garvey. Fearing the racism and lack of opportunity he would face in the United States, Arthur refused to go, and Kenneth grew up fatherless amid the street-corner oratory of UNIA officials and the literary outpouring of the Harlem Renaissance.[1] He then attended Howard University, where he met and married Arkansas-born Mamie Phipps, the daughter of a West Indian doctor. Together the couple went on to earn Ph.D.s in psychology at Columbia University and to collaborate on a series of research projects on racial inequality in the United States, including the doll test. The *Brown v. Board* decision was not the result of Kenneth Clark's efforts alone, to be sure. A range of factors contributed to the ruling, among them the discrediting of racist thought in the wake of World War II, the Cold War competition with the Soviet Union for world leadership, and the astute legal arguments of the NAACP.[2] Nevertheless, the important role played by Clark, the Canal Zone–born son of a black United Fruit employee, underscores the enduring ties between domestic racial dynamics and the U.S. empire in the postwar years.

Washington at the Helm

World War II transformed the United States' relationship with the world, and Central America was no exception. Even as the U.S. government armed its allies and projected its power across the Atlantic and Pacific, it became the dominant economic force in the broader Caribbean, as well as in much of South America. This role was not entirely new. Along with its numerous military occupations, Washington had a long history of intervening in the financial and commercial affairs of Central America and the rest of the Hispanic Caribbean, and the construction of the Panama Canal had powerfully influenced regional trade and migration patterns. Nevertheless, prior to World War II, it had been private capital, and above all United Fruit, that had served as the primary agent of American expansion and conveyor of U.S. imperial culture. In the early 1940s, however, Washington itself became the single most important purchaser, creditor, and employer in the region.[3]

    This trend was most apparent in nations where the U.S. government already had a permanent presence. In Panama, as fears of a European war grew in the late 1930s, Washington pushed ahead with plans for new construction and fortifications in and around the Canal Zone. Because American negotiators had refused to accept Panamanian immigration restrictions in the 1936 contract, U.S. officials were free to hire black immigrants. Jobs in the Canal Zone attracted thousands of West Indian workers from the British colonies as well as from United Fruit's decaying enclaves on Central America's Caribbean coast, particularly in neighboring Costa Rica. The ensuing influx of West Indians brought a resurgence of racial nationalism in Panama. In addition to demanding that black newcomers be confined to the Canal Zone and repatriated after their work was completed, the Panamanian government adopted a new constitution in 1941 that denied citizenship to West Indian immigrants as well as to their children born in Panamanian territory.[4]

The expansion of the U.S. naval base in Cuba's Guantánamo Bay likewise spurred labor migration. Although Washington had leased the territory since 1903, it was World War II that transformed it into a major military base. The intensive construction effort of the early 1940s created new job opportunities, especially for Cubans in the nearby town of Guantánamo. This proved a smooth transition for the many who had already worked in the sugar enclaves of United Fruit and other private firms in eastern Cuba. The corporate connections did not end there, however, for among the ranks of white American military officers and private contractors on the base were former United Fruit employees. The world they helped create in Guantánamo Bay must have seemed strikingly familiar. Not only did white personnel on the base enjoy the privileges of a colonial elite, but the U.S. government manipulated the racial tensions between Cuban and West Indian laborers. And although local Cubans drew upon the values of the Good Neighbor Policy to press for preferential hiring, U.S. base officials routinely placed English-speaking West Indians in positions of authority over Spanish-speaking coworkers.[5]

The U.S. government's expansion also had a profound impact on the British Caribbean itself. The Great Depression had devastated the economies of the British West Indies. In addition to collapsing export markets and declining financial support from London, the colonies found themselves shut out of employment in U.S. enclaves, which had previously served as critical outlets for out-of-work laborers. By the late 1930s, nearly every nation in Central America and the rest of the Hispanic Caribbean prohibited black immigration. Beginning in 1937, West Indian frustration boiled over in a wave of strikes that swept the British Caribbean, threatening colonial authority and social order. In this context, it is hardly surprising that British officials and West Indian workers alike welcomed not only the expanded hiring in the Canal Zone and Guantánamo Bay, but the construction of U.S. government enclaves in the British colonies themselves. The watershed moment came with the 1940 Destroyers for Bases agreement with Great Britain. In return for transferring 50 naval destroyers to London, Washington received the right to build bases on British colonies in the Western Hemisphere, most of them in the West Indies. The most important sites were in Trinidad, where both the U.S. Navy and Army established military enclaves, claimed exclusive rights to sites in Port of Spain, and built transit corridors not unlike those in Central America. In the process, they also sought to establish segregated space between Trinidadians and the overwhelmingly white American personnel. Despite efforts to limit interactions with local inhabitants, however, the U.S. government learned, like United Fruit before it, that it was almost impossible to isolate its enclaves from their host societies. Over the following years, these U.S. military bases inevitably played a role in the debate over empire and decolonization in the British Caribbean.[6]

A less visible aspect of Washington's wartime economic expansion was its impact on tropical agriculture. The driving force behind this change was the Japanese conquest of colonial Southeast Asia, which had cut off imports of critical products such as rubber, manila cordage, and quinine. To make up the shortfall, Washington extended loans and subsidies to countries and corporations throughout Central America and the Caribbean to encourage cultivation of the plants needed to produce these materials. In this effort, U.S. officials drew upon the expertise of United Fruit. In addition to supporting the company's experiments with strategic crops, Washington hired former United Fruit employees as tropical agriculture experts. Among them was Frances Emery-Waterhouse's husband, Russell, who had been fired from his job with United Fruit in Guatemala in 1941 after Frances published an article highlighting the Ubico regime's ties to Nazi Germany. Soon after, Russell accepted a U.S. government job on Costa Rica's Caribbean coast supervising the cultivation of abacá, the source of manila fiber and a relative of the banana plant. The accompanying injection of U.S. funds proved a welcome relief to the jobless West Indians still residing in Limón province, many of whom found themselves once again employed by United Fruit, albeit ultimately paid with U.S. government funds. Although the end of World War II prompted Washington to withdraw from this direct role in agricultural production, its economic power in Central America and the rest of the Caribbean had been permanently expanded.[7]

Costa Rica and Guatemala

The war years brought change to Costa Rica and Guatemala as well. In Costa Rica, the growing influence of the Communist Party in the late 1930s heightened anxieties among the political elite. Despite its defeat in the 1934 strike, the party had continued to gain strength, and several of its members held key positions in the administration of Rafael Calderón Guardia (1940–1944). By 1948, with Calderón poised to take power once again, an opposition movement led by the charismatic José María Figueres launched an armed rebellion. After a few weeks of fighting, the insurgents ousted the elected government and created a provisional junta. Figueres dominated Costa Rican politics for the following decade, serving as president in 1948–1949 and 1953–1958. Despite coming to power in a violent coup, he did more than any other figure to place Costa Rica on an exceptional course. In addition to disbanding the Costa Rican army, he nationalized the country's banking system, expanded social security, and instituted labor reforms. At the same time, his fiercely anti-Communist posture enabled him to avoid the fate of other Latin American reformers, including Guatemala's Jacobo Arbenz. Indeed, it was no coincidence that Figueres, who began his 1953 term by denouncing Costa Rica's status as a "banana republic" under United Fruit's "economic occupation," softened his rhetoric following the U.S.-sponsored overthrow of Arbenz the following year.[8]

Yet, if Figueres was unable to oust United Fruit, he went far toward healing Costa Rica's racial wounds. Especially striking were his attempts to reach out to West Indians. In the 1950s, the West Indian community remained deeply suspicious of Costa Rican Communists and their association with Hispanic racism. Figueres understood this dynamic and pushed to extend citizenship to black residents. By socializing with West Indian leaders and courting black voters in Limón, he built a new base of support in Limón province while isolating leftists. His efforts began the long process of incorporating West Indians into Costa Rican society.[9] Over the following decades, like their counterparts in the United States, blacks gained legal equality, including the right to seek employment anywhere in the nation, and Costa Rica itself remained free from the bloody conflicts that devastated the rest of Central America in the 1970s and 1980s. But the legacy of corporate and Hispanic racism remains. Black Costa Ricans still reside almost entirely on the Caribbean coast, where they suffer from widespread unemployment and poverty.[10] For their part, residents of the Central Valley continue to inform visitors that the nation owes its stability and prosperity to its unblemished whiteness, even as they claim to be free of U.S.-style racism. It was such thinking that enabled one Costa Rican host father to assure a U.S. exchange student in 1996 that "We Costa Ricans aren't racist like you Americans. We get along with blacks just fine. The only problem is that they are all lazy."[11]

The postwar period proved far more painful for Guatemala. It began with great hope, as a democratic movement known as the "October Revolution" overthrew Ubico in 1944. In addition to instituting universal male suffrage (and limited female suffrage), the new reformist president, Juan José Arévalo, abolished the vagrancy law and passed legislation granting workers the right to organize. Although the new labor law did not apply to most agricultural workers, political mobilization soon led to calls for reform of agrarian labor and land tenure. Not surprisingly, United Fruit's Pacific division proved a pivotal site in this struggle. By the 1940s, the Tiquisate Division on Guatemala's Pacific Coast had become the most productive part of United Fruit's empire, accounting for more than a quarter of the company's Latin American exports. But Ubico's fall, like that of Estrada Cabrera two decades earlier, left the firm exposed to nationalist criticism and labor mobilization. In contrast to earlier years, moreover, United Fruit faced a unified workforce. Due to immigration restrictions and the conditions of the 1936 contract, the company had been unable to impose an effective system of labor segmentation on its almost entirely Hispanic workforce, and by the late 1940s its laborers had struck for higher wages and organized the largest rural union in the nation.[12]

The firm's situation only worsened with the election of Jacobo Arbenz, a left-leaning former military officer. In Arbenz, United Fruit faced a leader not only supportive of workers' rights but also committed to dismantling the company's imperial hold on Guatemala. In addition to denouncing United Fruit's barely concealed rail monopoly, Arbenz signed a sweeping land redistribution law in 1952. Although the reform applied to all large estates, United Fruit claimed it was being singled out for persecution and denounced Arbenz as a closet Communist, which he may well have been. In this effort, even more than in earlier decades, the company benefited from close ties to the U.S. government. Secretary of State John Foster Dulles had previously served as United Fruit's attorney, and his brother, CIA Director Allen Dulles, had sat on the company's board. In addition, the firm's chief Washington lobbyist was married to President Dwight Eisenhower's personal secretary. Nevertheless, in the charged Cold War atmosphere of the

Figure 7. United Fruit Board of Directors, ca. 1950. Victor Cutter is seated at the back left.
Courtesy of Dartmouth College Library

early 1950s, Eisenhower likely needed little convincing of the threat posed by the Guatemalan revolution.[13] In 1954, he approved a CIA-sponsored coup that overthrew Arbenz and reversed the land reform. The operation set Guatemala on the path to a brutal civil war that lasted from 1961 to 1996. At the time, however, Arbenz's fall seemed a clear-cut victory for the U.S. government and United Fruit.

The company's celebration proved short-lived. Just months after the coup in Guatemala, the U.S. government filed an antitrust lawsuit against United Fruit. In light of its longstanding cooperation with Washington, the firm viewed the move as a betrayal. From the perspective of many U.S. officials, however, United Fruit was not only an abusive monopoly but an embarrassing holdover from an earlier age of corporate colonialism. Like segregation in the U.S. South, it had become a liability in the Cold War struggle for hearts and minds. As Secretary of State Dulles put it, "many of the Central American countries were convinced that the sole objective of United States foreign policy was to protect the fruit company."[14] By the late 1950s, facing slumping sales and stock prices, the company agreed to a settlement that required it to sell off many of its overseas assets, including the IRCA and the Compañía Agrícola. By the early 1970s, it no longer had holdings in Guatemala.[15]

The Postcolonial Turn

The U.S. government's decision to break up United Fruit was part of a larger postcolonial turn for the U.S. empire in the Caribbean. In the face of rising anti-Americanism throughout Latin America in the late 1950s and early 1960s, Washington became ever more determined to eliminate longstanding sources of nationalist resentment.[16] In Panama, for example, U.S. officials found themselves less able to justify the colonial character of the Canal Zone. In 1955, Washington had attempted to sooth the Panamanians by agreeing to end the silver and gold system. Over the following decade, however, even as the U.S. government struggled to respond to civil rights activism and white backlash at home, it faced mounting tensions in and around the Canal Zone. In January 1964, bloody clashes between American and Panamanian high school students helped set the U.S. government on the path to recognizing Panamanian sovereignty in the Canal Zone.[17]

The Cuban Revolution presented even greater challenges. By 1961, in addition to allying with the Soviet Union and confiscating U.S. investments (including those of United Fruit), Fidel Castro's regime was undercutting American claims to moral leadership by criticizing race relations in the United States and throughout its empire. Tensions between Washington and Havana had a profound impact on the relationship between the naval base in Guantánamo Bay and the surrounding Cuban communities. In the wake of the 1962 Cuban Missile Crisis, the U.S. government fired most of its local workers and began hiring British West Indians almost exclusively. Over the following decades, the base became a true enclave, closed off from its host state and sustained by Jamaican contract laborers. Like United Fruit officials in the 1910s, military commanders at GTMO combined often-demeaning attitudes toward West Indians with efforts to cultivate their loyalty, including annual celebrations of Jamaican Independence Day. Although described by one scholar as a new "postmodern" labor arrangement, these strategies had a long history in the U.S. empire.[18]

United Fruit itself underwent major transitions in this same period. In 1970, control of the struggling firm passed to investment banker Eli Black, who merged it with his meatpacking interests to form "United Brands."[19] Despite Black's efforts to revive the once-dominant company, he confronted a series of crises in the 1970s. In 1973, a new, more destructive banana disease, dubbed "Black Sigatoka," appeared in Central America, forcing United Brands and its competitors to expand their already heavy use of chemical pesticides. The following year, Hurricane Fifi flattened vast tracts of the company's banana farms and accelerated the spread of the disease.[20] Meanwhile, the successful oil embargo carried out by the Organization of Petroleum Exporting Countries (OPEC) helped inspire the banana-exporting countries to form their own cartel. Struggling to keep the firm afloat amid revelations that he had bribed the president of Honduras to lower his country's export taxes, Black committed suicide in 1975.

In the following decades, the corporation continued down its postcolonial path. In 1984, soon after ordering its overseas divisions to destroy their archives, it renamed itself "Chiquita Brands." This new incarnation of United Fruit accelerated the process of divestiture that had begun in the late 1950s. Although it still operated subsidiaries, it increasingly withdrew from direct cultivation of bananas in favor a system of contract farming pioneered a century before by Minor Keith. Under this arrangement, local planters hired and managed their own workers while relying on Chiquita and other North American corporations for credit, technology, pesticide, and access to U.S. markets. Although working and living conditions on Central American banana farms remained largely unchanged, laborers now directed their resentment primarily at the contract planters who were their direct employers, rather than the massive agribusinesses that stood in the background.[21]

Despite its lower profile in Central America, Chiquita continued to have the ear of the U.S. government. In the mid-1990s, it convinced the Clinton administration to file a grievance with the World Trade Organization against the European Union. Arguing that the EU's quota system gave an unfair advantage to banana farmers in the West Indies, Washington demanded that U.S. companies enjoy open access to the European market. The ensuing "banana wars" briefly captured headlines. While business groups viewed it as a test case for free trade, organizations such as Washington-based TransAfrica warned that the U.S. suit would undermine small-scale farmers in the West Indies without benefiting workers or consumers in the United States. By 2002, the WTO had ruled in favor of Chiquita, and the EU had agreed to dismantle its quota system.[22]

Bananas and Empire

By the time of these trade disputes in the late 1990s, few Americans associated bananas with overseas empire, and fewer still reflected on the long history of race, labor migration, and U.S. corporate colonialism that had shaped the Central American banana industry. If university students were assigned any reading at all on United Fruit, it invariably dealt with the 1954 overthrow of Arbenz in Guatemala, not the firm's pivotal role in U.S. imperial expansion in the early 1900s.[23] In the heyday of the company's power, however, observers routinely made such connections. After his 1916 visit to Costa Rica, for example, Count Vay von Vaya, the famed Hungarian travel writer, likened United Fruit to the British East India Company. In addition to controlling much of Central America's infrastructure and trade, he observed, the firm was the primary agent of American influence and seemed to be opening the way for more formal U.S. dominion. Due almost entirely to the company's prominence and power, he claimed, "the Yankees are not only becoming the masters of these people, but also their models. Everyone appears to imitate the invaders from the north," attempting to dress, speak, and act "like the American." Yet von Vaya also noted that this U.S. "conquest by means of the banana" depended upon British West Indian laborers. Declaring these black immigrant workers "people of great self-control and rare personal qualities," he implied that United Fruit's operations, and hence the U.S. empire in Central America, could not have taken shape without them.[24]

American observers, too, viewed the company as the vanguard of U.S. influence. In his celebratory 1914 account of United Fruit, *Conquest of the Tropics,* Frederick Adams observed that, although Americans "dwell with pride on the records of the pioneers who braved the wilderness and paved the way of our empire from the Atlantic to the Pacific," they had yet to appreciate the corporate pioneers who now braved the "invisible dangers" of Central America in that "instinctive spirit which ever has urged the American to face and conquer the frontier."[25] Writing over a decade later, Wallace Thompson could scarcely contain his enthusiasm for the firm's impact on Central America. Prior to the arrival of the ingenious Yankees, he insisted, the region's vast potential had remained untapped; but now, "wherever there are bananas, somewhere in the hot quiet about them is civilization."[26]

Of course, that "civilization" featured a corporate colonial culture based on racial hierarchy and labor segmentation. And although few American visitors grasped the importance of West Indian immigration and racial division to United Fruit's success, the ramifications of these labor strategies eventually proved impossible for the firm to ignore. In the years following Thompson's visit, the combination of Hispanic nationalism and anti-black xenophobia would force the company to forgo the employment of black immigrants in its quest for disease-free land on Central America's Pacific Coast. Although it was hardly apparent at the time, this abandonment of its labor segmentation system set United Fruit on the long road to withdrawing from direct cultivation and colonial control in Central America. By the time of the 1954 coup in Guatemala, the company was already a shadow of its imperial incarnation, and its earlier reliance on black immigrants had largely faded from memory. Yet its legacy remained, not only in the abandoned banana towns and unhealed racial wounds of Central America and the British Caribbean, but in the pivotal role that corporate power would continue to play in U.S expansion, in Latin America and beyond.[27]

Notes

Introduction

1. Smith to Sands, 20 December 1909, vol. 128, RG 84, United States National Archives II, College Park, Maryland (hereafter USNA); Haggard's report, enclosed in Carden to Grey, 31 January 1910, FO 371/837 (6083), United Kingdom National Archives, Kew (hereafter UKNA).

2. Herbert Bury, *A Bishop amongst Bananas* (London: Wells Gardner, Darton, 1911), 178–179, 196–198.

3. John L. Williams, "The Rise of the Banana Industry and Its Influence on Caribbean Countries" (Master's thesis, Clark University, 1925), 111.

4. Classic studies of white views of blacks include Winthrop D. Jordan, *White over Black: American Attitudes toward the Negro, 1550–1812* (Chapel Hill: University of North Carolina Press, 1968); and George M. Fredrickson, *The Black Image in the White Mind: The Debate on Afro-American Character and Destiny, 1817–1914* (New York: Harper Row, 1971). On the commodification of black bodies, see Walter Johnson, *Soul by Soul: Life inside the Antebellum Slave Market* (Cambridge, Mass.: Harvard University Press, 1999). An excellent study of the cotton frontier is Edward E. Baptist, *Creating an Old South: Middle Florida's Plantation Frontier before the Civil War* (Chapel Hill: University of North Carolina Press, 2002).

5. Dow to Allen, 10 July 1856, p. 12, box 3, folder 3, John M. Dow Papers, Kroch Library, Cornell University.

6. On the postwar South, See C. Vann Woodward, *Origins of the New South, 1877–1913* (Baton Rouge: Louisiana State University Press, 1971); Edward L. Ayers, *The Promise of the New South: Life after Reconstruction* (New York: Oxford University Press, 1992); and Leon F. Litwack, *Trouble in Mind: Black Southerners in the Age of Jim Crow* (New York: Alfred A. Knopf, 1998).

7. Studies of labor in the New England mills include William Moran, *The Belles of New England: The Women of the Textile Mills and the Families Whose Wealth They Wove* (New York: St. Martin's Press, 2002); and Thomas Dublin, *Transforming Women's Work: New England Lives in the Industrial Revolution* (Ithaca: Cornell University Press, 1994); quote from John R. Commons, *Races and Immigrants in America* (New York: Macmillan, 1907), 150.

8. On white workers and racial hierarchy, see David R. Roediger, *The Wages of Whiteness: Race and the Making of the American Working Class* (New York: Verso, 1991); Noel Ignatiev, *How the Irish Became White* (London: Routledge, 1995); and Jacqueline Jones, *American Work: Four Centuries of Black and White Labor* (New York: W. W. Norton, 1998).

9. Goethals as quoted in Michael L. Conniff, *Black Labor on a White Canal: Panama, 1904–1981* (Pittsburgh: University of Pittsburgh Press, 1985), 43.

10. Conniff, *Black Labor on a White Canal*, 44.

11. On the transition from slavery to freedom in Jamaica, see Thomas C. Holt, *The Problem of Freedom: Race, Labor, and Politics in Jamaica and Britain, 1832–1938* (Baltimore: Johns Hopkins University Press, 1992); on the rise of West Indian peasantries, see Sidney W. Mintz and Sally Price, eds., *Caribbean Contours* (Baltimore: Johns Hopkins, 1985), esp. 134–135.

12. "Trip to Jamaica" diary, 10–13 January 1850, John Bigelow Papers, New York Public Library, New York City. Bigelow published an account of his impressions entitled *Jamaica in 1850: Or, The Effects of Sixteen Years of Freedom on a Slavery Colony* (New York: George P. Putnam, 1851).

13. With respect to the distinctive racial culture of the British West Indies, historian Lancelot Lewis argues that "the West Indian black, unlike the American black, was never a minority in his country, and this meant that he never accepted the classic minority group psychology, the highly oppressive sense of being a black man in a white man's country. His very numerical superiority in the islands gave him a relaxed self-confidence, a freedom . . . from physical fear." Lancelot S. Lewis, *The West Indian in Panama: Black Labor in Panama, 1850–1914* (Washington, D.C.: University Press of America, 1980), 35.

14. Recent studies of the U.S. banana industry and West Indian immigration include Philippe I. Bourgois, *Ethnicity at Work: Divided Labor on a Central America Banana Plantation* (Baltimore: Johns Hopkins University Press, 1989); Paul J. Dosal, *Doing Business with the Dictators: A Political History of the United Fruit Company in Guatemala, 1899–1944* (Wilmington: Scholarly Resources, 1993); Trevor W. Purcell, *Banana Fallout: Class, Color, and Culture among West Indians in Costa Rica* (Los Angeles: UCLA/CAAS, 1993); Aviva Chomsky, *West Indian Workers and the United Fruit Company in Costa Rica, 1870–1940* (Baton Rouge: Louisiana State University Press, 1996); Mark Moberg, *Myths of Ethnicity and Nation: Immigration, Work, and Identity in the Belize Banana Industry* (Knoxville: University of Tennessee Press, 1997); Ronald N. Harpelle, *The West Indians of Costa Rica: Race, Class, and the Integration of an Ethnic Minority* (Kingston, Jamaica: Ian Randle, 2001); Steve Striffler, *In the Shadows of State and Capital: The United Fruit Company, Popular Struggle, and Agrarian Restructuring in Ecuador, 1900–1995* (Durham, N.C.: Duke University Press, 2002); John Soluri, *Banana Cultures: Agriculture, Consumption, and Environmental Change in Honduras and the United States* (Austin: University of Texas Press, 2005); Marcelo Bucheli, *Bananas and Business: The United Fruit Company in Colombia, 1899–2000* (New York: New York University Press, 2005); Frederick Douglass Opie, *Black Labor Migration in Caribbean Guatemala, 1882–1923* (Gainesville: University Press of Florida, 2009); and Glenn A. Chambers, *Race, Nation, and West Indian Immigration to Honduras, 1890–1940* (Baton Rouge: Louisiana State University Press, 2010). Two studies that attribute racial tensions primarily to the culture of host societies are Lara Putnam, *The Company They Kept: Migrants and the Politics*

of Gender in Caribbean Costa Rica, 1870–1960 (Chapel Hill: University of North Carolina Press, 2002); and Douglas W. Kraft, "Making West Indians Unwelcome: Bananas, Race, & the Immigrant Question in Izabal, Guatemala, 1900–1929" (Ph.D. diss., University of Miami, 2006). While both are superb, they rely almost exclusively on Costa Rican and Guatemalan archives, respectively.

15. Key contributions to the study of U.S. imperial culture include Amy Kaplan and Donald E. Pease, eds., *The Cultures of United States Imperialism* (Durham, N.C.: Duke University Press, 1993); Gilbert M. Joseph, Catherine C. LeGrand, and Ricardo D. Salvatore, eds. *Close Encounters of Empire: Writing the Cultural History of U.S.–Latin American Relations* (Durham, N.C.: Duke University Press, 1998); Kristin L. Hoganson, *Fighting for American Manhood: How Gender Politics Provoked the Spanish-American and Philippine-American Wars* (New Haven: Yale University Press, 1998); Eileen J. Suárez Findlay, *Imposing Decency: The Politics of Sexuality and Race in Puerto Rico, 1870–1920* (Durham, N.C.: Duke University Press, 1999); Mary A. Renda, *Taking Haiti: Military Occupation and the Culture of U.S. Imperialism, 1915–1940* (Chapel Hill: University of North Carolina Press, 2001); Paul A. Kramer, *The Blood of Government: Race, Empire, the United States, and the Philippines* (Chapel Hill: University of North Carolina Press, 2006). Two recent studies of work in U.S. government enclaves are Julia Greene, *The Canal Builders: Making America's Empire at the Panama Canal* (New York: Penguin, 2009); and Jana K. Lipman, *Guantánamo: A Working-Class History between Empire and Revolution* (Berkeley: University of California Press, 2009). Exceptions to the general exclusion of corporate empire include Thomas O'Brien, *The Revolutionary Mission: American Enterprise in Latin America, 1900–1945* (Cambridge: Cambridge University Press, 1996); idem, *The Century of U.S. Capitalism in Latin America* (Albuquerque: University of New Mexico Press, 1999); César J. Ayala, *American Sugar Kingdom: The Plantation Economy of the Spanish Caribbean, 1898–1934* (Chapel Hill: University of North Carolina Press, 1999); Aims McGuinness, *Path of Empire: Panama and the California Gold Rush* (Ithaca: Cornell University Press, 2008); and Greg Grandin, *Fordlandia: The Rise and Fall of Henry Ford's Forgotten Jungle City* (New York: Metropolitan Books, 2009).

16. Recent examples include Walter L. Hixson, *The Myth of American Diplomacy: National Identity and U.S. Foreign Policy* (New Haven: Yale University Press, 2008); and Brian Loveman, *No Higher Law: American Foreign Policy and the Western Hemisphere since 1776* (Chapel Hill: University of North Carolina Press, 2010).

17. Examples of seminal works with limited treatment of United Fruit include Emily S. Rosenberg, *Spreading the American Dream: American Economic and Cultural Expansion, 1890–1945* (New York: Hill & Wang, 1982); and idem, *Financial Missionaries to the World: The Politics and Culture of Dollar Diplomacy, 1900–1945* (Durham, N.C.: Duke University Press, 2003). Examples of "banana wars" scholarship that offer relatively little discussion of United Fruit include David Healy, *Drive to Hegemony: The United States in the Caribbean, 1898–1917* (Madison: University of Wisconsin Press, 1988); Ivan Musicant, *The Banana Wars: A History of United States Military Intervention in Latin America from the Spanish-American War to the Invasion of Panama* (New York: Macmillan, 1990); and Lester D. Langley, *The Banana Wars: United States Intervention in the Caribbean, 1898–1934* (Wilmington: Scholarly Resources, 2002). This criticism does not apply to studies of the international trade disputes of the late 1990s, such as Steve Striffler and Mark Moberg, eds., *Banana Wars: Power, Production, and History in the Americas* (Durham, N.C.: Duke University Press, 2003); and James Wiley, *The Banana: Empires, Trade Wars, and Globalization* (Lincoln: University of Nebraska Press, 2008).

18. Bourgois, *Ethnicity at Work*, xiii–xiv.

Chapter 1. Enterprise and Expansion, 1848–1885

1. "The Panama Railroad Completed," *New York Daily Times*, 9 February 1855.

2. Robert A. Naylor, *Penny Ante Imperialism: The Mosquito Shore and the Bay of Honduras, 1600–1914* (London: Associated University Presses, 1989), 137, 148–157. For a portrait of the Miskito region in this era, see C. Napier Bell, *Tangweera: Life and Adventures among Gentle Savages* (Austin: University of Texas Press, 1989 [1899]).

3. John L. Stephens, *Incidents of Travel in Central America, Chiapas and Yucatan* (New York: Dover, 1969 [1841]), 1:11–19. Like many U.S. visitors, Stephens used the familiar "Sambo" in place of the Central American word "*Zambo.*" A good introduction to Belizean history is O. Nigel Bolland, *Struggles for Freedom: Essays on Slavery, Colonialism, and Culture in the Caribbean and Central America* (Belize: Angelus Press, 1997), chaps. 2–3.

4. Nicaraguan government as quoted in Naylor, *Penny Ante Imperialism*, 176–177.

5. Wells to brother, 4 June 1850, Wells Letters, New-York Historical Society.

6. Clayton as quoted in Naylor, *Penny Ante Imperialism*, 187.

7. On Central America commercial patterns, see Lowell Gudmundson and Hector Lindo-Fuentes, *Central America: 1821–1871, Liberalism before Liberal Reform* (Tuscaloosa: University of Alabama Press, 1995), 31–43.

8. William Franklin Denniston, Travel Journal, 16 June 1849, Huntington Library; Squier to Edwards, 13 March 1853, Box 1, Folder 14, E. George Squier Collection, Huntington Library.

9. Denniston Journal, 21 June 1849, Huntington Library.

10. Wells to brother, 4 June 1850, Wells Letters, New-York Historical Society. Emphasis in original.

11. William O. Scroggs, *Filibusters and Financiers: The Story of William Walker and His Associates* (New York: Macmillan, 1916), 81; Wells to brother, 7 October 1851, Wells Letters, New-York Historical Society.

12. Squier to Edwards, 2 March 1853, box 1, folder 10, Squier Collection, Huntington Library. Emphasis in original.

13. Pierce as quoted in Lars Schoultz, *Beneath the United States: A History of U.S. Policy toward Latin America* (Cambridge, Mass.: Harvard University Press, 1998), 59.

14. Wells to Dr. Cyrus Wells, 5 December 1849, Wells Letters, New-York Historical Society.

15. McGuiness, *Path of Empire*, 42.

16. On Stephens's role, see Victor Von Hagen, *Maya Explorer: John Lloyd Stephens and the Lost Cities of Central America and Yucatán* (San Francisco: Chronicle Books, 1990 [1947]), 271–292. On the company's efforts to recruit workers, see McGuinness, *Path of Empire*, 57–71, Totten quoted on 62.

17. McGuinness, *Path of Empire*, 73–75.

18. Ibid., 125–147, 164–172.

19. Robert E. May, *The Southern Dream of Caribbean Empire, 1854–1861* (Gainesville: University Press of Florida, 2002), 30–34, 163–164; Ostend Manifesto reprinted in Robert H. Holden and Eric Zolov, eds., *Latin America and the United States: A Documentary History* (New York: Oxford University Press, 2000), 36–38.

20. On the racial and gendered motivations of filibustering, see Robert E. May, *Manifest Destiny's Underworld: Filibustering in Antebellum America* (Chapel Hill: University of North Carolina Press, 2002); and Amy S. Greenberg, *Manifest Manhood and the Antebellum American Empire* (Cambridge: Cambridge University Press, 2005).

21. A superb source for Walker's invasion of Mexico is Juan Bandini, "Report of the Invasion of Sonora," 25 May 1854, Box 7, Stearns-Gaffey Papers, Huntington Library.

22. Scroggs, *Filibusters and Financiers,* 85–100, 205–206, 134–140; May, *Southern Dream,* 96–101.

23. Scroggs, *Filibusters and Financiers,* 159–184, 207–208, 264–269, 296–302; May, *Southern Dream,* 96–109; Walker as quoted in Kyle Longley, *In the Eagle's Shadow: The United States and Latin America* (Wheeling: Harlan Davidson, 2002), 74.

24. Walker's *The War in Nicaragua* excerpted in Holden and Zolov, *Latin America and the United States,* 4.

25. Articles sent by Walker to an associate, box 24, folder 32, Samuel Barlow Collection, Huntington Library.

26. One example was famed journalist Richard Harding Davis, who reported in 1896 that "there is a statue of the Republic in the form of a young woman standing with her foot on the neck of General Walker, the American filibuster." Deeply offended, he declared, "it would have been a very good thing for Costa Rica if Walker, or any other man of force, had put his foot on the neck of every republic in Central America." Davis, *Three Gringos in Venezuela and Central America* (New York: Harper and Brothers, 1896), 146–147.

27. Wells to brother, 18 December 1858, 1 folder, Wells Letters, New-York Historical Society.

28. May, *Manifest Destiny's Underworld,* 243–247; idem, *Southern Dream,* 130–131; Scroggs, *Filibusters and Financiers,* 382–390.

29. Newspaper as quoted in May, *Southern Dream,* 238.

30. Lincoln as quoted in Fredrickson, *Black Image in the White Mind,* 150.

31. Blair as quoted in Eric Foner, *Free Soil, Free Labor, Free Men: The Ideology of the Republican Party before the Civil War* (New York: Oxford University Press, 1995 [1970]), 272.

32. *The Independent,* December 1861, Box 9, Scrapbook, Dow Papers, Kroch Library, Cornell University.

33. James D. Lockett, "Abraham Lincoln and Colonization: An Episode That Ends in Tragedy at L'Ile a Vache, Haiti, 1863–1864," *Journal of Black Studies* 21, no. 4 (June 1991): 428–444; Paul J. Scheips, "Lincoln and the Chiriqui Colonization Project," *Journal of Negro History* 37, no. 4 (October 1952): 418–453.

34. Gorgas as quoted in Leon F. Litwack, *Been in the Storm So Long: The Aftermath of Slavery* (New York: Vintage, 1979), 552.

35. Northern visitor as quoted in ibid., 257.

36. Eric Foner, *Reconstruction: America's Unfinished Revolution, 1863–1877* (New York: Harper and Row, 1988), 78–79, 102–110, 404–406. See also Demetrius L. Eudell, *The Political Languages of Emancipation in the British Caribbean and the U.S. South* (Chapel Hill: University of North Carolina Press, 2002).

37. David W. Blight, *Race and Reunion: The Civil War in American Memory* (Cambridge, Mass.: Harvard University Press, 2001), chap. 7; Logan as quoted in David Levering Lewis, *W. E. B. Du Bois: Biography of a Race, 1868–1919* (New York: Henry Holt, 1993), 123–124.

38. The classic study of this period is Walter LaFeber, *The New Empire: An Interpretation of American Expansion, 1860–1898* (Ithaca: Cornell University Press, 1998 [1963]). On the role of race in stymieing overseas territorial expansion, see Eric T. L. Love, *Race over Empire: Racism and U.S. Imperialism, 1865–1900* (Chapel Hill: University of North Carolina Press, 2004).

39. Love, *Race over Empire,* 35–65; Schurz as quoted in Robert L. Beisner, *Twelve against Empire: The Anti-Imperialists, 1898–1900* (New York: McGraw-Hill, 1968), 25.

40. On the new liberalism, see David Bushnell and Neill Macaulay, *The Emergence of Latin America in the Nineteenth Century* (New York: Oxford University Press, 1994), chaps. 9–10. For U.S. policy toward Mexico, see Thomas D. Schoonover, *Dollars over Dominion: The Triumph of Liberalism in Mexican–United States Relations, 1861–1867* (Baton Rouge: Louisiana State University Press, 1978); and John M. Hart, *Empire and Revolution: The Americans in Mexico since*

the Civil War (Berkeley: University of California Press, 2002). On railroads, see John Coatsworth, "Railroads, Landholding, and Agrarian Protest in the Early Porfiriato," *Hispanic American Historical Review* 54, no. 1 (February 1974): 48–71; and Daniel Lewis, *Iron Horse Imperialism: The Southern Pacific of Mexico, 1880–1951* (Tucson: University of Arizona Press, 2008).

41. Ralph Lee Woodward, *Central America: A Nation Divided* (New York: Oxford University Press, 1999), chaps. 5–6.

42. For a thoughtful discussion of Costa Rican exceptionalism, see Lowell Gudmundson, *Costa Rica before Coffee: Society and Economy on the Eve of the Export Boom* (Baton Rouge: Louisiana State University Press, 1986), 1–24.

43. For population estimates, see Carolyn Hall and Héctor Pérez Brignoli, *Historical Atlas of Central America* (Norman: University of Oklahoma Press, 2003), 76–77.

44. On pre-Columbian and early colonial history, see Eugenia Ibarra, *Las sociedades cacicales de Costa Rica* (San José: Universidad de Costa Rica, 1990); and Claudia Quirós, *La era de la encomienda* (San José: Universidad de Costa Rica, 1990); on slavery, see Rina Cáceres, *Negros, mulatos, esclavos y libertos en la Costa Rica del siglo XVII* (Mexico City: Institutuo Panamericano de Geografía e Historia, 2001); on the cacao industry, see Murdo J. MacLeod, *Spanish Central America: A Socioeconomic History, 1520–1720* (Berkeley: University of California Press, 1973), 330–340.

45. Héctor Pérez-Brignoli, *A Brief History of Central America,* trans. Ricardo B. Sawrey A. and Susana Stettri de Sawrey (Berkeley: University of California Press, 1989), 77, 91.

46. Stephens, *Incidents of Travel,* 1:353–359, 372–373.

47. Gudmundson, *Costa Rica before Coffee,* 29–40; Mario Samper, *Generations of Settlers: Rural Households and Markets on the Costa Rican Frontier, 1850–1935* (Boulder: Westview Press, 1990), 2–3, 48–58, 99.

48. Gudmundson, *Costa Rica before Coffee,* 3–4; Gordon Ireland, *Boundaries, Possessions, and Conflicts in Central and North America, and the Caribbean* (New York: Octagon Books, 1971), 12–24.

49. Mora as quoted in Scroggs, *Filibusters and Financiers,* 161–162.

50. Gudmundson and Lindo-Fuentes, *Central America,* 36–43; Pérez-Brignoli, *Brief History,* 83–97.

51. The 1862 legislation as cited in Harpelle, *West Indians,* 7.

52. Thomas D. Schoonover, *The United States in Central America, 1860–1911: Episodes of Social Imperialism and Imperial Rivalry in the World System* (Durham, N.C.: Duke University Press, 1991), 29–33.

53. Watt Stewart, *Keith and Costa Rica: The Biography of Minor Cooper Keith, American Entrepreneur* (Albuquerque: University of New Mexico Press, 1964), 9–13; Lawrence A. Clayton, *Grace: W. R. Grace and Co., The Formative Years, 1850–1930* (Ottowa, Ill.: Jameson Books, 1985), 75–77.

54. Nanne to Grace, 12 May 1872, box 26, bound correspondence #84, W. R. Grace Papers, Columbia University.

55. Norris to Grace, 21 February 1873, box 30, bound correspondence #93, Grace Papers, Columbia University.

56. Nanne to Grace, 28 February 1873, box 30, bound correspondence #93, Grace Papers, Columbia University.

57. Williamson as quoted in Stewart, *Keith and Costa Rica,* 31.

58. Keith to Grace, 7 September 1873, box 30, bound correspondence #93, Grace Papers, Columbia University.

59. Harpelle, *West Indians,* 57; Chomsky, *West Indian Workers,* 24.

60. The Keith anecdote is recounted in Stewart, *Keith and Costa Rica,* 52–53. In this transla-
tion, I have used "darkey" as the best approximation of "Negrito"—literally, "little black."
61. Keith to Flint, 17 March 1876, box 48, notebook 130, Grace Papers, Columbia University.
62. On race in colonial Guatemala, see Christopher H. Lutz, *Santiago de Guatemala: City,
Caste, and the Colonial Experience.* (Norman: University of Oklahoma Press, 1994); and Catherine
Komisaruk, "'The Work It Cost Me': The Struggles of Slaves and Free Africans in Guatemala,
1770–1825," *Urban History Workshop Review* 5, no. 3 (Fall 1999): 4–24. Prior to 1800, state orders
to provide labor were known as *repartimientos.* On the relationship between the Maya and the
state, see David J. McCreery, *Rural Guatemala, 1760–1940* (Stanford: Stanford University Press,
1994), 7–9, 93–95; and Carol A. Smith, ed., *Guatemalan Indians and the State, 1540–1988* (Austin:
University of Texas Press, 1990), 30–44, 74–77.
63. Smith, *Guatemalan Indians and the State,* 55–67; Stephens, *Incidents of Travel,* 1:224–232;
Hise as quoted in Naylor, *Penny Ante Imperialism,* 174.
64. On the Conservatives' limited use of *mandamientos,* see McCreery, *Rural Guatemala,* 126.
On Carrera's reign and policies, see Ralph Lee Woodward, Jr., *Rafael Carrera and the Emergence of
the Republic of Guatemala, 1821–1871* (Athens: University of Georgia Press, 1993).
65. McCreery, *Rural Guatemala,* 90. On the Garífuna, see Nancie L. Solien Gonzalez,
Sojourners in the Caribbean: Ethnogenesis and Ethnohistory of the Garífuna (Urbana: University of
Illinois Press, 1988).
66. Stephens, *Incidents of Travel,* 1:37–38.
67. Naylor, *Penny Ante Imperialism,* 110–111; William J. Griffith, *Empires in the Wilderness:
Foreign Colonization and Development in Guatemala, 1834–1844* (Chapel Hill: University of North
Carolina Press, 1965).
68. E. O. Crosby, "Memoirs and Reminiscences," 103, 99, Crosby Papers, Huntington
Library.
69. Ibid., 116, 97–99.
70. David J. McCreery, *Development and the State in Reforma Guatemala* (Athens: University
of Georgia, 1983), chap. 1; Don Francisco Gavarrete, printed in *Star and Herald,* Panama, 1867,
box 9, scrapbook, Dow papers, Kroch Library, Cornell University.
71. David J. McCreery, "'An Odious Feudalism': Mandamiento Labor and Commercial
Agriculture in Guatemala, 1858–1920," *Latin American Perspectives* 13, no. 1 (Winter 1986):
99–117. On the racial aspects of Liberal nation building, see René Reeves, *Ladinos with Ladinos,
Indians with Indians: Land, Labor, and Regional Ethnic Conflict in the Making of Guatemala* (Stanford:
Stanford University Press, 2006); and Smith, *Guatemalan Indians and the State,* 74–92.
72. McCreery, *Development and the State,* 91–96; Guatemala Sociedad de Inmigración to its
agents in San Francisco, 4 December 1877, Guatemala Sociedad de Inmigración Collection,
New York Public Library.
73. For a comparison of the German coffee planters and United Fruit, see Diane K. Stanley,
For the Record: The United Fruit Company's Sixty-Six Years in Guatemala (Guatemala City: Piedra
Santa, 1994), 6–11. On foreigners in Guatemala, see Thomas and Ebba Schoonover, "Statistics for
an Understanding of Foreign Intrusions into Central America from the 1820s to 1930," *Anuario
de Estudios Centroamericanos* 15, no. 1 (1989): 106.
74. William T. Brigham, *Guatemala, Land of the Quetzal* (New York: Charles Scribner's Sons,
1887), 78, 101, 276.
75. Ibid., 291, 321–322, 23.
76. Dosal, *Doing Business with the Dictators,* 18–27; McCreery, *Development and the State,* 38.
77. Minister as quoted in Kraft, "Making West Indians Unwelcome," 37.
78. McCreery, *Development and the State,* 71–82; Opie, *Black Labor Migration,* 33–34.

79. David Healy, *James G. Blaine and Latin America* (Columbia: University of Missouri Press, 2001), 24–27.

Chapter 2. Joining the Imperial World, 1885–1904

1. Frederick R. Karl, *Joseph Conrad, The Three Lives: A Biography* (New York: Farrar, Straus and Giroux, 1979), 125–130, 141–153.

2. Ian Watt, *Joseph Conrad, Nostromo* (Cambridge: Cambridge University Press, 1988), vii–x; Karl, *Joseph Conrad*, 280–289; Conrad as quoted in Adam Hochschild, *King Leopold's Ghost: A Story of Greed, Terror, and Heroism in Colonial Africa* (New York: Houghton Mifflin, 1998), 142.

3. John A. McClure, *Kipling and Conrad: The Colonial Fiction* (Cambridge: Harvard University Press, 1981), 142–145; Joseph Conrad, *Heart of Darkness*, ed. Robert Kimbrough (New York: W. W. Norton, 1988 [1899]), 10.

4. Joseph Conrad, *Nostromo* (New York: Alfred A. Knopf, 1957 [1904]), 14, 80.

5. Ibid., 149–150. Emphasis in original.

6. Ibid., 73–74.

7. On shifting imperial power, see LaFeber, *New Empire*, 176–177; Conrad to Cunninghame Graham, 26 December 1903, in Frederick R. Karl and Laurence Davies, eds., *The Collected Letters of Joseph Conrad*, vol. III (Cambridge: Cambridge University Press, 1988), 100–102. See also Watt, *Joseph Conrad*, 9–15.

8. Conrad, *Nostromo*, 33, 175–176. As John McClure observes, in *Nostromo* "imperialism is capitalism abroad." See McClure, *Kipling and Conrad*, 155.

9. On the relationship between capitalism and imperialism, see Eric Hobsbawm, *The Age of Capital, 1848–1875* (New York: Vintage, 1975); idem, *The Age of Empire, 1875–1914* (New York: Vintage, 1987).

10. The classic treatment of this period in U.S. foreign policy thought is LaFeber, *New Empire*. More recent attempts to place the United States in the broader imperial context include Matthew Frye Jacobson, *Barbarian Virtues: The United States Encounters Foreign Peoples at Home and Abroad, 1876–1917* (New York: Hill and Wang, 2000); and Thomas Bender, *A Nation among Nations: America's Place in World History* (New York: Hill and Wang, 2006), esp. chap. 4. On British rule in Egypt, see Eve M. Troutt Powell, *A Different Shade of Colonialism: Egypt, Great Britain, and the Mastery of the Sudan* (Berkeley: University of California Press, 2003).

11. Three years later, the Maritime Canal Company, a private U.S. firm, received a canal concession from Nicaragua. See Joseph Smith, *Illusions of Conflict: Anglo-American Diplomacy toward Latin America, 1865–1896* (Pittsburgh: University of Pittsburgh Press, 1979), 82–85.

12. David McCullough, *The Path between the Seas: The Creation of the Panama Canal: 1870–1914* (New York: Simon and Schuster, 1977), chaps. 5–6; Petras, *Jamaican Labor Migration*, 97–100.

13. A detailed breakdown of the French company's labor divisions and costs appeared in Colne to John Bigelow, n.d. (1886?), box 24, folder "questions pertaining to Panama Canal," John Bigelow Papers, New York Public Library.

14. Elizabeth Dow to John M. Dow, 22 April 1885, box 2, folder 4; John M. Dow to Bayard, 7 November 1885, Dow Papers, Kroch Library, Cornell University; Wright and Burt to U.S. and Colombian government, 1 April 1885, box 1, folder "1885–1887," E. Z. Penfield Papers, New York Public Library.

15. Irving King, "The Occupation of Panama," 8 May 1885, *New York Tribune*. See also John Lindsay-Poland, *Emperors in the Jungle: The Hidden History of the U.S. in Panama* (Durham, N.C.: Duke University Press, 2003), 18–21.

16. Colne to Bigelow, 11 March 1886, box 24, John Bigelow Papers, New York Public Library.

17. Charles Morrow Wilson, *Empire in Green and Gold: The Story of the American Banana Trade* (New York: Greenwood Press, 1968 [1947]), 1–30.

18. On U.S. adventurers, see Lester D. Langley and Thomas Schoonover, *Banana Men: American Mercenaries and Entrepreneurs in Central America, 1880–1930* (Lexington: University Press of Kentucky, 1995); on Burke, see C. Vann Woodward, *Origins of the New South: 1877–1913* (Baton Rouge: Louisiana University Press, 1951), 70–72.

19. O. Henry, *Cabbages and Kings* (New York: Exeter Books, 1986 [1904]), quote from 66.

20. Smith, *Illusions of Conflict*, 200–207; LaFeber, *New Empire*, 221–229; Charles R. Hale, *Resistance and Contradiction: Miskitu Indians and the Nicaraguan State, 1894–1987* (Stanford: Stanford University Press, 1994), 37–47.

21. Foster as quoted in Smith, *Illusions of Conflict*, 123; Louis A. Pérez, *Cuba between Empires, 1878–1902* (Pittsburgh: University of Pittsburgh Press, 1983), 30–31.

22. Atkins to mother, 8 January 1882, reprinted in Edwin F. Atkins, *Sixty Years in Cuba* (New York: Arno Press, 1980 [1926]), 75. On the end of Cuban slavery, see Rebecca J. Scott, *Slave Emancipation in Cuba: The Transition to Free Labor, 1860–1899* (Princeton: Princeton University Press, 1985). See also idem, "A Cuban Connection: Edwin F. Atkins, Charles Francis Adams Jr., and the Former Slaves of the Soledad Plantation," *Massachusetts Historical Review* 9 (2007): 7–34.

23. Rebecca J. Scott, *Degrees of Freedom: Louisiana and Cuba after Slavery* (Cambridge, Mass: Harvard University Press, 2005), 111–112.

24. Atkins, *Sixty Years*, 92.

25. On Atkins's hiring of Spanish veterans, see Scott, *Degrees of Freedom*, 121. On Soledad's labor system, see idem, "Race, Labor, and Citizenship in Cuba: A View from the Sugar District of Cienfuegos, 1886–1909," *Hispanic American Historical Review* 78, no. 4 (November 1998): 701; and Rebekah E. Pite, "The Force of Food: Life on the Atkins Family Sugar Plantation in Cienfuegos, Cuba, 1884–1900." *Massachusetts Historical Review* 5 (2003): 61–67.

26. Atkins, *Sixty Years*, 89, 90.

27. On the impact of the tariff, see Pérez, *Cuba between Empires*, 31–38; on Maceo's travels, see Scott, *Degrees of Freedom*, 127–128.

28. George Grantham Bain interview of Dupuy de Lôme, *New York Herald* in vol. 2/57, scrapbook April 14, 1895—Dec. 22, 1896, Atkins Papers, Massachusetts Historical Society.

29. Atkins interview, vol. 2/57, scrapbook April 14, 1896—Dec. 22, 1896, Atkins Papers, Massachusetts Historical Society; Edwin Atkins to Kate Atkins, Mar. 24, 1896, reprinted in Atkins, *Sixty Years*, 229.

30. The classic economic analysis is LaFeber, *New Empire*, esp. chap. 8. On prewar diplomacy, see John L. Offner, *An Unwanted War: The Diplomacy of the United States and Spain over Cuba, 1895–1898* (Chapel Hill: University of North Carolina Press, 1992). On the role of gender anxiety, see Hoganson, *Fighting for American Manhood*. The best analyses of the role of race in the U.S. intervention are Pérez, *Cuba between Empires;* and Ada Ferrer, *Insurgent Cuba: Race, Nation, and Revolution, 1868–1898* (Chapel Hill: University of North Carolina Press, 1999).

31. On the Cuban insurgents' war strategy, see John Lawrence Tone, *War and Genocide in Cuba, 1895–1898* (Chapel Hill: University of North Carolina Press, 2006).

32. Pérez, *Cuba between Empires*, 60–71, 173–187.

33. Speech by Albert J. Beveridge, "The March of the Flag," 17 September 1898, reprinted in Beveridge, *The Meaning of the Times and Other Speeches* (New York, 1908), 47–57; Schurz as quoted in Beisner, *Twelve against Empire*, 27.

34. Beveridge, "March of the Flag," *Meaning of the Times*, 49–50.

35. On the insular cases and Puerto Rico, see Christina Duffy Burnett and Burke Marshall, eds., *Foreign in a Domestic Sense: Puerto Rico, American Expansion, and the Constitution* (Durham, N.C.: Duke University Press, 2001).

36. Paul Kramer, "Race-Making and Colonial Violence in the U.S. Empire: The Philippine-American War as Race War." *Diplomatic History* 30, no. 2 (April 2006): 169–210.

37. Letter from black soldier in Philippines reprinted in Willard Gatewood, ed., *'Smoked Yankees' and the Struggle for Empire: Letters from Negro Soldiers, 1898–1902* (Urbana: University of Illinois Press, 1971), 279–280.

38. Soldier in Cuba as quoted in Litwack, *Trouble in Mind*, 465.

39. Poultney Bigelow, "Colonial Administration in Different Parts of the World," paper read at the 1899 International Geographical Congress of Berlin, box 42, "Writings, Lectures, and Notes" folder, Poultney Bigelow Papers, New York Public Library; Poultney Bigelow, *The Children of the Nations: A Study of Colonization and Its Problems* (New York: McClure, Philips, 1901), vii.

40. Kramer, *Blood of Government*, 155–161.

41. Healy, *Drive to Hegemony*, 44–50; Cuban rebel as quoted in Pérez, *Cuba between Empires*, 214.

42. Shafter as quoted in Louis A. Pérez, *Cuba under the Platt Amendment, 1902–1934* (Pittsburgh: University of Pittsburgh Press, 1986), 37.

43. Roosevelt as quoted in Pérez, *Cuba between Empires*, 274.

44. "Cleaning Up Santiago: Major Barbour Tells How That Pest-Hole Was Cleansed," 13 May 1899, box 132, George Kennan Papers, Library of Congress (hereafter LOC). On the intersection between disease control and U.S. power in Cuba, see Mariola Espinosa, *Epidemic Invasions: Yellow Fever and the Limits of Cuban Independence, 1878–1930* (Chicago: University of Chicago Press, 2009).

45. As Ada Ferrer argues, "in an age of ascendant racism, the United States opted to temper the victory of a multiracial movement [that was] explicitly antiracist." Ferrer, *Insurgent Cuba*, 5.

46. Pérez, *Cuba under the Platt Amendment*, 26–27.

47. Edwin F. Atkins, "The Commercial Argument for Cuban Annexation," *Boston Independent*, 1 Dec. 1898, vol. 2/59, scrapbook Aug. 1899–12 Dec. 1901; "The Business View of Cuba's Greatest Need," *Boston Transcript*, 15 June, 1899, vol. 2/60, scrapbook 3 Feb.–14 Dec. 1899, 22–23 May 1912, Atkins Papers, Massachusetts Historical Society.

48. "Gen. Wood on the Cubans," *New York Times*, 25 June 1899.

49. Louis A. Pérez, "The Pursuit of Pacification: Banditry and the United State's Occupation of Cuba, 1889–1902," *Journal of Latin American Studies* 18, no. 2 (November 1986): 329–333; idem, *Cuba between Empires*, 342–343.

50. Wood as quoted in Philip W. Kennedy, "Race and American Expansion in Cuba and Puerto Rico, 1895–1905" *Journal of Black Studies* 1, no. 3 (March 1971): 309.

51. On the struggle over suffrage in Cuba, see Scott, *Degrees of Freedom*, 201–206; Root's "ravish" quote in Pérez, *Cuba between Empires*, 279.

52. On the Platt Amendment, see Healy, *Drive to Hegemony*, 52–54; Root as quoted in Pérez, *Cuba between Empires*, 317–318.

53. Wood as quoted in Pérez, *Cuba between Empires*, 349.

54. Carlos Funtanellas et al., *United Fruit Company: Un Caso del Dominio Imperialista en Cuba* (Havana: Editorial de Ciencias Sociales, 1976), 53–60.

55. On Grace and the Nicaragua route, see Clayton, *Grace*, 240–241; and Healy, *Drive to Hegemony*, 78–82; Morgan as quoted in *New York Journal*, 15 November 1898.

56. McEnery as quoted in *New York Journal*, 12 December 1898.

57. Clayton, *Grace*, 242–248.

58. Bunau-Varilla to Martínez Silva, Colombian envoy to U.S., 7 February and 22 March 1902, box 24, "1901–1904" folder, John Bigelow Papers, New York Public Library.

59. McCullough, *Path between the Seas*, 330–338.

60. Roosevelt's "mandate from civilization" statement as quoted in Lindsay-Poland, *Emperors in the Jungle*, 27; his comparison to filibustering was recalled in Farrand to Turner, 29 January 1913, box 19, folder 9, Frederick Jackson Turner Papers, Huntington Library.

61. In Spanish, Central Americans often distinguish between "*Centroamérica*," which includes the original members of the Central American Federation (and sometimes Chiapas), and "*América Central*," which usually includes Panama along with Guatemala, El Salvador, Honduras, Nicaragua, and Costa Rica (and sometimes Belize).

62. Manuel Aragón, letter to editor, file clipping, T-35, reel 5, RG 59, USNA.

63. Toast of President Soto and Wingfield's response, 4 July 1887, M-17, MSS 696, Wingfield Papers, University of Virginia. Privately, U.S. diplomats were often less complimentary. In June 1892, Wingfield's successor, Bickford Mackey, dismissed Costa Ricans as "a primitive people," and when the Costa Rican president suspended the constitution three months later, Mackey expressed regret that the Costa Rican government "should degenerate into the sordid, hypocritical, and inglorious misrule which seems the foreordained destiny of the Spanish American so-called republics." Mackey to Wharton, 2 June and 3 September 1892, T-35, reel 5, RG 59, USNA.

64. Frank Vincent, *In and Out of Central America: And Other Sketches and Studies of Travel* (New York: Appleton, 1890), 6.

65. Munro, *Five Republics*, 138–143.

66. Particularly revealing was the controversy surrounding the figure of Juan Santamaría, a young *campesino* who died setting fire to Walker's headquarters. Although Santamaría was a *mulato*, official images transformed him into a symbol of national heroism and white racial purity. When Enrique Echandi's 1896 painting *La quema del mesón* ("The burning of the tavern") depicted a dark-skinned Santamaría, it so outraged the Costa Rican elite that they ruined the young painter's career. See Iván Molina Jiménez, *Costarricense por dicha: Identidad nacional y cambio cultural en Costa Rica durante los siglos XIX y XX* (San José: Editorial de La Universidad de Costa Rica, 2002), 56.

67. "Solicitud de Joseph Berth Casbolt y Moises Castro para establecer una colonia en Cahuita," 7 June 1895, Serie Congreso, no. 3512, Archivo Nacional de Costa Rica (hereafter ANCR). Because the site lay within the "maritime mile," which was required by law to remain public property, San José denied the proposal.

68. Joaquín Bernardo Calvo, *The Republic of Costa Rica* (Chicago: Kessinger, 1890), 267–268, 51–52.

69. On frontier anxiety, see David M. Wrobel, *The End of American Exceptionalism: Frontier Anxiety from the Old West to the New Deal* (Lawrence: University Press of Kansas, 1993); Ricardo Villafranca, *Costa Rica: The Gem of the American Republics, Its Resources and Its People* (New York: Sackett and Wilhems, 1895), 30, 134–138.

70. Ibid.

71. Wilson, *Empire in Green and Gold*, 53–55.

72. Noah's letter as quoted in Stewart, *Keith and Costa Rica*, 88–89.

73. The 1884 contract also granted Keith holdings in Guanacaste, which he parlayed into profitable timber, cattle, and gold mining enterprises. See Marc Edelman, *The Logic of the Latifundio: The Large Estates of Northwestern Costa Rica since the Late Nineteenth Century* (Stanford: Stanford University Press, 1992), 58.

74. Hochschild, *King Leopold's Ghost*, 91, 171; Stewart, *Keith and Costa Rica*, 48–59.

75. Putnam, *The Company They Kept*, 44–45; Keith's letter as quoted in Bourgois, *Ethnicity at Work*, 47–48.

76. On the Italian strike, see Stewart, *Keith and Costa Rica*, 67–75.

77. In noting the prominence of anti-Asian sentiment in Costa Rica, for example, Lara Putnam argues that Jamaicans enjoyed "a generally positive official image" until the 1930s. See Putnam, *Company They Kept*, 41.

78. Bross to Wingfield, 13 December 1888, box 11, folder 2, Wingfield Papers, University of Virginia.

79. Ibid.

80. Stewart, *Keith and Costa Rica*, 43–44.

81. Keith also partnered with Costa Rican Congressman and future dictator Federico Tinoco in a large sugar enterprise. Ibid., 137–143, 153–157.

82. Preston as quoted in Soluri, *Banana Cultures*, 40.

83. On the movement toward holding companies and trusts, see Robert H. Wiebe, *The Search for Order, 1877–1920* (New York: Hill and Wang, 1967), 181–186. On United Fruit's founding, see Wilson, *Empire in Green and Gold*, 101–112.

84. David McCreery, "Debt Servitude in Rural Guatemala, 1876–1936," *Hispanic American Historical Review* 63, no. 4 (November 1983): 735–759.

85. Government order as quoted in McCreery, *Rural Guatemala*, 181.

86. Virginia Garrard-Burnett, "Liberalism, Protestantism, and Indigenous Resistance in Guatemala, 1870–1920," *Latin American Perspectives* 24, no. 2 (March 1997): 44–45.

87. Dana G. Munro, *A Student in Central America, 1914–1916* (New Orleans: Middle American Research Institute, 1983), 42–43.

88. Byron to M. F. Tunnell, 15 July 1894, Tunnell Papers, Kroch Library, Cornell University.

89. Bella to M. F. Tunnell, 13 March 1895, Tunnell Papers, Kroch Library, Cornell University.

90. Bella to M. F. Tunnell, 1 and 15 March 1895, Tunnell Papers, Kroch Library, Cornell University.

91. W. Rodney Long, *The Railways of Central America and the West Indies* (Washington D.C.: Government Printing Office, 1925), 11.

92. Minister Young as quoted in Dosal, *Doing Business with the Dictators*, 31.

93. Estimate drawn from Opie, *Black Labor Migration*, 4–5.

94. Dosal, *Doing Business with the Dictators*, 122.

95. Opie, *Black Labor Migration*, 29–33.

96. Ibid., 16.

97. Ibid., 38–40.

98. Oscar de León Aragón, *Los contratos del la United Fruit Company y las compañías muelleras en Guatemala* (Guatemala City: Editorial del Ministerio de Educación Pública, 1950), 247–251.

99. Between 1901 and 1904, Keith's Central American Improvement Company had attempted and failed to complete the railroad under a different arrangement. On the 1904 contract, see ibid., 53–55. See also Dosal, *Doing Business with the Dictators*, 2–7, 42–50; and Stanley, *For the Record*, 31–40.

100. The best study of the banana trade in Belize is Mark Moberg, *Myths of Ethnicity and Nation: Immigration, Work, and Identity in the Belize Banana Industry* (Knoxville: University of Tennessee Press, 1997).

101. Petition of Fairweather, Cuthbert, and Woods, 6 March 1902, Colonial Office, 123/240, UKNA.

Chapter 3. Corporate Colonialism, 1904–1912

1. Hugh Wilson, *The Education of a Diplomat* (London: Longman's, Green, 1938), 8–19, 36–38.

2. Ibid., 39, 47, 64.

3. Ibid., 36–37.

4. Ibid., 71–72, 90.

5. David W. Southern, *The Progressive Era and Race: Reaction and Reform, 1900–1917* (Wheeling: Harlan Davidson, 2005). See also Gary Gerstle, *American Crucible: Race and Nation in the Twentieth Century* (Princeton: Princeton University Press, 2001), chaps. 1–2.

6. Tillman as quoted in Stephen Kantrowitz, *Ben Tillman and the Reconstruction of White Supremacy* (Chapel Hill: University of North Carolina Press, 2000), 270.

7. On the Springfield riot, see Roberta Senechal, *The Sociogenesis of a Race Riot: Springfield, Illinois, in 1908* (Urbana: University of Illinois Press, 1990).

8. Geoffrey C. Ward, *Unforgivable Blackness: The Rise and Fall of Jack Johnson* (New York: Vintage, 2006); Gail Bederman, *Manliness and Civilization: A Cultural History of Gender and Race in the United States* (Chicago: University of Chicago Press, 1995), 1–5; Litwack, *Trouble in Mind*, 440–444.

9. Williams, "Rise and Influence of the Banana Industry," 119–121.

10. Root as quoted in Philip C. Jessup, *Elihu Root* (New York: Dodd, Mead, 1938), vol. 1, 471.

11. Presidential Message, *Congressional Record*, 39 (6 December 1904), 1:19.

12. Cyrus Veeser, *A World Safe for Capitalism: Dollar Diplomacy and America's Rise to Global Power* (New York: Columbia University Press, 2002); Schoultz, *Beneath the United States*, 189; Healy, *Drive to Hegemony*, 22–23, 121–122; Knox as quoted in Longley, *Eagle's Shadow*, 131.

13. A good account of events in Nicaragua in this period is Healy, *Drive to Hegemony*, 152–160. Knox had signed a similar treaty with Honduras in January 1911. See Rosenberg, *Financial Missionaries*, 61–66.

14. William Bayard Hale, "With the Knox Mission in Central America," *World's Work* (June 1912): 181–186.

15. Lewis Einstein, Policy Report, 22 April 1912, box 17, bound correspondence, Knox Papers, LOC. See also Healy, *Drive to Hegemony*, 166–167, 260.

16. Davis, *Three Gringos*, 194.

17. On the racial symbolism of the canal, see Stephen Frenkel, "Geography, Empire, and Environmental Determinism." *Geographical Review* 82, no. 2 (April 1992): 147.

18. Shonts as quoted in Greene, *Canal Builders*, 48.

19. Conniff, *Black Labor on a White Canal*, 25–32.

20. Lewis, *West Indian in Panama*, 35.

21. Poultney Bigelow, "Our Mismanagement at Panama," *The Independent,* 4 January 1906, 17–18.

22. Davis to Wallace, 3 May 1905, submitted to the April 1906 Isthmian Canal hearings, 2661, reel 10, John Tyler Morgan Papers, LOC.

23. Isthmian Canal hearings, 20 April 1906, 2766, reel 10, Morgan Papers, LOC.

24. McCullough, *Path between the Seas,* chap. 15; Lindsey-Poland, *Emperors in the Jungle,* 33.

25. Roosevelt's statement to Congress, reprinted in *New York Times,* 18 December 1906.

26. Deeks as quoted in A. Grenfell Price, "White Settlement in the Panama Canal Zone," *Geographical Review* 25, no. 1 (January 1935): 9.

27. For the British view on the silver and gold system, see Mallet to Foreign Office, 15 February 1909, FO 371 708/no. 11908, UKNA. See also Conniff, *Black Labor on a White Canal,* 31–36.

28. Bigelow, "Our Mismanagement," 13–19.

29. Lewis, *West Indians,* 30–31; Conniff, *Black Labor on a White Canal,* 31–34; Harry A. Franck, *Zone Policeman 88: A Close Range Study of the Panama Canal and Its Workers* (New York: Century, 1913), 12, 29–30, 64, 91.

30. In 1913, Clifford's other son was crippled in a similar rail accident. Clifford to Foreign Office, 4 January 1914, FO 371, 2058/no. 6159; Mallet to Foreign Office, 16 March 1914, FO 371, 2058/no. 16213; Clifford to Foreign Office, 13 April 1914, FO 371, 2058/no. 19473, UKNA.

31. U.S. medical official as quoted in Lindsay-Poland, *Emperors in the Jungle,* 35.

32. British report and U.S. prosecution documents enclosed in Mallet to Grey, 6 June 1910, FO 371 944/no. 23240, UKNA. On the legal system in the Canal Zone, see Greene, *Canal Builders,* 283–285.

33. Lewis, *West Indian in Panama,* 45–46; Greene, *Canal Builders,* chap. 7; Franck, *Zone Policeman 88,* 108. An example of racial enforcement among whites was U.S. Minister to Panama Thomas C. Dawson, who found himself unwelcome in the social circles of the Canal Zone because of his Brazilian wife. See Mallet to Foreign Office, 28 January 1911, FO 371, 1176/no. 6536, UKNA.

34. William F. Sands, *Our Jungle Diplomacy* (Chapel Hill: University of North Carolina Press, 1944), 47.

35. On the riot, see Greene, *Canal Builders,* chap. 8.

36. Ibid., 144–150; Bigelow, "Our Mismanagement," 11–12.

37. Mallet to Grey, 17 May 1910, FO 371, 944/no. 21176, UKNA.

38. Cox to Grey, 8 December 1910, FO 371 944/no. 46879, UKNA.

39. For a discussion of this organizational structure, see Williams, "Rise of the Banana Industry," 25–27.

40. Victor M. Cutter, "The Philippines as a Commercial Investment for the United States" (Master's thesis, Dartmouth College, 1904), 23, Victor M. Cutter Papers, Dartmouth College (hereafter Cutter Papers).

41. "How Victor Cutter Became Head of $150,000,000 Company at 43," *Boston Sunday Post,* 12 October 1924; Schweppe to Brounger, 5 January 1906, INCOFER #4760, Archivo Nacional de Costa Rica, Zapote, Costa Rica (hereafter ANCR).

42. "Zent Section: General Plan," Engineer and Farm Maps, box 2, folder 15, Cutter Papers.

43. "How Victor Cutter Became Head."

44. Paula Palmer, *Transcripciones de Paula Palmer sobre Entrevistas a Indígenas,* tomo 1, 55, Fondo Grabaciones, ANCR. See also Bourgois, *Ethnicity at Work,* chap. 3.

45. Schweppe to Harton, 23 July 1909; Schweppe to Trott, 15 August 1909, INCOFER #4833.

46. Mullins to Cooper, 8 March 1913, INCOFER #4942, ANCR. See also Chomsky, *West Indian Workers,* 44–47.

47. Mullins to Lynn, "confidential," 12 July 1913, INCOFER #4855.

48. Schweppe to Dietz, 25 August 1910, INCOFER #4936, ANCR; Schweppe to Cobben, New York City, 21 July 1910, INCOFER #4953, ANCR.

49. Bury, *Bishop amongst Bananas,* 156.

50. In December 1913, for example, Mullins instructed the company's agent in Colón to purchase larvecide and crude oil from the U.S. government for the poisoning of mosquito breeding grounds in Limón. Mullins to Wilford, 3 December 1913, INCOFER #5040.

51. U.S. consular reports from the 1899–1905 period are replete with death certificates for victims of yellow fever and malaria, many of whom were Civil War veterans who had settled in the region decades before. In November 1902, for example, U.S. Consul Chas Caldwell reported, "On Oct. 16, 1902, John H. Darling, American citizen and veteran of the Civil War, died of pernicious malaria at Cartago. He left some personal effects, a little ready money, and a document giving him the monthly rent of a banana farm." Caldwell to Pierce, 10 November 1902, T-35, reel 6, RG 59, USNA.

52. A good discussion of United Fruit's health policies is Chomsky, *West Indian Workers,* chaps. 4–5.

53. Williams, "Rise of the Banana Industry," 46.

54. Seaman to Schweppe, 27 June 1906, INCOFER #4760, ANCR.

55. In August 1909, for example, Schweppe informed one subordinate that all squatters who "refuse to sign this contract should be reported to the Auditor, with the amount of land that they occupy, so that he may notify the Cashier to deduct the amount of rent due upon payment of banana checks. This, of course, when the cultivations are bananas; but where they be yams and other fruit, you must see to the collection of the rent yourself, and if necessary, call in the Agent of Police to assist you." Schweppe to Burdette, 22 August 1909, INCOFER #4833, ANCR.

56. Long, *Railways of Central America,* 113–118.

57. A 1925 U.S. consular report described this system as debt peonage, cited in Harpelle, *West Indians,* 18.

58. Jiménez's speech as quoted in Chomsky, *West Indian Workers,* 213–214.

59. Williams, "Rise of the Banana Industry," 40.

60. Root as quoted in Healy, *Drive to Hegemony,* 148.

61. Banana growers' petition in "Exposición del Señor Secretario del Fomento," 16 May 1908, Serie Congreso, no. 10278, ANCR.

62. Mallet to Foreign Office, 17 December 1908, FO 371, 708/no. 1498, UKNA. One official in the Foreign Office reported that Costa Rican officials preferred that the loans not be held by Americans. Chalky memorandum, 30 October 1909, FO 371, 708/no. 43733, UKNA; Merry to Knox, 29 January 1910, vol. 34, RG 84, USNA.

63. Mullins to Montejo, 21 July 1909, INCOFER #4833, ANCR.

64. Schweppe to Keith, 24 July 1910, INCOFER #4953, ANCR.

65. Schweppe to Henderson, 28 July 1910, INCOFER #4953, ANCR; Mullins to Keith, 24 July 1910, INCOFER #4953, ANCR.

66. Schweppe to Keith, 24 July 1910, INCOFER #4953; two weeks later, he again stressed that "the labor itself is really not at fault but unfortunately we have had a few agitators among us." Schweppe to Field, 6 August 1910, INCOFER #4953, ANCR.

67. Schweppe to Keith, 29 July 1910, INCOFER #4953, ANCR. See also Harpelle, *West Indians,* 28.

68. Schweppe to Keith, 24 July 1910, INCOFER #4953, ANCR.

69. Schweppe to Keith, 2 and 6 August 1910, INCOFER #4953, ANCR.

70. Cables and reports enclosed in Cox to Grey, 8 December 1910, FO 371 944/no. 46879, UKNA.

71. As Cox put it, McGrigor's "position on the staff of the United Fruit Company renders it impossible for him to hold the confidence of British West Indian labourers." Ibid.

72. Octavio Montero, "Pobres negros!" *Hoja Obrera* (San José), 6 December 1910, as quoted in Chomsky, *West Indian Workers,* 217.

73. Martin, *Race First,* 3–4; Harpelle, *West Indians,* 28–35.

74. Mallet to Foreign Office, 11 July 1911, FO 371, 1176/no. 31097, UKNA.

75. Sydney Olivier, *White Capital and Coloured Labour* (London: Independent Labour Party, 1906); Mallet to Foreign Office, 25 November 1911, FO 371, 1176/no. 51704, UKNA.

76. Lionel Carden, "Annual Report, 1909," 18 January 1910, FO 371 837, UKNA. See also Dosal, *Doing Business with the Dictators.*

77. Under Estrada Cabrera's orders, local officials required planters in the surrounding departments to contribute workers to the railroad, a demand that sometimes threatened to disrupt other foreign enterprises. In September 1906, for example, one mayor ordered the American-owned Kensett, Champney & Co. in Alta Verapaz to "send 10 mozos" for work on the railroad. Although the U.S. legation secured an exemption for the company, the regime forced hundreds of Guatemalans to labor on the project. Argueta to Kensett, Champney, 10 September 1906; and Barrios to *Jéfe Político,* Cobán, 11 October 1906, in vol. 124, RG 84, USNA. On the terms of the 1904 agreement, see Kraft, "Making West Indians Unwelcome," 62.

78. Winter, *Guatemala,* 144.

79. Reed to Kent, 22 September 1907; affidavit of Simon Shine, 13 November 1907; affidavit of George Fitzgerald, 21 December 1907, vol. 125, RG 84, USNA.

80. Shine's letter as quoted in Schoonover, *United States and Central America,* 121.

81. Arias as quoted in Sands, *Our Jungle Diplomacy,* 109.

82. Ibid., 99–100.

83. Reed as quoted in Schoonover, *United States in Central America,* 124. This tension played out in the June 1909 issue of *Literary Digest,* which reported Guatemalan abuses of Americans. Although the article cited Shine's case specifically, it elided all references to his race, referring to him only as an American "hotel-keeper." In the eyes of the magazine's editors, Shine's claims to protection as a U.S. citizen apparently hinged upon his implied whiteness. See "Our Citizens Mistreated in Central America," *The Literary Digest* 38, no. 24 (12 June 1909): 999–1000.

84. McCreery, *Development and the State,* 57–60; J. J. Ordoñez, "Cuestionario," 30 March 1905, paquete #1 (1905), Jefatura Política de Izabal (hereafter JPI), Archivo General de Centroamérica (hereafter AGCA). One measure of local banana growing was the rising number of land claims (*denuncios*) on public lands (*baldíos*) in the department of Izabal. By 1905, they accounted for most paperwork in the governor's office.

85. Kraft, "Making West Indians Unwelcome," 58–60.

86. Cutter to father, 25 September 1907, box 2, folder 9, Cutter Papers; Wilson, *Education of a Diplomat,* 64.

87. This first small hospital was located on the Dartmouth plantation. Although the company focused its medical efforts on its employees, Guatemalan officials allowed it to carry out vaccinations and quarantines of the local population. In January 1909, for example, authorities in

Morales assisted with vaccinations despite the resistance of local *ladinos*. Andrade to *Comandante* Puerto Barrios, 5, 17 January 1909, "Telegrafos al Comandante," paquete #1 (1909), JPI, AGCA; Steven S. Gillick, "Life and Labor in a Banana Enclave: Bananeros, the United Fruit Company, and the Limits of Trade Unionism in Guatemala, 1906 to 1931" (Ph.D. diss., Tulane University, 1994), 133–139; on Macphail, see Stanley, *For the Record*, 125–127.

88. "How Victor Cutter Became Head"; Williams, "Rise of the Banana Industry," 24–27.

89. Bury, *Bishop amongst Bananas*, 203.

90. Williams, "Rise of the Banana Industry," 118–119. With Cutter clearly in mind, Sands described United Fruit managers in Guatemala as "handpicked men from the New England colleges, principally Dartmouth." Sands, *Our Jungle Diplomacy*, 97.

91. Smith to Sands, 20 December 1909, vol. 128, RG 84, USNA.

92. Haggard's report, enclosed in Carden to Grey, 31 January 1910, FO 371/837 (6083), UKNA; Tennison to Knox, 3 January 1910, M-862, reel 1142, RG 59, USNA; "Negroes Cause Trouble: Clash with American and Jamaican Blacks in Guatemala," *New Orleans Times-Picayune*, 24 December 1909.

93. Cutter to Sands, 17 December 1909, included in Carden to Grey, 31 January 1910, FO 371/837 (6083), UKNA.

94. Lionel Carden to Grey, 31 January 1910, FO 371/837 (6083); Reed to Owen, 24 December 1909, vol. 128, RG 84, USNA.

95. Haggard's report, enclosed in Carden to Grey, 31 January 1910, FO 371/837 (6083), UKNA.

96. Cutter to Sands, 10 January 1910, vol. 128, RG 84, USNA.

97. Cutter to Sands, 25 February 1910; Cutter to Sands, 7 March 1910, vol. 128, RG 84, USNA.

98. Cutter to Carden, 14 March 1910, vol. 128, RG 84, USNA.

99. Mendoza to Jéfe Político, 31 May 1909, paquete #1 (1909), JPI, AGCA; "Republica de Guatemala Fuerza Ordenaria," paquete #1 (1909), JPI, AGCA.

100. Williams, "Rise of the Banana Industry," 120.

101. Ruhl also noted that, as in other colonial settings, white women gained a reputation for snobbishness and abuse of domestic workers. Encouraged by the enclave's racial hierarchy and their own elevated status, such women welcomed the chance to "play the lady." Ruhl described one woman who "spoke a complacent but awful Spanish" yet "was afflicted with that superiority complex which, amongst Americans who go to live in 'backward' tropical neighborhoods, seems to attack the females of the species more virulently than it does their husbands." See Arthur J. Ruhl, *The Central Americans: Adventures and Impressions between Mexico and Panama* (New York: Charles Scribner's Sons, 1929), 270–271.

Chapter 4. Divided Workers, 1912–1921

1. Guatemalan telegrams included in Young to Grey, 1 June 1914, FO 371/1921 (27762), UKNA; Ayala to Jefe Político, 14 May 1914, paquete #3 (1914), JPI, AGCA.

2. Testimony of John Dessart, 16 May 1914, enclosed in Young to Grey, 1 June 1914, FO 371/1921 (27762), UKNA.

3. Haggard report, Young to Grey, 1 June 1914, FO 371/1921 (27762), UKNA.

4. See, for example, Langley, *Banana Wars*.

5. Palmer, *Transcripciones*, tomo IV, 1–10, ANCR.

6. As British Consul Claude Mallet observed, this employment would "relieve the congestion of an over-crowded labour market that would otherwise arise if a large number of men should be without work and unwilling to return to the West Indies." Mallet to Foreign Office, 21 August 1913, FO 1703/no. 42435, UKNA.

7. A British diplomat later recalled that in one incident seventeen West Indians were summarily executed by machine gun. Haggard to Foreign Office, 8 June 1923, "Treatment of West Indians in Cuba," FO 371, A3865/2333/14, UKNA; Healy, *Drive to Hegemony,* 198–199.

8. Conniff, *Black Labor,* 42, 57–60; Lindsay-Poland, *Emperors in the Jungle,* 40.

9. Martin, *Race First,* 5–11. In one writing, Garvey denounced corporations in the Caribbean that "stir up local agitation" in weaker nations and then "call upon the home authorities for protection," and he declared Dollar Diplomacy "a disgrace to our civilization." Marcus Garvey, "An Exposé of the Caste System among Negroes," 31 August 1923, reprinted in Amy Jacques-Garvey, ed., *Philosophy and Opinions of Marcus Garvey* (New York: Atheneum, 1992), 72–73.

10. UNIA Membership Records, Micro R 1571, reel 1, a22, Schomburg Center for Black Studies, New York Public Library. Although these records are drawn from the 1924–1926 period, they probably reflect basic patterns of concentration of UNIA branches in the early 1920s. For useful tables on U.S. and overseas membership, see Martin, *Race First,* 15–16. The first copies of *Negro World* seem to have appeared in Costa Rica in August 1919. See Montgomery to Secretary of State, 24 August 1919, M-669, reel 18, RG 59, USNA.

11. Martin, *Race First,* 151–167. For a celebratory account of United Fruit's steam line, see John H. Melville, *The Great White Fleet* (New York: Vantage Press, 1976).

12. United Fruit counsel as quoted in David Levering Lewis, *When Harlem Was in Vogue* (New York: Penguin, 1997), 43.

13. Bennett to Lindsay, 11 March 1920, FO 371 4536/A1921/986/32, UKNA.

14. Walter to Armstrong, 11 August 1919, FO 252, 571/no. 145, UKNA; O'Brien, *Revolutionary Mission,* 85; Darío A. Euraque, *Reinterpreting the Banana Republic: Region and State in Honduras, 1870–1972* (Chapel Hill: University of North Carolina Press, 1996), 43–50. The best account of the clashes over the Motagua valley is Dosal, *Doing Business with the Dictators,* chaps. 5 and 8.

15. Darío A. Euraque, "The Banana Enclave, Nationalism, and Mestizaje in Honduras, 1910s–1930s," in Aviva Chomsky and Aldo Lauria-Santiago, eds., *Identity and Struggle at the Margins of the Nation-State: The Laboring Peoples of Central America and the Hispanic Caribbean* (Durham, N.C.: Duke University Press, 1998), 155–160.

16. Armstrong to Haggard, 2 October 1913, FO 252 477/no. 278, UKNA.

17. Frances Emery-Waterhouse, *Banana Paradise* (New York: Stephen-Paul, 1947), 249.

18. Edward to Mrs. W. M. Thornton, 23 May 1910, 16 October 1919, 28 January 1920, 12 January 1920, box 4, Thornton Family Papers, University of Virginia.

19. Euraque, "The Banana Enclave," in Chomsky and Lauria-Santiago, eds., *Identity and Struggle,* 140–143; Gerberich to State Department, 15 June 1920, M-647, reel 33, RG 59, USNA; "Honduras Bars Jamaica Negroes," *New York Times,* 25 June 1920; in August 1920, U.S. consul Jim Garrety warned of the UNIA's "Negro anti-white propaganda" among West Indians in La Ceiba; see Garrety to State Department, 17 August 1920, M-647, reel 32, RG 59, USNA.

20. Merrill to Chittenden, 8 July 1912, INCOFER #5036, ANCR.

21. Mullins to Chittenden, 6 July 1912, INCOFER #5036; Mullins to Schermerhorn, 3 September 1912, INCOFER #4857.

22. Donaldson to Bryan, 12 May 1914, M-669, reel 30, RG 59, USNA.

23. Meily to State Department, 18 March 1925, vol. 152, RG 84, USNA.

24. Frederick Upham Adams, *Conquest of the Tropics: The Story of the Creative Enterprises Conducted by the United Fruit Company* (Garden City, N.Y.: Page, 1914), 106–107.

25. Chomsky, *West Indian Workers,* 50–51; Bourgois, *Ethnicity at Work,* chap. 6.

26. George P. Putnam, *The Southland of North America: Rambles and Observations in Central America during the Year 1912* (New York: Knickerbocker Press, 1913), 43–44, 92–100; Adams, *Conquest of the Tropics,* 59.

27. Ministro de Hacienda to Administrador de Aduana, Limón, 24 August 1914, Fondo Hacienda, #30877, ANCR.

28. Chaukley to Foreign Office, 15 August 1914; and Cox to Chaukley, 5 September 1914, both in FO 371, 2058/no. 54348, UKNA.

29. According to local lore, González granted land to the residents of Cahuita despite its location within the maritime mile.

30. Schermerhorn to Cutter, 21 August 1915, box 3, scrapbook 2, Cutter Papers; *El Imparcial* (San José), 2 October 1915. Other Costa Rican newspapers applauded Cutter's handling of the strikes. See, for example, *La información* (San José), 23 November 1915.

31. Schermerhorn to Cutter, 6 June 1916. Just over a year later, Cutter was appointed vice president and transferred back to Boston. See Preston to Cutter, 9 October 1917. Both in box 3, scrapbook 2, Cutter Papers.

32. Healy, *Drive to Hegemony,* 230–231.

33. Harpelle, *West Indians,* 44.

34. Murray to McFarland, 16 May 1919, as quoted in Bourgois, *Ethnicity at Work,* 55–56.

35. George W. Baker Jr., "Woodrow Wilson's Use of the Non-Recognition Policy in Costa Rica," *The Americas* 22, no. 1 (July 1965): 3–21.

36. Blair to Murray, 11 June 1919, FO 371/3865, 530–531, UKNA.

37. Montgomery to Lansing, 24 August 1919, M-669, reel 18, RG 59, USNA.

38. Chittenden to Cutter, 21 December 1919, reprinted in Striffler and Moberg, *Banana Wars,* 120–121.

39. In February 1921, for example, West Indian stevedores in Puerto Limón struck for higher wages and were immediately fired and blacklisted by the company. The U.S. consul approved of this action. Rather than being forced into concessions, he noted, the company had "been able to keep the whip hand" with its laborers. U.S. Consulate Limon to State Department, special report: "Labor Troubles in Limon," 15 February 1921, M-607, reel 33, RG 59, USNA.

40. Harpelle, *West Indians,* 57; Chittenden to Blair, April 1921, reprinted in Striffer and Moberg, *Banana Wars,* 123–125.

41. Chittenden to Cutter, 22 April 1921, reprinted in Striffer and Moberg, *Banana Wars,* 123–125.

42. UNIA Estrada, Costa Rica, to U.S. Attorney General, 1 November 1925, box 1160A, folder 42–792 (8), RG 204, USNA; on the UNIA's demobilizing effect, see Chomsky, *West Indian Workers,* 198–206.

43. In May 1912, for example, United Fruit's steamship *Cartago* arrived at Puerto Barrios from Colon, Panama. Ordinarily, the ship carried between seven and ten cabin passengers and eight to fifteen deck passengers. On this voyage, the passenger manifest listed seven cabin passengers and 234 "deckers," nearly all of whom bore English surnames. Around the same time, United Fruit's steamship *Heredia* carried thirty-three cabin passengers and 168 deckers: "United Fruit Steamship Service," passenger manifests, SS *Cartago,* 13 May 1912, SS *Heredia* (n.d.), paquete #2 (1912), JPI, AGCA. In March 1914, British Vice Consul Haggard reported that "approximately 600 West Indians have arrived in Guatemala since August 1st, 1913, about 30% of which were women and children," and he added that "about 300 left for the ports of Puerto

Cortes and Tela in the Republic of Honduras, for Puerto Limon in Costa Rica and for the island of Jamaica within the same period." Haggard to Foreign Office, 8 March 1914, FO 371 2058/ no. 13692, UKNA.

44. *La Campaña,* 5 July 1913, enclosed in Wilson to State Department, 16 July 1913, vol. 163.

45. Haggard, "Report on the Quiriguá Incident," 20 May 1914 telegrams enclosed in Young to Grey, 1 June 1914, FO 371/1921 (27762), UKNA.

46. Moreno to Monzón, 21 April 1916, paquete #4 (1916), JPI, AGCA.

47. Adams, *Conquest of the Tropics,* 273–274.

48. Williams, "Rise of the Banana Industry," 121. Texan writer Eugene Cunningham caught a glimpse of the racialized mentality of company employees in 1920, when he met an American blacksmith named "California" Jack Dempsey who had recently quit his job with United Fruit: "Loud-mouthed, obscene, with the mentality of a grammar-school boy and the senseless obstinacy of an army mule, he possessed a deep contempt for the 'niggers' about him. Their inability to speak English he regarded as a personal affront." To Dempsey, Hispanics as well as blacks were "niggers." Eugene Cunningham, *Gypsying through Central America* (New York: E. P. Dutton, 1922), 240.

49. Davis to Estrada Cabrera, 28 February, 2 March 1914, vol. 204, RG 84, USNA. See also Dosal, *Doing Business with the Dictators,* 22–23, 42–45, 63–68.

50. Haggard, "Report on the Quiriguá Incident," 20 May 1914 telegrams enclosed in Young to Grey, 1 June 1914, FO 371/1921 (27762), UKNA.

51. Young to Grey, 1 June 1914, FO 371/1921 (27762); Young to Grey, 15 June 1914, FO 371/1921 (30123), UKNA.

52. *La República,* 14 May 1914.

53. Lipton to State Department, 14 September 1914, M-655, reel 29, RG 59, USNA; Robins to State Department, 10 November 1914, vol. 165, RG 84, USNA.

54. Gillick, "Life and Labor in a Banana Enclave," 30–31.

55. For an extensive discussion of this local harassment, see Kraft, "Making West Indians Unwelcome," 135–153.

56. White's correspondence and deposition contained in "Criminal: Cornelio Ortega por Abuso de Autoridad," Rf. No. 854-d, paquete #3 (1916), JPI, AGCA.

57. The investigation file includes several documents given to such women by Ortega himself, declaring, for example, "Fidelia Ochoa will not be bothered by my garrison for three months because she has completed her term of service." The fact that Ortega was investigated, removed, and incarcerated is a striking aspect of this case. Ortega's incarceration may indicate that his practices were not accepted by higher officials, such as Izabal's governor, Luis Monzón. Ortega to Ochoa, 18 October 1915; testimony of Cornelio Ortega, 31 December 1915, in "Criminal: Cornelio Ortega por Abuso de Autoridad," Rf. No. 854-d, paquete #3 (1916), JPI, AGCA.

58. Fajardo to Juez Municipal, Morales, 12 February 1917, "Criminal: Contra el capitan de trabajadores de Dartmouth James Dempster," paquete #3 (1917), JPI, AGCA.

59. Testimonies of James Dempster and Samuel Cooper in "Criminal: contra del capitán de trabajadores de Dartmouth," 12 February 1917, paquete #3 (1917), JPI, AGCA. The testimonies themselves underscore the demographic patterns in the enclave. Dempster was thirty-seven years old, literate, and likely a longtime employee of the company. In contrast, the three *ladinos* whom Fajardo impressed into service were in their early twenties, illiterate, and originally from other parts of Guatemala.

60. Reed to Armstrong, 3 January 1918, FO 252 (543), UKNA.

61. Shaw to Monzón, 11 June 1919, as quoted in Kraft, "Making West Indians Unwelcome," 190.
62. Shaw to Leavell, 20 January 1915, vol. 169, RG 84, USNA.
63. Reed to Haggard, 4 December 1918, FO 252 (543), UKNA.
64. "Report on Guatemala, 1920–1921," FO 371 (9523), UKNA.
65. On 8 April, Governor Monzón sent police to disrupt a Unionist meeting in Livingston. See "Criminal: Contra los reos Carlos Rendon V. Gustavo Aguilar, Alberto Lemus y Francisco Alfredo Alarcon por insultos vertidos contra el Presidente de la Republica," 9 April 1920, Livingston, paquete #1 (1920), JPI, AGCA; Adams to McMillin, 12 April 1920, vol. 198, RG 84, USNA. See also Dosal, *Doing Business with the Dictators*, 95–100. Only days before the strike, Victor Cutter had traveled through his old stomping grounds on the way back from Honduras. See "United Fruit Steamship Service," SS *Saramacca*, passenger manifest, Tela to Puerto Barrios, 1 April 1920, paquete #1 (1920), JPI, AGCA.
66. Bourne handled many of the black community's legal disputes and commercial transactions. Also prominent was businessman George C. Reneau, who owned a trading house and hotel in Puerto Barrios and served as mayor in the 1920s. In October 1920, Reneau petitioned the Guatemalan authorities to grant the municipality of Puerto Barrios all the land that United Fruit's original city plan had called for. See Reneau to *Juez Político Departamental*, 16 October 1920, paquete #1 (1920), JPI, AGCA.
67. "Reports of the Convention," 3 August 1920, in Robert A. Hill, ed., *The Marcus Garvey and Universal Negro Improvement Association Papers* (Berkeley: University of California Press, 1983–), vol. II, 514–515.

Chapter 5. The Rise of Hispanic Nationalism, 1921–1929

1. Beaulac to State Department, 14–16 July 1924, vol. 125, RG 84, USNA.
2. Photostats of fliers enclosed in Beaulac to State Department, 16 July 1924, vol. 125, RG 84, USNA.
3. Beaulac to State Department 21 July 1924, vol. 125, RG 84, USNA.
4. Beaulac to State Department, 16 July 1924, vol. 125, RG 84, USNA.
5. Beaulac to Morales, 15 July 1924, vol. 125, RG 84, USNA.
6. Beaulac to State Department, 14–16 July 1924, vol. 125, RG 84, USNA.
7. On the rise of Latin American nationalism, see Richard V. Salisbury, *Anti-Imperialism and International Competition in Central America, 1920–1929* (Wilmington: Scholarly Resources, 1989); and Michael L. Krenn, *U.S. Policy toward Economic Nationalism in Latin America, 1917–1929* (Wilmington: Scholarly Resources, 1990). On the shifting definitions of "imperialism" in the 1920s, see Rosenberg, *Financial Missionaries*, 130.
8. Robert Freeman Smith, *The United States and Revolutionary Nationalism in Mexico, 1916–1932* (Chicago: University of Chicago Press, 1972); José Vasconcelos, *La raza cósmica, mission de la raza iberoamericana* (Baltimore: Johns Hopkins University Press, 1997 [1925]). Vasconcelos also presented his ideas in José Vasconcelos and Manuel Gamio, "The Latin-American Basis of Mexican Civilization," *Aspects of Mexican Civilization* (Chicago: University of Chicago Press, 1926), 3–102. On the racial dimensions of the Mexican Revolution, see Alan Knight, "Racism, Revolution, and *Indigenismo*: Mexico, 1910–1940," in Richard Graham, ed., *The Idea of Race in Latin America, 1870–1940* (Austin: University of Texas Press, 1990), esp. 84–88; on Haya, see

Richard V. Salisbury, "The Middle American Exile of Víctor Raúl Haya de la Torre," *The Americas* 40, no. 1 (July 1983): 1–15.

9. Sandino related some of his story to interviewer José Román in 1933, reprinted in Augusto C. Sandino, *Sandino: The Testimony of a Nicaraguan Patriot, 1921–1934*, ed. Robert Edgar Conrad (Princeton: Princeton University Press, 1990), 27–31. He voiced his discontent with life in company towns in a 1922 letter to his father; see Augusto Sandino to Don Gregorio Sandino, ibid., 34–35. On the Tampico oil industry, see Hart, *Empire and Revolution*, 154–164. For a good treatment of Sandino's life in Tampico, see Neill Macaulay, *The Sandino Affair* (Chicago: Quadrangle, 1967), 48–54.

10. On Mexican aid to the Nicaraguan Liberals, see Richard V. Salisbury, "Mexico, the United States, and the 1926–1927 Nicaraguan Crisis," *Hispanic American Historical Review* 66, no. 2 (May 1986): 317–339. On the Sandino rebellion, see Macauley's *Sandino Affair;* and Michael J. Schroeder, "The Sandino Rebellion Revisited: Civil War, Imperialism, Popular Nationalism, and State Formation Muddied Up Together in the Segovias of Nicaragua, 1926–1934," in Joseph et al., *Close Encounters of Empire*, 208–251. On U.S. perceptions of the Havana conference, see Lewis S. Gannett, "The Indispensable Mr. Hughes," *Nation* (15 February 1928): 182–183. A good account of this shift in U.S.–Latin American relations is Schoultz, *Beneath the United States*, 290–315. Later that year, the radical Committee on Cultural Relations with Latin America organized demonstrations against the war, including one outside the White House. Soon after, a series of articles on Sandino by journalist Carleton Beals in the *Nation* magazine raised opposition to the war within the United States. Beals, "With Sandino in Nicaragua," *Nation* (22 February–28 March 1928): 204–205, 232–233, 260–261, 288–289, 314–317, 340–341. On Beals, see John A. Britton, *Carleton Beals: A Radical Journalist in Latin America* (Albuquerque: University of New Mexico Press, 1987).

11. Barry Carr, "Identity, Class, and Nation: Black Immigrant Workers, Cuban Communism, and the Sugar Insurgency, 1925–1933," *Hispanic American Historical Review* 78, no. 1 (1998): 83; O'Brien, *Revolutionary Mission*, 212–221; *Heraldo de Cuba* as quoted in Funtanellas, *United Fruit Company*, 248.

12. Like many West Indians, Lugg drew upon his status as both a British subject and a World War I veteran to solicit support from London. See Lugg to Secretary of State for the Colonies, 8 December 1924, FO 371 10618/A122/22/14, UKNA.

13. Morris to Foreign Office, 23 December 1924, FO 371, 10618/A206/22/14, UKNA.

14. Turcios as quoted in Euraque, "The Threat of Blackness," Striffler and Moberg, *Banana Wars*, 243; Honduran official quoted in Gerberich to State Department, 20 July 1921, M-647, reel 33, RG 59, USNA.

15. "Murder of Mr. Herbert Leslie Forbes in Honduras," 29 October 1924, FO 371, 9523, UKNA.

16. Beaulac to State Department, 23 August 1923, M-647, reel 32, RG 59, USNA.

17. British officials hoped the U.S. government would assist in the repatriation of unemployed British West Indians, but they recognized that this was unlikely due to "high fares, and the reluctance of most of the companies, both British and foreign, to carry negro passengers." British Embassy to State Department, 6 December 1921, M-607, reel 33, RG 59, USNA.

18. South to State Department, 13 December 1926; South to State Department, 7 February 1927, M-607, reel 33, RG 59, USNA. See also Conniff, *Black Labor*, 64–66.

19. On Panama disease, see Soluri, *Banana Cultures*, 53–55.

20. United Fruit celebrated its innovations in its glossy new magazine, *Unifruitco*, which began publication in 1925.

21. On Ford's scheme in Brazil, see Grandin, *Fordlandia*.

22. Proclaiming United Fruit the "advance agent in subduing disease, developing . . . resources, and ultimately leading the way to political and social order," Anderson added that "as an American citizen and a New Englander I was immensely gratified at what I saw." Anderson to Cutter, 7 September 1922, M-672, reel 13, RG 59, USNA.

23. On Cutter's depiction in the press, see, for example, "How Victor Cutter Became Head of $150,000,000 Company at 43," *Boston Sunday Post*, 12 October 1924; and George Kent, "Head of $150,000,000 Corporation Rose from Obscure Post in Jungle," news clipping, box 3, scrapbook 1924–1926, Cutter Papers; "We Greet the New President of the United Fruit Company," *Fruit Dispatch* (November 1924), box 1, folder 8.

24. Victor M. Cutter, "Trade Relations with Latin America," Boston, 7 August 1925, box 2, folder 14, Cutter Papers.

25. Salisbury, *Anti-Imperialism and International Competition*, chaps. 3–4.

26. "Latin-American Policy Needed: United Fruit Head Tells 20th Century Club," *Boston Post*, 4 October 1925, box 3, scrapbook 3 1924–1926, Cutter Papers.

27. Victor M. Cutter, "Relations of United States Companies with Latin America," 23 April 1927, box 2, folder 14, Cutter Papers.

28. Victor M. Cutter, "Our Greatest Economic Problem," *Current History* (October 1927): 74–76. In the wake of anti-imperialist rhetoric at the Havana conference, the firm continued to push this line, emphasizing the $24 million in wages it paid annually to its workers. "United Fruit Reports on Foreign Business," *New York Times*, 16 February 1928. In a March 1928 speech to the Bond Club of New York, Cutter emphasized that "manufactured goods have been made available to the laboring classes in the coast towns at lower prices than ever before, making possible an appreciable improvement in the standards of living." See Cutter, "Destiny and Development in Latin America," 29 March 1928, box 2, folder 14, Cutter Papers.

29. Kraft, "Making West Indians Unwelcome," 236.

30. On the labor conflict in Santa Marta, see Bucheli, *Bananas and Business*, chap. 5; and Catherine C. LeGrand, "Living in Macondo: Economy and Culture in a United Fruit Company Enclave in Colombia," in Joseph et al., *Close Encounters of Empire*, 333–368.

31. Salisbury, *Anti-Imperialism and International Competition*, 100–101, 40–41.

32. Ibid., 45–51.

33. Meily to State Department, 22 May 1925, vol. 157, RG 84, USNA.

34. Meily to State Department, 18 March 1925, vol. 152, RG 84, USNA.

35. Ibid.

36. Putnam, *Company They Kept*, 69–71; Chomsky, *West Indian Workers*, 234–238.

37. Putnam, *Company They Kept*, 167. There were, of course, Costa Ricans who embraced the "uplifting" effect of United Fruit. See Waterman to Division of Latin American Affairs, 5 November 1925, U.S. Legation, San José, to State Department, 20 April 1926, M-669, reel 29, RG 59, USNA.

38. Putnam, *Company They Kept*, 65–72; Harpelle, *West Indians of Costa Rica*, 105.

39. Thompson, *Rainbow Countries*, 19–25; Ruhl, *Central Americans*, 30.

40. On elite responses to radical nationalism, see Chomsky, *West Indian Workers*, 234–238; a good treatment of the negotiations in the late 1920s is Harpelle, *West Indians*, 67–68.

41. Marco A. Zumbado R., "Un aspecto del asunto: Una visión del problema," 15 November 1926, memorandum to Costa Rican Congress, Serie Congreso, no. 15400, ANCR; memorandum to Costa Rican Congress, "Sociedad Económica de Amigos del Pais: Exposicion sobre el Problema Bananero," 6 January 1927, Serie Congreso, no. 15400, ANCR.

42. Public statement printed in *La Gaceta—Diario Oficial*, 10 February 1927, Serie Congreso, no. 15400, ANCR.

43. Salisbury, *Anti-Imperialist and International Competition*, 103–106.

44. Salisbury, "Middle American Exile," 10–14.

45. De Lambert to State Department, 21 August 1928, M-669, reel 30, RG 59, USNA.

46. U.S. Chargé d'Affaires Herbert Gould as quoted in Dosal, *Doing Business with the Dictators*, 100.

47. Opie, *Black Labor Migration*, 75–76.

48. Keith to McMillan, 23 May 1921, vol. 204, RG 84, USNA; Frost to State Department, 12 July 1921, M-655, reel 29, RG 59, USNA; Aguirre to McMillan, 28 October 1921, vol. 204, RG 84, USNA.

49. The same envoy described General Jorge Ubico as "almost pure, if not absolutely pure, white." Curtis to Munro, 19, 31 January 1922, vol. 206, RG 84, USNA.

50. Cruse to Weeks (forwarded to Secretary of State Charles E. Hughes), 2 December 1922, M-672, reel 13, RG 59, USNA.

51. Curtis to State Department, 6 February 1922, vol. 206, RG 84, USNA.

52. Geissler to State Department, 6 February 1923, M-655, reel 20, RG 59, USNA.

53. Frost to State Department, 7 February 1923, M-655, reel 20, RG 59, USNA; Thomas to Geissler, 7 March 1923, vol. 210, RG 84, USNA.

54. *El Excelsior* was owned and published by Eduardo Aguirre Velásquez, the Guatemalan consul in New York City. Its editorial is enclosed in Geissler to State Department, 6 February 1923, M-655, reel 20, RG 59, USNA.

55. A week into the strike, Geissler reported that "200 native stevedores at Porto Barrios and 800 native farm laborers of United Fruit Company are striking for higher wages and because of alleged preference for negroes and that strikers prevent about 2,000 negro plantation workers, nearly all from Belize and Jamaica, from working and prevent movement of freight between United Fruit Company ships and railroad." Geissler to Hughes, 10 February 1923, M-655, reel 20, RG 59, USNA; Thomas, memorandum, 4 March 1923, vol. 210, RG 84, USNA.

56. Dosal, *Doing Business with the Dictators*, 134–135.

57. For the 1924 contract, see De León Aragón, *Los Contratos*, 252–257; see also Stanley, *For the Record*, 50–53.

58. For several examples of *ladino* workers' complaints against black foremen and use of patriotic rhetoric, see Kraft, "Making West Indians Unwelcome," 191–197, 219–224.

59. Geissler to State Department, 21 April 1926, M-655, reel 20, RG 59, USNA.

60. Both quotations from Ellis to State Department, 14 October 1926, vol. 225, RG 84, USNA.

61. For a discussion of the various development efforts on the Pacific Coast, see Frost to State Department, 5 May 1923, vol. 210, RG 84, USNA.

62. Geissler to State Department, 15 April 1926, vol. 226, RG 84, USNA.

63. Holland to State Department, 4 November 1925, vol. 220, RG 84, USNA; Hambly to Holland, 15 April 1926, vol. 226, RG 84, USNA.

64. Dosal, *Doing Business with the Dictators*, 162–170.

65. For a good account of the border clash, see ibid., chap. 8.

66. Salisbury, *Anti-Imperialism and International Competition*, 142–146; Salisbury, "Middle American Exile," 7.

67. For a discussion of the bribery of local editors, coordinated by United Fruit official Joaquín Hecht, see Geissler to Hughes, 22 May 1928, M-655, reel 40, RG 59, USNA.

68. Cindy Forster, "Reforging National Revolution," in Chomsky and Lauria-Santiago, *Identity and Struggle*, 200–201.

Chapter 6. Reframing the Empire, 1929–1940

1. Emery-Waterhouse, *Banana Paradise,* 103, 11, 19.
2. Ibid., 11–12. This was likely a reference to the case of Gabriela Carranza de Lima, a Guatemalan woman who claimed that two West Indians had thrown her and her two-month-old baby from a moving train in February 1914. In September 1914, she identified her attacker as Jamaican Daniel Lindsay, who had served jail time for his role in the December 1909 labor uprising against United Fruit. At the time Carranza accused him, Lindsay, now a foreman at the firm's El Pilar farm, was being charged with involvement in the Quiriguá incident. Although apparently innocent of both charges, Lindsay became a bogeyman-like figure for *ladinos* in Izabal, who blamed him for a range of killings. Because the Quiriguá incident came less than three months after the death of Carranza's infant, the two likely blurred in popular memory. On Lindsay's legal troubles and Carranza's testimony, see Kraft, "Making West Indians Unwelcome," 162–174.
3. Emery-Waterhouse, *Banana Paradise,* 40, 4.
4. Ibid., 94–96, 124–125, 2. As in other colonial spheres, white residents sought to limit the influence of the tropics on their children. "At the age of nine or ten," Emery-Waterhouse explained, "the banana children must be sent away to become educated, else they become over-bearing and conceited little savages." Ibid., 20.
5. For critical views of the Good Neighbor Policy, see David Green, *The Containment of Latin America: A History of the Myths and Realities of the Good Neighbor Policy* (Chicago: Quadrangle, 1971); and David F. Schmitz, *Thank God They're on Our Side: The United States and Right-Wing Dictatorships, 1921–1965* (Chapel Hill: University of North Carolina Press, 1999), chap. 3. See also Grandin, *Empire's Workshop,* 33–35.
6. Conversation with British Consul F. Nutter Cox recounted in Eberhardt to Stimson, 26 March 1930, vol. 188, RG 84, USNA.
7. On the global significance of the Italo-Ethiopian War, see Brenda Gayle Plummer, *Rising Wind: Black Americans and U.S. Foreign Affairs, 1935–1960* (Chapel Hill: University of North Carolina Press, 1996), 37–56.
8. On the massacre, see Eric Paul Roorda, *The Dictator Next Door: The Good Neighbor Policy and the Trujillo Regime in the Dominican Republic, 1930–1945* (Durham, N.C.: Duke University Press, 1998), 127–144; and Richard Lee Turits, "A World Destroyed, a Nation Imposed: The 1937 Haitian Massacre in the Dominican Republic," *Hispanic American Historical Review* 82, no. 3 (August 2002): 589–635.
9. Carr, "Identity, Class, and Nation," 83–116; Marc C. Macleod, "Undesirable Aliens: Race, Ethnicity, and Nationalism in the Comparison of Haitian and British West Indian Immigrant Workers in Cuba, 1912–1939," *Journal of Social History* 31, no. 3 (Spring 1998): 599–623.
10. Walter LaFeber, *The Panama Canal: The Crisis in Historical Perspective* (New York: Oxford University Press, 1989 [1978]), 67–69; Conniff, *Black Labor on a White Canal,* 84–88.
11. Panamanian negotiator Ricardo Alfaro as quoted in Conniff, *Black Labor on a White Canal,* 87.
12. The treaty was not ratified by the U.S. Senate until 1939. See LaFeber, *Panama Canal,* 68–70.
13. On the shifting political context within Latin America, see Bucheli, *Bananas and Business,* chap. 3.
14. Wilson, *Education of a Diplomat,* 37.

15. The best account of the clash between Cutter and Zemurray is Wilson, *Empire in Green and Gold*, 257–266. A description of Cutter's "Musa" estate appeared in "And Did You Know?" *The Highlander*, 15 July 1930, box 4, scrapbook 1930, Cutter Papers.

16. Chambers, *Race, Nation, and West Indian Immigration*, chap. 6. See also Euraque, "Banana Enclave," Chomsky and Lauria-Santiago, eds., *Identity and Struggle*, 151–168.

17. Harpelle, *West Indians*, 70–71.

18. Eberhardt to Stimson, 26 March 1930, vol. 188, RG 84, USNA.

19. José Guerrero, "Cómo se quiere que sea Costa Rica, blanca, o negra? El problema racial del negro y las actuales contrataciones bananeras," *La Tribuna*, 13 August 1930. For an excellent analysis of his article, see Putnam, *Company They Kept*, 73.

20. W. A. Petgrave, "A Reply to Audacity," 20 August 1930, *The Searchlight*, copy in Charles C. Eberhardt to State Department, 23 August 1930, box 5581, folder 1, RG 59, USNA.

21. Harpelle, *West Indians*, 70–71. Some West Indians sought to take advantage of this anti-black sentiment. In March 1931, for example, 2,000 West Indian residents petitioned the Costa Rican Congress for funds to return to Jamaica. They emphasized that such an exodus would "assure steady employment for those remaining, both native and Jamaicans." Eberhardt to State Department, 31 March 1931, box 5587, folder 3, RG 59, USNA.

22. Marsh to Heads of All Departments, 29 September 1930, INCOFER #729, ANCR.

23. Petition to Congress by residents of Limón, signed by 574 Hispanics, July 1933, Serie Congreso, no. 16753, ANCR. See also Chomsky, *West Indian Workers*, 234–238.

24. Harpelle, *West Indians*, 84–85.

25. Crosby to Simon, 9 April 1934, CO 318/413/1, UKNA.

26. Holler to State Department, 25 April 1934, box 5581, folder 1, RG 59, USNA.

27. Chomsky, *West Indian Workers*, 239–243.

28. Harpelle, *West Indians*, 78–81.

29. Ibid., 82–83.

30. Chomsky, *West Indian Workers*, 244–253.

31. On the impact of the exclusion on the West Indians of Limón, see Harpelle, *West Indians*, chaps. 7–8; and Purcell, *Banana Fallout*.

32. Vallejo to Hatch, 5 October 1934, INCOFER #852, ANCR.

33. Robinson to Sheehy, 7 November 1936; Montero to Sheehy, 16 November 1936, INCOFER #852, ANCR.

34. "Plano de la Finca Orozco," 15 November 1936, no. 18985, fondo mapas, ANCR.

35. Between the censuses of 1927 and 1950, the Hispanic population of the province tripled from 9,970 to 30,260. The best demographic study of the region during this era is Ronny José Viales Hurtado, *Después del Enclave: 1927–1950* (San José, Editorial de la Universidad de Costa Rica, 1998). See also Jeffrey Casey Gaspar, *Limón: 1880–1940* (San José: Universidad de Costa Rica, 1979), 239.

36. Putnam, *Company They Kept*, 168; Harpelle, *West Indians*, 95. Such policies also had an international dimension. At the League of Nations, for example, Costa Rica refused to condemn Italy's 1935 invasion of Ethiopia, and the following year the Italian government presented San José with 175 submachine guns in gratitude.

37. On Sigatoka, see Soluri, *Banana Cultures*, 105–112.

38. Martin Luther quoted in Palmer, *Entrevistas*, vol. 3, 49–52, ANCR.

39. "Los Estados Unidos y Machado," 24 September 1929, *Nuestro Diario*.

40. The official announcement of restrictions appeared in *El Guatemalteco*, 5 February 1930.

41. De León Aragón, *Los contratos*, 252–257.

42. The best English-language study of Ubico is Kenneth J. Grieb, *Guatemalan Caudillo: The Regime of Jorge Ubico, Guatemala, 1931–1944* (Athens: Ohio University Press, 1979).

43. On the massacre in El Salvador, see Jeffrey L. Gould, *To Rise in Darkness: Revolution, Repression, and Memory in El Salvador* (Durham, N.C.: Duke University Press, 2008); on U.S. rule in Nicaragua and the rise of Somoza, see Michel Gobat, *Confronting the American Dream: Nicaragua under U.S. Imperial Rule* (Durham, N.C.: Duke University Press, 2005); on U.S. policy toward authoritarian rule, see Schmitz, *Thank God They're on Our Side.*

44. "Victor M. Cutter Talks to International Students," *Boston Globe,* 21 November 1932, box 4, scrapbook 4 1931–1934, Cutter Papers.

45. The best analysis of Ubico's relationship with United Fruit is Dosal, *Doing Business with the Dictators;* on Ubico's policy toward foreign capital, see Grieb, *Guatemalan Caudillo,* chap. 12.

46. "Decreto Numero 1995," *Diario de Centro America,* 11 May 1934, and "Decreto Numero 1996," *Diario de Centro America,* 12 May 1934, enclosed in Hanna to State Department, 17 May 1934, M-1280, reel 7, RG 59, USNA. On the labor law reform, see McCreery, *Rural Guatemala,* 316–322. An excellent concise study of Ubico's rule is Paul J. Dosal and Oscar Peláez Almengor, *Jorge Ubico: Dictadura, economía y "La tacita de Plata"* (Guatemala City: University of San Carlos, 2002).

47. Dosal, *Doing Business with the Dictators,* chap. 9.

48. Grieb, *Guatemalan Caudillo,* 85–89. In a careful statistical analysis, Doug Kraft estimates that by the time of the 1940 census, the West Indian population was less than half of its height in the early 1910s. See Kraft, "Making West Indians Unwelcome," 97–98.

49. Stanley, *For the Record,* 83–84.

50. Cindy Forster, *The Time of Freedom: Campesino Workers in Guatemala's October Revolution* (Pittsburgh: University of Pittsburgh Press, 2001), 18–21.

Epilogue

1. On the politics of the black diaspora in Harlem, see Lewis, *When Harlem Was in Vogue;* and Winston James, *Holding Aloft the Banner of Ethiopia: Caribbean Radicalism in Early Twentieth-Century America* (London: Verso, 1998).

2. On the interplay between the Cold War and Civil Rights, see Thomas Borstelmann, *The Cold War and the Color Line: American Race Relations in the Global Arena* (Cambridge, Mass.: Harvard University Press, 2001); and Mary Dudziak, *Cold War Civil Rights: Race and the Image of American Democracy* (Princeton: Princeton University Press, 2000).

3. On wartime U.S.–Latin American relations, see Green, *Containment of Latin America,* esp. chaps. 4–6; David Rock, ed., *Latin American in the 1940s: War and Postwar Transitions* (Berkeley: University of California, 1994), esp. chaps. 1–2.

4. Conniff, *Black Labor on a White Canal,* chap. 5; Harpelle, *West Indians,* 144–146.

5. The most visible example of the personnel connection between United Fruit and the naval base was the case of Kid Chicle, a local boxer and aspiring base worker who drowned in Guantánamo Bay after being struck by a U.S. army lieutenant, who was himself a former United Fruit manager. See Lipman, *Guantánamo,* 34–36. Lipman argues that "the naval base elevated the position of West Indians and effectively transformed the social order of Guantánamo." Ibid., 50.

6. On Trinidad's wartime encounter with the U.S. empire, see Harvey R. Neptune, *Caliban and the Yankees: Trinidad and the United States Occupation* (Chapel Hill: University of North Carolina Press, 2007). On the long-term implications of the U.S. presence in Jamaica and Trinidad, see Jason C. Parker, *Brother's Keeper: The United States, Race, and Empire in the British Caribbean* (New York: Oxford University Press, 2008).

7. Emery-Waterhouse, *Banana Paradise*, 250–257.

8. On U.S.–Costa Rican relations during the 1940s and 1950s, see Kyle Longley, *The Sparrow and the Hawk: Costa Rica and the United States during the Rise of José Figueres* (Tuscaloosa: University of Alabama Press, 1997).

9. On Figueres's efforts to court West Indians, see Chomsky, *West Indian Workers*, 236–250; and Harpelle, *West Indians*, 180–183.

10. Purcell, *Banana Fallout*.

11. That student was, of course, me.

12. On the impact of revolutionary labor mobilization, particularly in United Fruit's Pacific enclave, see Forster, *Time of Freedom*.

13. On the connections between United Fruit and the Eisenhower administration, see Schoultz, *Beneath the United States*, 337–338. The best account of Arbenz's political leanings and the U.S. response to the Guatemalan revolution is Piero Gleijeses, *Shattered Hope: The Guatemalan Revolution and the United States, 1944–1954* (Princeton: Princeton University Press, 1991).

14. Dulles as quoted in Stephen G. Rabe, *Eisenhower and Latin America: The Foreign Policy of Anticommunism* (Chapel Hill: University of North Carolina Press, 1988), 58.

15. In 1972, the company sold the remainder of its holdings in Guatemala to Del Monte. On the antitrust lawsuit, see Dosal, *Doing Business with the Dictators*, 229–231; and Peter Chapman, *Bananas: How the United Fruit Company Shaped the World* (New York: Canongate, 2007), 146–151.

16. On nationalism in this period, see Alan McPherson, *Yankee No!: Anti-Americanism in U.S.–Latin American Relations* (Cambridge, Mass.: Harvard University Press, 2003).

17. Conniff, *Black Labor on a White Canal*, chap. 7.

18. Lipman, *Guantánamo*, 194–199.

19. United Brands had interests in agricultural production within the United States as well. As part of the domestic agribusiness boom, the company clashed with Mexican-American farm workers in the Southwest before coming to terms with labor leader César Chávez in the late 1960s. See Chapman, *Bananas*, 169.

20. On Black Sigatoka, see Soluri, *Banana Cultures*, 199–206.

21. For a superb analysis of the divestiture process, see Marcelo Bucheli, "United Fruit Company in Latin America," in Striffler and Moberg, *Banana Wars*, 80–100; and idem, *Bananas and Business*, esp. chap. 7.

22. See Striffler and Moberg, *Banana Wars*; and Wiley, *The Banana*.

23. The most popular accounts of the 1954 coup are Stephen Schlesinger and Stephen Kinzer, *Bitter Fruit: The Untold Story of the American Coup in Guatemala* (Garden City: Doubleday, 1982); and Richard H. Immerman, *The CIA in Guatemala: The Foreign Policy of Intervention* (Austin: University of Texas Press, 1982).

24. "The Banana Called a Weapon of Conquest," *New York Times*, 18 June 1916.

25. Adams, *Conquest of the Tropics*, 10, 53.

26. Thompson, *Rainbow Countries*, 15.

27. This was especially evident in the oil industry. See Miguel Tinker Salas, *The Enduring Legacy: Oil, Culture, and Society in Venezuela* (Durham, N.C.: Duke University Press, 2009); and Robert Vitalis, *America's Kingdom: Mythmaking on the Saudi Oil Frontier* (Stanford: Stanford University Press, 2007).

Bibliography

Archives and Other Repositories

Costa Rica
Archivo Nacional de Costa Rica, Zapote, Costa Rica (ANCR).

Great Britain
United Kingdom National Archives, Kew (UKNA).

Guatemala
Archivo General de Centro América, Guatemala City, Guatemala (AGCA).

United States
Columbia University, Rare Books and Manuscripts, New York City.
Cornell University, Kroch Library, Ithaca, New York.
Dartmouth College, Rauner Special Collections, Hanover, New Hampshire.
Harvard Business School, Baker Library, Cambridge, Massachusetts.
Huntington Library, San Marino, California.
Massachusetts Historical Society, Boston.
New-York Historical Society, New York City.
New York Public Library, Special Collections, New York City.
Schomburg Center for Black Studies, New York City.

United States Library of Congress, Washington, D.C. (LOC).
United States National Archives II, College Park, Maryland (USNA).
University of Texas at Arlington, Special Collections, Arlington, Texas.
University of Virginia, Alderman Library, Charlottesville, Virginia.
University of Washington, Special Collections, Seattle, Washington.

Newspapers

The American (Bluefields, Nicaragua).
Diario de Centro América (Guatemala City, Guatemala).
El Excelsior (Guatemala City, Guatemala).
El Guatemalteco (Guatemala City, Guatemala).
El Imparcial (San José, Costa Rica).
La República (Guatemala City, Guatemala).
La Tribuna (San José, Costa Rica).
New York Journal
New York Times
New York Tribune
Nuestro Diario (San José, Costa Rica).
The Searchlight (Limón, Costa Rica).

Printed Primary Sources

Adams, Frederick Upham. *Conquest of the Tropics: The Story of the Creative Enterprises Conducted by the United Fruit Company.* Garden City: Page, 1914.
Amaya Amador, Ramón. *Prisión Verde.* Tegucigalpa: Universidad Nacional Autónoma de Honduras, 1950.
Asturias, Miguel Angel. *Papa Verde.* Buenos Aires: Editorial Losada, 1954.
——. *El Señor Presidente.* 1946. Guatemala City: Piedra Santa Editorial, 2002.
Atkins, Edwin F. *Sixty Years in Cuba.* 1926. New York: Arno Press, 1980.
Beals, Carleton. *Banana Gold.* Philadelphia: J. B. Lippincott, 1932.
Beaulac, Willard L. *Career Diplomat: A Career in the Foreign Service of the United States.* New York: Macmillan, 1964.
Bell, C. Napier. *Tangweera: Life and Adventures among Gentle Savages.* 1899. Austin: University of Texas Press, 1989.
Bennett, Hugh H. "Agriculture in Central America." *Annals of the Association of American Geographers* 16, no. 2 (1926): 63–84.
Beveridge, Albert J. *The Meaning of the Times and Other Speeches.* New York: Bobbs-Merrill, 1908.
Bigelow, John. *Jamaica in 1850: Or, The Effects of Sixteen Years of Freedom on a Slave Colony.* New York: George P. Putnam, 1851.
Bigelow, Poultney. "Our Mismanagement at Panama." *The Independent* 60 (4 January 1906): 9–21.

Blanshard, Paul. *Democracy and Empire in the Caribbean.* New York: Macmillan, 1947.

Brigham, William T. *Guatemala, Land of the Quetzal.* New York: Charles Scribner's Sons, 1887.

Bury, Herbert. *A Bishop amongst Bananas.* London: Wells Gardner, Darton, 1911.

Calvo, Joaquín Bernardo. *The Republic of Costa Rica.* Chicago: Kessinger, 1890.

Charles, Cecil. *Honduras: The Land of Great Depths.* Chicago: Rand, McNally, 1890.

Commons, John R. *Races and Immigrants in America.* New York: Macmillan, 1907.

Conrad, Joseph. *The Collected Letters of Joseph Conrad.* Ed. Frederick R. Karl and Laurence Davies. Cambridge: Cambridge University Press, 1988.

———. *Heart of Darkness.* 1899. New York: W. W. Norton, 1988.

———. *Nostromo.* 1904. New York: Alfred A. Knopf, 1957.

Croly, David G., and David Goodman. *Miscegenation: The Theory of the Blending of the Races, Applied to the American White Man and Negro.* New York, H. Dexter, Hamilton, 1864.

Crowther, Samuel. *The Romance and Rise of the American Tropics.* Garden City: Doubleday, Doran, 1929.

Cunningham, Eugene. *Gypsying through Central America.* New York: E. P. Dutton, 1922.

Curtis, William E. "The Smallest of American Republics." *Harper's Magazine* 75 (October 1887): 668–682.

Cutter, Victor M. "Caribbean Tropics in Commercial Transition." *Economic Geography* 2, no. 4 (October 1926): 494–507.

Davis, Richard Harding. *Three Gringos in Venezuela and Central America.* New York: Harper and Brothers, 1896.

Deutsch, Hermann. *The Incredible Yanqui: The Career of Lee Christmas.* London: Longmans, Green, 1931.

Elliot, L. E., *Central America: New Paths in Ancient Lands.* London: Methuen, 1924.

Emery-Waterhouse, Frances. *Banana Paradise.* New York: Stephen-Paul, 1947.

Franck, Harry A. *Roaming through the West Indies.* New York: Blue Ribbon Books, 1920.

———. *Zone Policeman 88: A Close Range Study of the Panama Canal and Its Workers.* New York: Century, 1913.

Fraser, Edwin R. "Where Our Bananas Come From." *National Geographic Magazine* 23, no. 7 (July 1912): 713–730.

Gage, Thomas. *The English-American, His Travail by Sea and Land; or, A New Survey of the West-Indias.* London: R. Cotes, 1648.

Gann, Thomas W. *Ancient Cities and Modern Tribes: Exploration and Adventure in Maya Lands.* London: Duckworth, 1926.

Garvey, Marcus. *Philosophy and Opinions of Marcus Garvey.* Ed. Amy Jacques-Garvey. New York: Atheneum, 1992.

Hale, William Bayard. "With the Knox Mission in Central America," *World's Work* (June 1912): 181–186.

Henry, O. *Cabbages and Kings.* 1904. New York, Exeter Books, 1986.

Hill, Robert A., ed. *The Marcus Garvey and Universal Negro Improvement Association Papers.* Berkeley: University of California Press, 1983.

Hobson, J. A. *Imperialism*. London: George Allen and Unwin, 1902.

Johnson, James Weldon. *Along This Way*. 1933. New York: Da Capo Press, 2000.

———. "Self-Determining Haiti." *The Nation* 11 (28 August–11 September 1920): 236–239, 265–267, 295–297, 345–347.

Jones, Chester Lloyd. "Bananas and Diplomacy." *North American Review* 198 (August 1913): 188–194.

———. *Costa Rica and Civilization in the Caribbean*. 1935. New York: Russell and Russell, 1967.

———. *Guatemala Past and Present*. Minneapolis: University of Minnesota Press, 1940.

Kepner, Charles David, Jr. *Social Aspects of the Banana Industry*. New York: Columbia University Press, 1936.

———, and Jay Henry Soothill. *The Banana Empire: A Case Study of Economic Imperialism*. New York: Vanguard Press, 1935.

Kidd, Benjamin. *The Control of the Tropics*. New York: Macmillan, 1898.

Long, W. Rodney. *The Railways of Central America and the West Indies*. Washington, D.C.: Government Printing Office, 1925.

Martí, José. *José Martí: Selected Writings*. Ed. Ester Allen. New York: Penguin, 2002.

McFee, William. *The Gates of the Caribbean: The Story of a Great White Fleet Caribbean Cruise*. Boston: United Fruit Company Steamship Service, 1922.

Munro, Dana G. *The Five Republics of Central America: Their Political and Economic Development and Their Relations with the United States*. New York: Oxford University Press, 1918.

———. *A Student in Central America, 1914–1916*. New Orleans: Middle American Research Institute, 1983.

———. *The United States and the Caribbean Area*. Boston: World Peace Foundation, 1934.

Nichols, Francis H. "Cuban Character." *Outlook* (29 July 1899): 707–713.

Olivier, Sydney. *White Capital and Coloured Labour*. London: Independent Labour Party, 1906.

Palmer, Jesse T. "The Banana in Caribbean Trade." *Economic Geography* 8, no. 3 (June 1932): 262–273.

Perry, Edward. "Anti-American Propaganda in Hispanic America." *Hispanic American Historical Review* 3, no. 1 (February 1920): 17–40.

Pollan, Arthur A. *The United Fruit Company and Middle America*. New York: New School for Social Research, 1944.

Price, A. Grenfell. "White Settlement in the Panama Canal Zone." *The Geographical Review* 25, no. 1 (January 1935): 1–11.

Putnam, George Palmer. *The Southland of North America: Rambles and Observations in Central America during the Year 1912*. New York: Knickerbocker Press, 1913.

Rippy, J. Fred. "Justo Rufino Barrios and the Nicaraguan Canal." *Hispanic American Historical Review* 20, no. 2 (May 1940): 190–197.

———. "Pan-Hispanic Propaganda in Hispanic America." *Political Science Quarterly* 37, no. 3 (September 1922): 389–414.

———. "Relations of the United States and Costa Rica during the Guardia Era." *Bulletin of the Pan American Union* 77, no. 2 (February 1943): 61–68.

———. "Relations of the United States and Guatemala during the Epoch of Justo Rufino Barrios." *Hispanic American Historical Review* 22, no. 4 (November 1942): 595–605.

Root, Elihu. *Latin America and the United States. Collected Speeches.* Cambridge, Mass.: Harvard University Press, 1917.

———. *The Military and Colonial Policy of the United States. Collected Speeches.* Cambridge, Mass.: Harvard University Press, 1916.

Rothery, Agnes E. *Central America and the Spanish Main.* Boston: Houghton Mifflin, 1929.

Ruhl, Arthur J. *The Central Americans: Adventures and Impressions between Mexico and Panama.* New York: Charles Scribner's Sons, 1929.

Sandino, Augusto C. *Sandino: The Testimony of a Nicaraguan Patriot, 1921–1934.* Trans. Robert Edgar Conrad. Princeton: Princeton University Press, 1990.

Sands, William F. "Mysterious Temples of the Jungle: The Prehistoric Ruins of Guatemala." *National Geographic Magazine* 24, no. 3 (March 1913): 324–338.

———. *Our Jungle Diplomacy.* Chapel Hill: University of North Carolina Press, 1944.

Scott, James Brown. "The Central American Peace Conference of 1907." *American Journal of International Law* 2, no. 1 (January 1908): 121–143.

Scroggs, William O. *Filibusters and Financiers: The Story of William Walker and His Associates.* New York: Macmillan, 1916.

Showalter, William J. "The Countries of the Caribbean." *National Geographic Magazine* 24, no. 2 (February 1913): 227–250.

Stephens, John Lloyd. *Incidents of Travel in Central America, Chiapas, and Yucatan.* 2 vols. 1840–1841. New York: Dover, 1969.

Swayne, Eric. "British Honduras." *Geographical Journal* 50, no. 3 (September 1917): 161–175.

Thompson, Wallace. *Greater America: An Interpretation of Latin America in Relation to Anglo-Saxon America.* New York: E. P. Dutton, 1932.

———. *Rainbow Countries of Central America.* Chautauqua, N.Y.: Chautauqua Press, 1927.

United Fruit Company. *Proceedings of the International Conference on Health Problems in Tropical America.* Boston: United Fruit Company, 1924.

———. *Unifruitco.* Boston: United Fruit Company, 1925–1954.

Vasconcelos, José. *Aspects of Mexican Civilization.* Chicago: University of Chicago Press, 1926.

———. *La raza cósmica, misión de la raza iberoamericana.* 1925. Baltimore: Johns Hopkins University Press, 1997.

Villafranca, Ricardo. *Costa Rica: The Gem of the American Republics, Its Resources and Its People.* New York: Sackett and Wilhems, 1895.

Vincent, Frank. *In and Out of Central America: And Other Sketches and Studies of Travel.* New York: Appleton, 1890.

Waibel, Leo. "White Settlement in Costa Rica." *Geographical Review* 29, no. 4 (October 1939): 529–560.

Weisinger, Nina. "A Summer Vacation in Costa Rica." *Hispania* 4, no. 3 (May 1921): 138–140.

Wilson, Charles Morrow. *Central America: Challenge and Opportunity.* New York: Henry Holt, 1941.

———. *Empire in Green and Gold: The Story of the American Banana Trade.* 1947. New York: Greenwood Press, 1968.

Wilson, Hugh. *The Education of a Diplomat.* London: Longmans, Green, 1938.

Winter, Nevin O. *Guatemala and Her People of Today.* Boston: Page, 1909.

Youngblood, F. J. "A Little Journey in Honduras." *National Geographic Magazine* 30, no. 2 (August 1916): 177–184.

Secondary Sources

Adams, David P. "Malaria, Labor, and Population Distribution in Costa Rica: A Biohistorical Perspective." *Journal of Interdisciplinary History* 27, no. 1 (Summer 1996): 75–85.

Adas, Michael. *Dominance by Design: Technological Imperatives and America's Civilizing Mission.* Cambridge, Mass.: Harvard University Press, 2006.

———. *Machines as the Measure of Men: Science, Technology, and the Ideologies of Western Dominance.* Ithaca: Cornell University Press, 1989.

Aguilar Rivera, José Antonio. *El manto liberal: Los poderes de emergencia en México, 1821–1876.* Mexico City: Universidad Nacional Autónoma de México, 2001.

Amaya Banegas, Jorge Alberto. *Los Arabes y Palestinos en Honduras, 1900–1950.* Tegucigalpa: Estudios Históricos Rey Juan Carlos I, 1995.

Andrews, George Reid. *Afro-Latin America, 1800–2000.* New York: Oxford University Press, 2004.

Ardao, Arturo. *América Latina y la latinidad.* Mexico City: Universidad Nacional Autónoma de México, 1993.

Arnesen, Eric. *Waterfront Workers of New Orleans: Race, Class, and Politics, 1863–1923.* Urbana: University of Illinois Press, 1991.

Augelli, John P. "The Rimland-Mainland Concept of Cultural Areas in Middle America." *Annals of the Association of American Geographers* 52, no. 2 (June 1962): 119–129.

Ayala, César J. *American Sugar Kingdom: The Plantation Economy of the Spanish Caribbean, 1898–1934.* Chapel Hill: University of North Carolina Press, 1999.

Ayers, Edward L. *The Promise of the New South: Life after Reconstruction.* New York: Oxford University Press, 1992.

Balharry, Eugenio Herrera. "Los inmigrantes y el poder en Costa Rica." *Revista de Historia* 6, no. 2 (January–June 1985): 131–155.

Bancroft, Frederic. *Frederic Bancroft: Historian: The Colonization of American Negroes from 1801 to 1865.* Ed. Jacob E. Cooke. Norman: University of Oklahoma Press, 1957.

Baptist, Edward E. *Creating an Old South: Middle Florida's Plantation Frontier before the Civil War.* Chapel Hill: University of North Carolina Press, 2002.

Bederman, Gail. *Manliness and Civilization: A Cultural History of Gender and Race in the United States.* Chicago: University of Chicago Press, 1995.

Beisner, Robert L. *Twelve against Empire: The Anti-Imperialists, 1898–1900.* New York: McGraw-Hill, 1968.

Bender, Thomas. *A Nation among Nations: America's Place in World History.* New York: Hill and Wang, 2006.

Benjamin, Jules R. *The United States and the Origins of the Cuban Revolution: An Empire of Liberty in an Age of National Liberation.* Princeton: Princeton University Press, 1990.

Bergquist, Charles. *Labor and the Course of American Democracy: U.S. History in Latin American Perspective.* London: Verso, 1996.

———. *Labor in Latin America: Comparative Essays on Chile, Argentina, Venezuela, and Colombia.* Stanford: Stanford University Press, 1986.

Biesanz, John. "Race Relations in the Canal Zone." *Phylon* 11, no. 1 (1st Qtr. 1950): 23–30.

Blight, David W. *Race and Reunion: The Civil War in American Memory.* Cambridge, Mass.: Harvard University Press, 2001.

Bolland, O. Nigel. *Struggles for Freedom: Essays on Slavery, Colonialism, and Culture in the Caribbean and Central America.* Belize City: Angelus Press, 1997.

Bolster, W. Jeffrey. *Black Jacks: African American Seamen in the Age of Sail.* Cambridge, Mass.: Harvard University Press, 1997.

Borstelmann, Thomas. *The Cold War and the Color Line: American Race Relations in the Global Arena.* Cambridge, Mass.: Harvard University Press, 2001.

Bourgois, Philippe I. *Ethnicity at Work: Divided Labor on a Central American Banana Plantation.* Baltimore: The Johns Hopkins University Press, 1989.

Briggs, Laura. *Reproducing Empire: Race, Sex, Science, and U.S. Imperialism in Puerto Rico.* Berkeley: University of California Press, 2002.

Britton, John A. *Carleton Beals: A Radical Journalist in Latin America.* Albuquerque: University of New Mexico Press, 1987.

Bucheli, Marcelo. *Bananas and Business: The United Fruit Company in Colombia, 1899–2000.* New York: New York University Press, 2005.

Bulmer-Thomas, Victor. *The Political Economy of Central America since 1920.* Cambridge: Cambridge University Press, 1987.

Burns, E. Bradford. *Patriarch and Folk: The Emergence of Nicaragua, 1798–1858.* Cambridge, Mass., Harvard University Press, 1991.

———. *The Poverty of Progress: Latin America in the Nineteenth Century.* Berkeley: University of California Press, 1980.

Bushell, David, and Neill Macaulay. *The Emergence of Latin America in the Nineteenth Century.* New York: Oxford University Press, 1994.

Cáceres, Rina. *Negros, mulatos, esclavos y libertos en la Costa Rica del siglo XVII.* Mexico City: Institutuo Panamericano de Geografía e Historia, 2001.

Carr, Barry. "Identity, Class, and Nation: Black Immigrant Workers, Cuban Communism, and the Sugar Insurgency, 1925–1934." *Hispanic American Historical Review* 78, no. 1 (1998): 83–116.

Cecelski, David S., and Timothy B. Tyson, eds. *Democracy Betrayed: The Wilmington Race Riot of 1898 and Its Legacy.* Chapel Hill: University of North Carolina Press, 1998.

Chambers, Glenn A. *Race, Nation, and West Indian Immigration to Honduras, 1890–1940.* Baton Rouge: Louisiana State University Press, 2010.

Chapman, Peter. *Bananas: How the United Fruit Company Shaped the World.* New York: Canongate, 2007.

Charlip, Julie A. *Cultivating Coffee: The Farmers of Carazo, Nicaragua, 1880–1930.* Athens: Ohio University Press, 2003.

Chomsky, Aviva. "'Barbados or Canada?' Race, Immigration, and Nation in Early-Twentieth-Century Cuba." *Hispanic American Historical Review* 80, no. 3 (2000): 415–462.

——. *Linked Labor Histories: New England, Colombia, and the Making of a Global Working Class.* Durham, N.C.: Duke University Press, 2008.

——. *West Indian Workers and the United Fruit Company in Costa Rica, 1870–1940.* Baton Rouge: Louisiana State University Press, 1996.

——, and Aldo Lauria-Santiago, eds. *Identity and Struggle at the Margins of the Nation-State: The Laboring Peoples of Central America and the Hispanic Caribbean.* Durham, N.C.: Duke University Press, 1998.

Clayton, Lawrence A. *Grace: W. R. Grace and Co., The Formative Years, 1850–1930.* Ottowa, Ill: Jameson Books, 1985.

——. "The Nicaraguan Canal in the Nineteenth Century: Prelude to American Empire in the Caribbean." *Journal of Latin American Studies* 19, no. 2 (November 1987): 323–352.

Coatsworth, John H. "Railroads, Landholding, and Agrarian Protest in the Early Porfiriato." *Hispanic American Historical Review* 54, no. 1 (February 1974): 48–71.

Cohen, Lizabeth. *Making a New Deal: Industrial Workers in Chicago, 1919–1939.* Cambridge: Cambridge University Press, 1990.

Cohen, Robin. *Frontiers of Identity: The British and the Others.* London: Longman, 1994.

Colby, Jason M. "'Banana Growing and Negro Management': Race, Labor, and Jim Crow Colonialism in Guatemala, 1884–1930." *Diplomatic History* 30, no. 4 (September 2006): 595–621.

——. "Race, Empire, and New England Capital in the Caribbean, 1890–1930." *Massachusetts Historical Review* (2009): 1–25.

Connell-Smith, Gordon. "The United State and the Caribbean: Colonial Patterns, Old and New." *Journal of Latin American Studies* 4, no. 1 (May 1972): 113–122.

Conniff, Michael L. *Black Labor on a White Canal: Panama, 1904–1981.* Pittsburgh: University of Pittsburgh Press, 1985.

——, and Thomas J. Davis. *Africans in the Americas: A History of the Black Diaspora.* New York: St. Martin's Press, 1994.

Cooper, Frederick, Allen Isaacman, Florencia E. Mallon, William Roseberry, and Steven J. Stern, eds. *Confronting Historical Paradigms: Peasants, Labor, and*

the Capitalist World System in Africa and Latin America. Madison: University of
Wisconsin Press, 1993.

Cooper, Frederick, and Ann Laura Stoler, eds., *Tensions of Empire: Colonial Cultures in
a Bourgeois World*. Berkeley: University of California Press, 1997.

Cowie, Jefferson. *Capital Moves: RCA's 70-Year Quest for Cheap Labor*. Ithaca: Cornell
University Press, 1999.

Crapol, Edward P. *James G. Blaine: Architect of Empire*. Wilmington: Scholarly
Resources, 2000.

Cronon, William. *Nature's Metropolis: Chicago and the Great West*. New York: W. W.
Norton, 1991.

Crowell, Jackson. "The United States and a Central American Canal, 1869–1877."
Hispanic American Historical Review 49, no. 1 (February 1969): 27–52.

Davids, Jules. *American Political and Economic Penetration of Mexico, 1877–1920*. New
York: Arno Press, 1976.

DeConde, Alexander. *Ethnicity, Race, and American Foreign Policy*. Boston:
Northeastern University Press, 1992.

Deere, Carmen Diana. "Here Come the Yankees! The Rise and Decline of United
States Colonies in Cuba, 1898–1930." *Hispanic American Historical Review* 78, no. 4
(November 1998): 729–765.

De la Fuente, Alejandro. "Myths of Racial Democracy: Cuba, 1900–1912." *Latin
American Research Review* 34, no. 3 (1999): 39–73.

De León, Arnoldo. *The Called Them Greasers: Anglo Attitudes toward Mexicans in Texas,
1821–1900*. Austin: University of Texas Press, 1983.

De León Aragón, Oscar, ed. *Los contratos de la United Fruit Company y las compañías
muelleras en Guatemala*. Guatemala City: Editorial de Ministerio del Educación
Pública, 1950.

Dore, Elizabeth. "Debt Peonage in Granada, Nicaragua, 1870–1930: Labor in a
Noncapitalist Transition." *Hispanic American Historical Review* 83, no. 3 (August
2003): 521–559.

Dosal, Paul J. *Doing Business with the Dictators: A Political History of United Fruit in
Guatemala, 1899–1944*. Wilmington: Scholarly Resources, 1993.

———. "The Political Economy of Guatemalan Industrialization, 1871–1948: The
Career of Carlos P. Novella." *Hispanic American Historical Review* 68, no. 2 (2000):
321–358.

———, and Oscar Peláez Almengor. *Jorge Ubico: Dictadura, Economía y 'La Tacita de
Plata'*. Guatemala City: Universidad de San Carlos, Centro de Estudios Urbanos y
Regionales, 2002.

Douglas, Ann. *Terrible Honesty: Mongrel Manhattan in the 1920s*. New York: Noonday
Press, 1995.

Drinnon, Richard. *Facing West: The Metaphysics of Indian Hating and Empire Building*.
New York: Schocken Books, 1980.

Dublin, Thomas. *Transforming Women's Work: New England Lives in the Industrial
Revolution*. Ithaca: Cornell University Press, 1994.

Du Bois, W. E. B. *Black Reconstruction in America*. 1935. New York: The Free Press, 1998.

Dudziak, Mary. *Cold War Civil Rights: Race and the Image of American Democracy.* Princeton: Princeton University Press, 2000.

Duffy Burnett, Christina. "The Edges of Empire and the Limits of Sovereignty: American Guano Islands." *American Quarterly* 57, no. 3 (September 2005): 779–803.

———, and Burke Marshall, eds. *Foreign in a Domestic Sense: Puerto Rico, American Expansion, and the Constitution*. Durham, N.C.: Duke University Press, 2001.

Dunkerley, James. *Americana: The Americas in the World, around 1850*. London: Verso, 2000.

———. *Power in the Isthmus: A Political History of Modern Central America*. London: Verso, 1988.

Echeverri-Gent, Elisavinda. "Forgotten Workers: British West Indians and the Early Days of the Banana Industry in Costa Rica and Honduras." *Journal of Latin American Studies* 24, no. 2 (May 1992): 275–308.

Edelman, Marc. *The Logic of the Latifundio: The Large Estates of Northwestern Costa Rica since the Late Nineteenth Century*. Stanford: Stanford University Press, 1992.

Edgerly, Peter. *Envisioning Africa: Racism and Imperialism in Conrad's* Heart of Darkness. Lexington: University Press of Kentucky, 2000.

Espinosa, Mariola. *Epidemic Invasions: Yellow Fever and the Limits of Cuban Independence, 1878–1930*. Chicago: University of Chicago Press, 2009.

Eudell, Demetrius L. *The Political Languages of Emancipation in the British Caribbean and the U.S. South*. Chapel Hill: University of North Carolina Press, 2002.

Euraque, Darío A. *Reinterpreting the Banana Republic: Region and State in Honduras, 1870–1972*. Chapel Hill: University of North Carolina Press, 1996.

———. "Social, Economic, and Political Aspects of the Carías Dictatorship in Honduras: The Historiography." *Latin American Research Review* 29, no. 1 (1994): 238–248.

Evans, Sterling. "At Union's Brink: Ideals and Problems in Restoring the United Provinces of Central America, 1920–1922." *Latin American Research Review* 32, no. 1 (1997): 69–87.

Ferrer, Ada. *Insurgent Cuba: Race, Nation, and Revolution, 1868–1898*. Chapel Hill: University of North Carolina Press, 1999.

Fifer, J. Valerie. *United States Perceptions of Latin America, 1850–1930: A New West South of Capricorn*. Manchester: Manchester University Press, 1991.

Foner, Eric. *Free Soil, Free Labor, Free Men: The Ideology of the Republican Party before the Civil War*. 1970. New York: Oxford University Press, 1995.

———. *Reconstruction: America's Unfinished Revolution, 1863–1877*. New York: Harper and Row, 1988.

Foner, Nancy. "West Indian Identity in the Diaspora: A Comparative and Historical Perspective." *Latin American Perspectives* 25, no. 3 (May 1998): 173–188.

Forster, Cindy. *The Time of Freedom: Campesino Workers in Guatemala's October Revolution*. Pittsburgh: University of Pittsburgh Press, 2001.

Frederickson, George M. *The Black Image in the White Mind: The Debate on Afro-American Character and Destiny, 1817–1914*. Hanover: Wesleyan University Press, 1987.

——. *Black Liberation: A Comparative History of Black Ideologies in the United States and South Africa*. New York: Oxford University Press, 1995.

——. *White Supremacy: A Comparative Study in American and South African History*. New York: Oxford University Press, 1981.

Frenkel, Stephen. "Geography, Empire, and Environmental Determinism." *Geographical Review* 82, no. 2 (April 1992): 143–153.

——. "Jungle Stories: North American Representations of Tropical Panama." *Geographical Review* 86, no. 3 (July 1996): 317–333.

Fry, Joseph A. *Dixie Looks Abroad: The South and U.S. Foreign Relations, 1789–1973*. Baton Rouge: Louisiana State University Press, 2002.

——. *John Tyler Morgan and the Search for Southern Autonomy*. Knoxville, University of Tennessee Press, 1992.

Funtanellas, Carlos, ed. *United Fruit Company: Un Caso del Dominio Imperialista en Cuba*. Havana: Editorial de Ciencias Sociales, 1976.

Gardner, Lloyd. *Economic Aspects of New Deal Diplomacy*. Madison: University of Wisconsin Press, 1964.

Garrard-Burnett, Virginia. "Liberalism, Protestantism, and Indigenous Resistance in Guatemala, 1870–1920." *Latin American Perspectives* 24, no. 2 (March 1997): 35–55.

——. "Protestantism in Rural Guatemala, 1872–1954." *Latin American Research Review* 24, no. 2 (1989): 127–142.

Gaspar, Jeffrey Casey. *Limón: 1880–1940*. San José: Universidad de Costa Rica, 1979.

Gatewood, Willard B., Jr. *Black Americans and the White Man's Burden, 1898–1903*. Urbana: University of Illinois Press, 1975.

——, ed. '*Smoked Yankees' and the Struggle for Empire: Letters from Negro Soldiers, 1898–1902*. Urbana: University of Illinois Press, 1971.

Gerstle, Gary. *American Crucible: Race and Nation in the Twentieth Century*. Princeton: Princeton University Press, 2001.

Gilmore, Glenda Elizabeth. *Gender and Jim Crow: Women and the Politics of White Supremacy in North Carolina, 1896–1920*. Chapel Hill: University of North Carolina Press, 1996.

Gilroy, Paul. *The Black Atlantic: Modernity and Double Consciousness*. Cambridge, Mass.: Harvard University Press, 1993.

Gleijeses, Piero. *Shattered Hope: The Guatemalan Revolution and the United States, 1944–1954*. Princeton: Princeton University Press, 1991.

Gobat, Michel. *Confronting the American Dream: Nicaragua under U.S. Imperial Rule*. Durham, N.C.: Duke University Press, 2005.

Gould, Jeffrey L. *To Die in This Way: Nicaraguan Indians and the Myth of Mestizaje, 1880–1960*. Durham, N.C.: Duke University Press, 1998.

——. *To Lead as Equals: Rural Protest and Political Consciousness in Chinandega, Nicaragua, 1912–1979*. Chapel Hill: University of North Carolina, 1990.

———. *To Rise in Darkness: Revolution, Repression, and Memory in El Salvador.* Durham, N.C.: Duke University Press, 2008.

Graham, Richard. *Britain and the Onset of Modernization in Brazil.* New York: Cambridge University Press, 1968.

———, ed. *The Idea of Race in Latin America, 1870–1940.* Austin: University of Texas Press, 1990.

Grandin, Greg. *The Blood of Guatemala: A History of Race and Nation.* Durham, N.C.: Duke University Press, 2000.

———. *Empire's Workshop: Latin America, the United States, and the Rise of the New Imperialism.* New York: Owl Books, 2006.

———. *Fordlandia: The Rise and Fall of Henry Ford's Forgotten Jungle City.* New York: Metropolitan Books, 2009.

Green, David. *The Containment of Latin America: A History of the Myths and Realities of the Good Neighbor Policy.* Chicago: Quadrangle, 1971.

Greenberg, Amy S. *Manifest Manhood and the Antebellum American Empire.* Cambridge: Cambridge University Press, 2005.

Greene, Julie. *The Canal Builders: Making America's Empire at the Panama Canal.* New York: Penguin, 2009.

Gresham, Luveta W. "Colonization Proposals for Free Negroes and Contrabands during the Civil War." *Journal of Negro Education* 16, no. 1 (Winter 1947): 28–33.

Grieb, Kenneth J. *Guatemalan Caudillo: The Regime of Jorge Ubico, Guatemala, 1931–1944.* Athens: Ohio University Press, 1979.

Griffith, William J. *Empires in the Wilderness: Foreign Colonization and Development in Guatemala, 1834–1844.* Chapel Hill: University of North Carolina Press, 1965.

Gudmundson, Lowell. *Costa Rica before Coffee: Society and Economy on the Eve of the Export Boom.* Baton Rouge: Louisiana State University Press, 1986.

———, and Héctor Lindo-Fuentes. *Central America, 1821–1871: Liberalism before Liberal Reform.* Tuscaloosa: University of Alabama Press, 1995.

Guterl, Matthew Pratt. *The Color of Race in America, 1900–1940.* Cambridge, Mass.: Harvard University Press, 2001.

Hahn, Peter L., and Mary Ann Heiss, eds. *Empire and Revolution: The United States and the Third World since 1945.* Columbus: Ohio State University Press, 2001.

Hale, Charles R. *Resistance and Contradiction: Miskitu Indians and the Nicaraguan State, 1894–1987.* Stanford: Stanford University Press, 1994.

Hall, Carolyn, and Héctor Pérez Brigloli. *Historical Atlas of Central America.* Tulsa: University of Oklahoma Press, 2003.

Hall, Jacquelyn Dowd, et al. *Like a Family: The Making of a Southern Cotton Mill World.* Chapel Hill: University of North Carolina Press, 1987.

Halperín Donghi, Tulio. *The Contemporary History of Latin America.* Trans. John Chasteen. Durham, N.C.: Duke University Press, 1993.

Handy, Jim. "Efrentándose al pulpo: Nacionalismo económico y cambio político en Guatemala y Costa Rica en la década de 1920." *Mesoamérica* 17, no. 31 (June 1996): 11–39.

———. *Gift of the Devil: A History of Guatemala.* Boston: South End Press, 1984.

———. *Revolution in the Countryside: Rural Conflict and Agrarian Reform in Guatemala, 1944–1954*. Chapel Hill: University of North Carolina Press, 1994.

Harpelle, Ronald N. "The Social and Political Integration of West Indians in Costa Rica: 1930–1950." *Journal of Latin American Studies* 25, no. 1 (February 1993): 103–120.

———. *The West Indians of Costa Rica: Race, Class, and the Integration of an Ethnic Minority*. Kingston: Ian Randle, 2001.

Hart, John Mason. *Empire and Revolution: The Americans in Mexico since the Civil War*. Berkeley: University of California Press, 2002.

Haynes, Douglas M. *Imperial Medicine: Patrick Manson and the Conquest of Tropical Disease*. Philadelphia: University of Pennsylvania Press, 2001.

Headrick, Daniel R. *The Tools of Empire: Technology and European Imperialism in the Nineteenth Century*. New York: Oxford University Press, 1981.

Healy, David. *Drive to Hegemony: The United States in the Caribbean, 1898–1917*. Madison: University of Wisconsin Press, 1988.

———. *James G. Blaine and Latin America*. Columbia: University of Missouri Press, 2001.

Helg, Aline. *Our Rightful Share: The Afro-Cuban Struggle for Equality, 1886–1912*. Chapel Hill: University of North Carolina Press, 1995.

Hellwig, David J. "The Afro-American Press and Woodrow Wilson's Mexican Policy, 1913–1917." *Phylon* 48, no. 4 (4th Qtr. 1987): 261–270.

Hietala, Thomas R. *Manifest Design: American Exceptionalism and Empire*. Ithaca: Cornell University Press, 2003.

Hill, Roscoe R. "The Nicaraguan Canal Idea to 1913." *Hispanic American Historical Review* 28, no. 2 (May 1948): 197–211.

Hixon, Walter L. *The Myth of American Diplomacy: National Identity and U.S. Foreign Policy*. New Haven: Yale University Press, 2008.

Hobsbawm, Eric. *The Age of Capital, 1848–1875*. New York: Vintage, 1975.

———. *The Age of Empire, 1875–1914*. New York: Vintage, 1987.

———. *The Age of Revolution, 1789–1848*. Cleveland: World, 1962.

Hochschild, Adam. *King Leopold's Ghost: A Story of Greed, Terror, and Heroism in Colonial Africa*. New York: Houghton Mifflin, 1998.

Hodes, Martha Elizabeth. *White Women, Black Men: Illicit Sex in the 19th-Century South*. New Haven: Yale University Press, 1997.

Hoganson, Kristin L. *Consumer's Imperium: The Global Production of American Domesticity, 1865–1920*. Chapel Hill: University of North Carolina Press, 2007.

———. *Fighting for American Manhood: How Gender Politics Provoked the Spanish-American and Philippine-American Wars*. New Haven: Yale University Press, 1998.

Holden, Robert H., and Eric Zolov, eds. *Latin America and the United States: A Documentary History*. New York: Oxford University Press, 2000.

Holloway, Thomas. *Immigrants on the Land: Coffee and Society in São Paulo, 1886–1934*. Chapel Hill: University of North Carolina Press, 1980.

Holt, Thomas C. *The Problem of Freedom: Race, Labor, and Politics in Jamaica and Britain, 1832–1938*. Baltimore: Johns Hopkins University Press, 1992.

Horsman, Reginald. *Race and Manifest Destiny: The Origins of Racial Anglo-Saxonism.* Cambridge, Mass.: Harvard University Press, 1981.

Hunt, Michael H. *Ideology and U.S. Foreign Policy.* New Haven: Yale University Press, 1987.

Ibarra, Eugenia. *La sociedades cacicales de Costa Rica.* San José: Universidad de Costa Rica, 1990.

Ignatiev, Noel. *How the Irish Became White.* London: Routledge, 1995.

Immerman, Richard H. *The CIA in Guatemala: The Foreign Policy of Intervention.* Austin: University of Texas Press, 1982.

Ireland, Gordon. *Boundaries, Possessions, and Conflicts in Central and North America and the Caribbean.* New York: Octagon Books, 1971.

Jacobson, Matthew Frye. *Barbarian Virtues: The United States Encounters Foreign Peoples at Home and Abroad, 1876–1917.* New York: Hill and Wang, 2000.

———. *Whiteness of a Different Color: European Immigrants and the Alchemy of Race.* Cambridge, Mass.: Harvard University Press, 1998.

James, C. L. R. *The Black Jacobins: Toussaint L'Ouverture and the San Domingo Revolution.* New York: Vintage, 1963.

James, Lawrence. *Raj: The Making and Unmaking of British India.* New York: St. Martin's Griffin, 1997.

James, Winston. *Holding Aloft the Banner of Ethiopia: Caribbean Radicalism in Early Twentieth-Century America.* London: Verso, 1998.

Jessup, Philip C. *Elihu Root.* 2 vols. New York: Dodd, Mead, 1938.

Johnson, Walter. *Soul by Soul: Life inside the Antebellum Slave Market.* Cambridge: Mass.: Harvard University Press, 1999.

Jones, Clarence F., and Paul C. Morrison. "Evolution of the Banana Industry of Costa Rica." *Economic Geography* 28, no. 1 (June 1952): 1–19.

Jones, Jacqueline. *American Work: Four Centuries of Black and White Labor.* New York: W.W. Norton, 1998.

Jordan, Winthrop D. *White over Black: American Attitudes toward the Negro, 1550–1812.* Chapel Hill: University of North Carolina Press, 1968.

Joseph, Gilbert M., and Jeffery T. Brannon, eds. *Land, Labor, and Capital in Modern Yucatan: Essays in Regional History and Political Economy.* Tuscaloosa: University of Alabama Press, 1991.

Joseph, Gilbert M., Catherine C. LeGrand, and Ricardo D. Salvatore, eds. *Close Encounters of Empire: Writing the Cultural History of U.S.–Latin American Relations.* Durham, N.C.: Duke University Press, 1998.

Joseph, Gilbert M., and Daniel Nugent, eds. *Everyday Forms of State Formation: Revolution and the Negotiation of Rule in Modern Mexico.* Durham, N.C.: Duke University Press, 1994.

Kantrowitz, Stephen. *Ben Tillman and the Reconstruction of White Supremacy.* Chapel Hill: University of North Carolina Press, 2000.

Kaplan, Amy, and Donald Pease, eds. *Cultures of United States Imperialism.* Durham, N.C.: Duke University Press, 1993.

Karl, Frederick R. *Joseph Conrad, The Three Lives: A Biography.* New York: Farrar, Straus, and Giroux, 1979.

Karnes, Thomas L. *Tropical Enterprise: The Standard Fruit and Steamship Company in Latin America.* Baton Rouge: Louisiana State University Press, 1978.

Keen, Benjamin. *Essays in the Intellectual History of Colonial Latin America.* Boulder: Westview Press, 1998.

Kennedy, Philip W. "Race and American Expansion in Cuba and Puerto Rico, 1895–1905." *Journal of Black Studies* 1, no. 3 (March 1971): 306–316.

Klubock, Thomas Miller. *Contested Communities: Class, Gender, and Politics in Chile's El Teniente Copper Mine, 1904–1948.* Durham, N.C.: Duke University Press, 1998.

Knight, Franklin W. *The Caribbean: The Genesis of a Fragmented Nationalism.* New York: Oxford University Press, 1990.

Komisaruk, Catherine. "'The Work It Cost Me': The Struggles of Slaves and Free Africans in Guatemala, 1770–1825." *Urban History Workshop Review* no. 5 (Fall 1999): 4–24.

Kramer, Paul A. *The Blood of Government: Race, Empire, the United States, and the Philippines.* Chapel Hill: University of North Carolina Press, 2006.

———. "Race-Making and Colonial Violence in the U.S. Empire: The Philippine-American War as Race War." *Diplomatic History* 30, no. 2 (April 2006): 169–210.

Krenn, Michael L. *U.S. Policy toward Economic Nationalism in Latin America, 1917–1929.* Wilmington: Scholarly Resources, 1990.

LaFeber, Walter. *The American Search for Opportunity, 1865–1913.* Cambridge: Cambridge University Press, 1993.

———. *Inevitable Revolutions: The United States in Central America.* New York: W. W. Norton, 1993.

———. *The New Empire: An Interpretation of American Expansion, 1860–1898.* 1963. Ithaca: Cornell University Press, 1998.

———. *The Panama Canal: The Crisis in Historical Perspective.* New York: Oxford University Press, 1989.

Langley, Lester. *The Banana Wars: United States Intervention in the Caribbean, 1898–1934.* Wilmington: Scholarly Resources, 2002.

———, and Thomas Schoonover. *Banana Men: American Mercenaries and Entrepreneurs in Central America, 1880–1930.* Lexington: University Press of Kentucky, 1995.

Lauren, Paul Gordon. *Power and Prejudice: The Politics and Diplomacy of Racial Discrimination.* Boulder: Westview Press, 1988.

Lauria-Santiago, Aldo A. *An Agrarian Republic: Commercial Agriculture and the Politics of Peasant Communities in El Salvador, 1823–1914.* Pittsburgh: University of Pittsburgh Press, 1999.

Levy, Eugene. *James Weldon Johnson: Black Leader, Black Voice.* Chicago: University of Chicago Press, 1973.

Lewis, Daniel. *Iron Horse Imperialism: The Southern Pacific of Mexico, 1880–1951.* Tucson: University of Arizona Press, 2008.

Lewis, David Levering. *W. E. B. Du Bois: Biography of a Race, 1868–1919.* New York: Henry Holt, 1993.

———. *W. E. B. Du Bois: The Fight for Equality and the American Century, 1919–1963.* New York: Henry Holt, 2000.

———. *When Harlem Was in Vogue.* New York: Penguin, 1997.

Lewis, James E. *The American Union and the Problem of Neighborhood: The United States and the Collapse of the Spanish Empire, 1783–1829*. Chapel Hill: University of North Carolina Press, 1997.

Lewis, Lancelot S. *The West Indian in Panama: Black Labor in Panama, 1850–1914*. Washington D.C.: University Press of America, 1980.

Lindsay-Poland, John. *Emperors in the Jungle: The Hidden History of the U.S. in Panama*. Durham, N.C.: Duke University Press, 2003.

Lipman, Jana K. *Guantánamo: A Working-Class History between Empire and Revolution* (Berkeley: University of California Press, 2009).

Litwack, Leon F. *Been in the Storm So Long: The Aftermath of Slavery*. New York: Vintage, 1979.

———. *North of Slavery: The Negro in the Free States, 1790–1860*. Chicago: University of Chicago Press, 1961.

———. *Trouble in Mind: Black Southerners in the Age of Jim Crow*. New York: Alfred A. Knopf, 1998.

Lockett, James D. "Abraham Lincoln and Colonization: An Episode That Ends in Tragedy at L'Ile à Vache, Haiti, 1863–1864." *Journal of Black Studies* 21, no. 4 (June 1991): 428–444.

Logan, Rayford W. *The Betrayal of the Negro: From Rutherford B. Hayes to Woodrow Wilson*. New York: Da Capo Press, 1997.

———. *The Diplomatic Relations of the United States with Haiti, 1776–1891*. Chapel Hill: University of North Carolina Press, 1941.

Longley, Kyle. *In the Eagle's Shadow: The United States and Latin America*. Wheeling: Harlan Davidson, 2002.

———. *The Sparrow and the Hawk: Costa Rica and the United States during the Rise of José Figueres*. Tuscaloosa: University of Alabama Press, 1997.

Look Lai, Walton. *Indentured Labor, Caribbean Sugar: Chinese and Indian Migrants to the British West Indies, 1838–1918*. Baltimore: Johns Hopkins University Press, 1993.

Love, Eric T. L. *Race over Empire: Racism and U.S. Imperialism, 1865–1900*. Chapel Hill: University of North Carolina Press, 2004.

Loveman, Brian. *No Higher Law: American Foreign Policy and the Western Hemisphere since 1776*. Chapel Hill: University of North Carolina Press, 2010.

Lutz, Christopher H. *Santiago de Guatemala: City, Caste, and the Colonial Experience*. Norman: University of Oklahoma Press, 1994.

Macaulay, Neill. *The Sandino Affair*. Chicago: Quadrangle, 1967.

Mack, Gerstle. *The Land Divided: A History of the Panama Canal and Other Isthmian Canal Projects*. New York: Knopf, 1944.

Maclean, Nancy. *Behind the Mask of Chivalry: The Making of the Second Ku Klux Klan*. New York: Oxford University Press, 1994.

Macleod, Marc C. "Undesirable Aliens: Race, Ethnicity, and Nationalism in the Comparison of Haitian and British West Indian Immigrant Workers in Cuba, 1912–1939." *Journal of Social History* 31, no. 3 (Spring 1998): 599–623.

MacLeod, Murdo J. *Spanish Central America: A Socioeconomic History, 1520–1720*. Berkeley: University of California Press, 1973.

Madigan, Tim. *The Burning: Massacre, Destruction, and the Tulsa Race Riot of 1921.* New York: St. Martin's Press, 2001.

Major, John. *Prize Possession: The United States Government and the Panama Canal, 1903–1979.* Cambridge: Cambridge University Press, 1993.

Manela, Erez. *The Wilsonian Moment: Self-Determination and the International Origins of Anticolonial Nationalism.* New York: Oxford University Press, 2007.

Marquardt, Steve. "'Green Havoc': Panama Disease, Environmental Change, and Labor Process in the Central American Banana Industry." *American Historical Review* 106, no. 1 (February 2001): 49–80.

Martin, Tony. *Race First: The Ideological and Organizational Struggles of Marcus Garvey and the Universal Negro Improvement Association.* Dover: Majority Press, 1976.

May, Robert E. *Manifest Destiny's Underworld: Filibustering in Antebellum America.* Chapel Hill: University of North Carolina Press, 2002.

———. *The Southern Dream of Caribbean Empire, 1854–1861.* Gainesville: University Press of Florida, 2002.

———. "Young American Males and Filibustering in the Age of Manifest Destiny: The United States Army as a Cultural Mirror." *Journal of American History* 78, no. 3 (December 1991): 857–886.

May, Stacy, and Galo Plaza. *The United Fruit Company in Latin America.* New York: National Planning Association, 1958.

McCann, Thomas P. *An American Company: The Tragedy of United Fruit.* New York: Crown, 1976.

McCardell, John. *The Idea of a Southern Nation: Southern Nationalists and Southern Nationalism, 1830–1860.* New York: W. W. Norton, 1979.

McClure, John A. *Kipling and Conrad: The Colonial Fiction.* Cambridge, Mass.: Harvard University Press, 1981.

McCormick, Thomas J. *China Market: America's Quest for Informal Empire, 1893–1901.* Chicago: Quadrangle, 1967.

McCreery, David J. "Coffee and Class: The Structure of Development in Liberal Guatemala." *Hispanic American Historical Review* 56, no. 3 (1976): 438–460.

———. "Debt Servitude in Rural Guatemala, 1876–1936." *Hispanic American Historical Review* 63, no. 4 (November 1983): 735–759.

———. "'An Odious Feudalism': Mandamiento Labor and Commercial Agriculture in Guatemala, 1858–1920." *Latin American Perspectives* 13, no. 1 (Winter 1986): 99–117.

———. *Rural Guatemala, 1760–1940.* Stanford: Stanford University Press, 1994.

McCullough, David. *The Path between the Seas: The Creation of the Panama Canal, 1870–1914.* New York: Simon and Schuster, 1977.

McGerr, Michael. *A Fierce Discontent: The Rise and Fall of the Progressive Movement in America.* New York: Oxford University Press, 2003.

McGuinness, Aims. *Path of Empire: Panama and the California Gold Rush.* Ithaca: Cornell University Press, 2008.

McMillen, Neil R. *Dark Journey: Black Mississippians in the Age of Jim Crow.* Urbana: University of Illinois Press, 1989.

McPherson, Alan. "Courts of World Opinion: Trying the Panama Flag Riots of 1964." *Diplomatic History* 28, no. 1 (January 2004): 83–112.

———. *Yankee No!: Anti-Americanism in U.S.–Latin American Relations.* Cambridge, Mass: Harvard University Press, 2003.

McWilliams, Tennant S. *The New South Faces the World: Foreign Affairs and the Southern Sense of Self, 1877–1950.* Baton Rouge: Louisiana State University Press, 1988.

Melville, John H. *The Great White Fleet.* New York: Vantage Press, 1976.

Mintz, Sidney W. *Caribbean Transformations.* New York: Columbia University Press, 1974.

———. *Sweetness and Power: The Place of Sugar in Modern History.* New York: Penguin, 1985.

———, and Sally Price, eds. *Caribbean Contours.* Baltimore: Johns Hopkins University Press, 1985.

Mitchell, Pablo. *Coyote Nation: Sexuality, Race, and Conquest in Modernizing New Mexico, 1880–1920.* Chicago: University of Chicago Press, 2005.

Moberg, Mark. "Crown Colony as Banana Republic: The United Fruit Company in British Honduras, 1900–1920." *Journal of Latin American Studies* 28, no. 2 (May 1996): 357–381.

———. *Myths of Ethnicity and Nation: Immigration, Work, and Identity in the Belize Banana Industry.* Knoxville: University of Tennessee Press, 1997.

Molina Jiménez, Iván. *Costarricense por dicha: Identidad nacional y cambio cultural en Costa Rica durante los siglos XIX y XX.* San José: Editorial de la Universidad de Costa Rica, 2002.

———, and Steven Palmer. *Historia de Costa Rica: Breve, actualizada y con ilustraciones.* San José: Editorial de la Universidad de Costa Rica, 2002.

Montgomery, David. *Beyond Equality: Labor and the Radical Republicans, 1863–1872.* New York: Knopf, 1967.

Moran, William. *The Belles of New England: The Women of the Textile Mills and the Families Whose Wealth They Wove.* New York: St. Martin's Press, 2002.

Morgan, Edmund S. *American Slavery, American Freedom: The Ordeal of Colonial Virginia.* New York: W.W. Norton, 1975.

Morrison, Michael A. *Slavery and the American West: The Eclipse of Manifest Destiny and the Coming of the Civil War.* Chapel Hill: University of North Carolina Press, 1997.

Muñoz, Jorge Luján. *Guatemala: Breve Historia Contemporánea.* Mexico City: Fondo de Cultura Económica, 1998.

Musicant, Ivan. *The Banana Wars: A History of United States Military Intervention in Latin America from the Spanish-American War to the Invasion of Panama.* New York: Macmillan, 1990.

Naylor, Robert A. *Penny Ante Imperialism: The Mosquito Shore and the Bay of Honduras, 1600–1914.* London: Associated University Presses, 1989.

Neptune, Harvey R. *Caliban and the Yankee: Trinidad and the United States Occupation.* Chapel Hill: University of North Carolina Press, 2007.

Newton, Velma. *The Silver Men: West Indian Labor Migration to Panama.* Kingston: Ian Randle, 2004.

Nightingale, Carl. "Historical Geographies of the Color Line in Early Colonial Madras and New York." *American Historical Review* 113 (2008): 48–71.
———. "The Transnational Contexts of Early Twentieth-Century American Urban Segregationism." *Journal of Social History* 39 (Spring 2006): 668–702.
Nugent, Daniel, ed. *Rural Revolt in Mexico: U.S. Intervention and the Domain of Subaltern Politics.* Durham, N.C.: Duke University Press, 1998.
O'Brien, Thomas F. *The Century of U.S. Capitalism in Latin America.* Albuquerque: University of New Mexico Press, 1999.
———. *Making the Americas: The United States and Latin America from the Age of Revolutions to the Era of Globalization.* Albuquerque: University of New Mexico Press, 2007.
———. *The Revolutionary Mission: American Enterprise in Latin America, 1900–1945.* Cambridge: Cambridge University Press, 1999.
Offner, John L. *An Unwanted War: The Diplomacy of the United States and Spain over Cuba, 1895–1898.* Chapel Hill: University of North Carolina Press, 1992.
Oliva Medina, Mario. *Artesanos y obreros costarricenses, 1880–1914.* San José: Editorial Universidad de Costa Rica, 1985.
Opie, Frederick Douglass, *Black Labor Migration in Caribbean Guatemala, 1882–1923.* Tallahassee: University Press of Florida, 2009.
Ott, Thomas O. *The Haitian Revolution: 1789–1804.* Knoxville: University of Tennessee Press, 1973.
Paige, Jeffery M. *Coffee and Power: Revolutions and the Rise of Democracy in Central America.* Cambridge, Mass.: Harvard University Press, 1997.
Painter, Nell Irving. *Standing at Armageddon: The United States, 1877–1919.* New York: W. W. Norton, 1987.
Palmer, Steven. *From Popular Medicine to Medical Populism: Doctors, Healers, and Public Power in Costa Rica, 1800–1940.* Durham, N.C.: Duke University Press, 2003.
———. "Getting to Know the Unknown Soldier: Official Nationalism in Liberal Costa Rica, 1880–1920." *Journal of Latin American Studies* 25, no. 1 (February 1993): 45–72.
Parker, Jason C. *Brother's Keeper: The United States, Race, and Empire in the British Caribbean, 1937–1962.* New York: Oxford University Press, 2008.
Pérez, Louis A., Jr. *Cuba between Empires, 1878–1902.* Pittsburgh: University of Pittsburgh Press, 1983.
———. *Cuba under the Platt Amendment, 1902–1934.* Pittsburgh: University of Pittsburgh Press, 1986.
———, ed. *José Martí in the United States: The Florida Experience.* Tempe: Arizona State University Center for Latin American Studies, 1995.
———. *On Becoming Cuba: Identity, Nationality, and Culture.* Chapel Hill: University of North Carolina Press, 1999.
———. "The Pursuit of Pacification: Banditry and the United States Occupation of Cuba, 1889–1902." *Journal of Latin American Studies* 18, no. 2 (November 1986): 313–332.

———. *The War of 1898: The United States and Cuba in History and Historiography.* Chapel Hill: University of North Carolina Press, 1998.

Pérez-Brignoli, Héctor. *A Brief History of Central America.* Trans. Ricardo B. Sawrey A. and Susana Stettri de Sawrey. Berkeley: University of California Press, 1989.

Petras, Elizabeth McLean. *Jamaican Labor Migration: White Capital and Black Labor, 1850–1930.* Boulder: Westview Press, 1988.

Pike, Frederick B. *FDR's Good Neighbor Policy: Sixty Years of Generally Gentle Chaos.* Austin: University of Texas Press, 1995.

———. *The United States and Latin America: Myths and Stereotypes of Civilization and Nature.* Austin: University of Texas Press, 1992.

Pite, Rebekah E. "The Force of Food: Life on the Atkins Family Sugar Plantation in Cienfuegos, Cuba, 1884–1900." *Massachusetts Historical Review* 5 (2003): 58–93.

Plummer, Brenda Gayle. "The Afro-American Response to the Occupation of Haiti, 1915–1934." *Phylon* 43, no. 2 (2nd Qtr. 1982): 125–143.

———. *Haiti and the Great Powers, 1902–1915.* Baton Rouge: Louisiana State University Press, 1988.

———. *Haiti and the United States: The Psychological Moment.* Athens: University of Georgia Press, 1992.

———. *Rising Wind: Black Americans and U.S. Foreign Affairs, 1935–1960.* Chapel Hill: University of North Carolina Press, 1996.

Powell, Eve M. Troutt. *A Different Shade of Colonialism: Egypt, Great Britain, and the Mastery of the Sudan.* Berkeley: University of California Press, 2003.

Pratt, Mary Louise. *Imperial Eyes: Travel Writing and Transculturation.* New York: Routledge, 1992.

Purcell, Trevor W. *Banana Fallout: Class, Color, and Culture among West Indians in Costa Rica.* Los Angeles: UCLA/CAAS, 1993.

Putnam, Lara. *The Company They Kept: Migrants and the Politics of Gender in Caribbean Costa Rica, 1870–1960.* Chapel Hill: University of North Carolina Press, 2002.

Quirós, Claudia. *La era de la encomienda.* San José: Editorial Universidad de Costa Rica, 1990.

Rabe, Stephen G. *Eisenhower and Latin America: The Foreign Policy of Anticommunism.* Chapel Hill: University of North Carolina Press, 1988.

———. *The Most Dangerous Area in the World: John F. Kennedy Confronts Communist Revolution in Latin America.* Chapel Hill: University of North Carolina Press, 1999.

Ramos, Julio. *Divergent Modernities: Culture and Politics in Nineteenth-Century Latin America.* Trans. John D. Blanco. Durham, N.C.: Duke University Press, 2001.

Reeves, René. *Ladinos with Ladinos, Indians with Indians: Land, Labor, and Regional Ethnic Conflict in the Making of Guatemala.* Stanford: Stanford University Press, 2006.

Renda, Mary A. *Taking Haiti: Military Occupation and the Culture of U.S. Imperialism.* Chapel Hill: University of North Carolina Press, 2001.

Rock, David, ed. *Latin American in the 1940s: War and Postwar Transitions.* Berkeley: University of California Press, 1994.

Roediger, David R. *The Wages of Whiteness: Race and the Making of the American Working Class.* New York: Verso, 2002.

Roldán de Montaud, Inés. *La restauración en Cuba: El fracaso de un proceso reformista.* Madrid: Consejo Superior de Investigaciones Científicas, 2000.

Rook, Robert. "Race, Water, and Foreign Policy: The Tennessee Valley Authority's Global Agenda Meets 'Jim Crow'." *Diplomatic History* 28, no. 1 (January 2004): 55–81.

Roorda, Eric Paul. *The Dictator Next Door: The Good Neighbor Policy and the Trujillo Regime in the Dominican Republic, 1930–1945.* Durham, N.C.: Duke University Press, 1998.

Rose, Susan D., and Steve Brouwer. "The Export of Fundamentalist Americanism: U.S. Evangelical Education in Guatemala." *Latin American Perspectives* 17, no. 4 (1990): 42–56.

Roseberry, William, Lowell Gudmundson, and Mario Samper Kutschback, eds. *Coffee, Society, and Power in Latin America.* Baltimore: Johns Hopkins University Press, 1995.

Rosenberg, Emily S. *Financial Missionaries to the World: The Politics and Culture of Dollar Diplomacy, 1900–1930.* Durham, N.C.: Duke University Press, 2003.

——. "From Colonialism to Professionalism: The Public-Private Dynamic in United States Foreign Advising, 1898–1929." *Journal of American History* 74, no. 1 (June 1987): 59–82.

——. *Spreading the American Dream: American Economic and Cultural Expansion, 1890–1945.* New York: Hill and Wang, 1982.

Rydell, Robert W. *All the World's A Fair: Visions of Empire at American International Expositions, 1876–1916.* Chicago: University of Chicago Press, 1984.

Said, Edward W. *Culture and Imperialism.* New York: Vintage, 1994.

——. *Orientalism.* New York: Vintage, 1979.

Salas, Miguel Tinker, *The Enduring Legacy: Oil, Culture, and Society in Venezuela.* Durham, N.C.: Duke University Press, 2009.

Salisbury, Richard V. *Anti-Imperialism and International Competition in Central America, 1920–1929.* Wilmington: Scholarly Resources, 1989.

——. "Mexico, the United States, and the 1926–1927 Nicaraguan Crisis." *Hispanic American Historical Review* 66, no. 2 (May 1986): 317–339.

——. "The Middle American Exile of Víctor Raúl Haya de la Torre," *The Americas* 40, no. 1 (July 1983): 1–15.

Samper, Mario. *Generations of Settlers: Rural Households and Markets on the Costa Rican Frontier, 1850–1935.* Boulder: Westview Press, 1990.

Scheips, Paul J. "Lincoln and the Chiriqui Colonization Project." *Journal of Negro History* 37, no. 4 (October 1952): 418–453.

Schlesigner, Stephen, and Stephen Kinzer. *Bitter Fruit: The Untold Story of the American Coup in Guatemala.* New York: Doubleday, 1982.

Schmitz, David F. *Henry L. Stimson: The First Wise Man.* Wilmington: Scholarly Resources, 2001.

——. *Thank God They're On Our Side: The United States and Right-Wing Dictatorships, 1921–1965.* Chapel Hill: University of North Carolina Press, 1999.

Schoonover, Thomas D. "Central American Commerce and Maritime Activity in the Nineteenth Century: Sources for a Quantitative Approach." *Latin American Research Review* 13, no. 2 (1978): 157–169.

——. *Dollars over Dominion: The Triumph of Liberalism in Mexican–United States Relations, 1861–1867.* Baton Rouge: Louisiana State University Press, 1978.

——. *Uncle Sam's War of 1898 and the Origins of Globalization.* Lexington: University Press of Kentucky, 2003.

——. *The United States in Central America, 1860–1911: Episodes of Social Imperialism and Imperial Rivalry in the World System.* Durham, N.C.: Duke University Press, 1991.

——, and Ebba Schoonover. "Statistics for an Understanding of Foreign Intrusions into Central America from the 1820s to 1930." *Anuario de Estudios Centroamericanos* 15, no. 1 (1989): 93–117.

Schoultz, Lars. *Beneath the United States: A History of U.S. Policy toward Latin America.* Cambridge, Mass.: Harvard University Press, 1998.

Scott, Rebecca J. "A Cuban Connection: Edwin F. Atkins, Charles Francis Adams Jr., and the Former Slaves of the Soledad Plantation." *Massachusetts Historical Review* 9 (2007): 7–34.

——. *Degrees of Freedom: Louisiana and Cuba after Slavery.* Cambridge, Mass.: Harvard University Press, 2005.

——. "Race, Labor, and Citizenship in Cuba: A View from the Sugar District of Cienfuegos, 1886–1909." *Hispanic American Historical Review* 78, no. 4 (November 1998): 687–728.

——. *Slave Emancipation in Cuba: The Transition to Free Labor, 1860–1899.* Princeton: Princeton University Press, 1985.

Sealy, Theodore. *Jamaica's Banana Industry: A History of the Banana Industry with Particular Reference to the Part Played by the Jamaica Banana Producers Association, Ltd.* Kingston: The Association, 1984.

Senechal, Roberta, *The Sociogenesis of a Race Riot: Springfield, Illinois, in 1908.* Urbana: University of Illinois Press, 1990.

Simmons, Charles Willis. "Racist Americans in a Multi-Racial Society: Confederate Exiles in Brazil." *Journal of Negro History* 67, no. 1 (Spring 1982): 34–39.

Skowronek, Stephen. *Building a New American State: The Expansion of National Administrative Capacities, 1877–1920.* Cambridge: Cambridge University Press, 1982.

Smith, Carol A., ed. *Guatemalan Indians and the State: 1540–1988.* Austin: University of Texas Press, 1990.

——. "Race-Class-Gender Ideology in Guatemala: Modern and Anti-Modern Forms." *Comparative Studies in Society and History* 37, no. 4 (October 1995): 723–749.

Smith, Henry Nash. *Virgin Land: The American West as Symbol and Myth.* Cambridge, Mass.: Harvard University Press, 1978.

Smith, Joseph. *Illusions of Conflict: Anglo-American Diplomacy toward Latin America, 1865–1896*. Pittsburgh: University of Pittsburgh Press, 1979.

Smith, Robert Freeman. *The United States and Revolutionary Nationalism in Mexico, 1916–1932*. Chicago: University of Chicago Press, 1972.

Solien Gonzalez, Nancie L. *Sojourners of the Caribbean: Ethnogenesis and Ethnohistory of the Garifuna*. Urbana: University of Illinois Press, 1988.

Sollis, Peter. "The Atlantic Coast of Nicaragua: Development and Autonomy." *Journal of Latin American Studies* 21, no. 3 (October 1989): 481–520.

Soluri, John. "People, Plants, and Pathogens: The Eco-social Dynamics of Export Banana Production in Honduras, 1875–1950." *Hispanic American Historical Review* 80, no. 3 (August 2000): 463–501.

———. *Banana Cultures: Agriculture, Consumptions, and Environmental Change in Honduras and the United States* (Austin: University of Texas Press, 2005).

Southern, David W. *The Progressive Era and Race: Reaction and Reform, 1900–1917*. Wheeling: Harlan Davidson, 2005.

Speck, Mary. "Closed-Door Imperialism: The Politics of Cuban-U.S. Trade, 1902–1933." *Hispanic American Historical Review* 85, no. 3 (August 2005): 449–483.

Spenser, Daniela. *The Impossible Triangle: Mexico, Soviet Russia, and the United States in the 1920s*. Durham, N.C.: Duke University Press, 1999.

Spurr, David. *The Rhetoric of Empire: Colonial Discourse in Journalism, Travel Writing, and Imperial Administration*. Durham, N.C.: Duke University Press, 1993.

Stanley, Diane K. *For the Record: The United Fruit Company's Sixty-Six Years in Guatemala*. Guatemala City: Piedra Santa, 1994.

Stansifer, Charles L. "E. George Squier and the Honduras Interoceanic Railroad Project." *Hispanic American Historical Review* 46, no. 1 (February 1966): 1–27.

Stein, Stanley J., and Barbara H. Stein, *The Colonial Heritage of Latin America: Essays on Economic Dependence in Perspective*. New York: Oxford University Press, 1970.

Stewart, Watt. *Keith and Costa Rica: The Biography of Minor Cooper Keith, American Entrepreneur*. Albuquerque: University of New Mexico Press, 1964.

Stocking, George. *Race, Culture, and Evolution: Essays in the History of Anthropology*. New York: Free Press, 1968.

Stoler, Ann Laura. *Capitalism and Confrontation in Sumatra's Plantation Belt, 1870–1979*. New Haven: Yale University Press, 1985.

———. *Carnal Knowledge and Imperial Power: Race and the Intimate in Colonial Rule*. Berkeley: University of California Press, 2002.

———, ed. *Haunted by Empire: Geographies of Intimacy in North American History*. Durham, N.C.: Duke University Press, 2006.

———. "Rethinking Colonial Categories: European Communities and the Boundaries of Rule." *Comparative Studies in Society and History* 31, no. 1 (1989): 134–161.

———. "Sexual Affronts and Racial Frontiers: European Identities and the Politics of Exclusion in Colonial Southeast Asia." *Comparative Studies in Society and History* 34, no. 3 (1992): 514–551.

Stone, Ralph. *The Irreconcilables*. Lexington: University Press of Kentucky, 1970.

Stouse, Pierre A.D., Jr. "Instability of Tropical Agriculture: The Atlantic Lowlands of Costa Rica." *Economic Geography* 46, no. 1 (January 1970): 78–97.

Striffler, Steve. *In the Shadows of State and Capital: The United Fruit Company, Popular Struggle, and Agrarian Restructuring in Ecuador, 1900–1995.* Durham, N.C.: Duke University Press, 2002.

——, and Mark Moberg, eds. *Banana Wars: Power, Production, and History in the Americas.* Durham, N.C.: Duke University Press, 2003.

Suárez Findlay, Eileen J. *Imposing Decency: The Politics of Sexuality and Race in Puerto Rico, 1870–1920.* Durham, N.C.: Duke University Press, 1999.

Sullivan, Patricia. *Days of Hope: Race and Democracy in the New Deal Era.* Chapel Hill: University of North Carolina Press, 1996.

Takaki, Ronald T. *Strangers from a Different Shore: A History of Asian Americans.* Boston: Little, Brown, 1989.

Taracena Arriola, Arturo. *Invención criolla, sueño ladino, pesadilla indígena: Los Altos de Guatemala: de región a estado, 1740–1871.* Antigua, Guatemala: Centro de Investigaciones Regionales de Mesoamérica, 1999.

Taylor, Alan. *American Colonies: The Settling of North America.* New York: Penguin, 2001.

Thurner, Mark, and Andrés Guerrero, eds., *After Spanish Rule: Postcolonial Predicaments of the Americas.* Durham, N.C.: Duke University Press, 2003.

Tolbert, Emory. "Outpost Garveyism and the UNIA Rank and File." *Journal of Black Studies* 5, no. 3 (March 1975): 233–253.

Tone, John Lawrence. *War and Genocide in Cuba, 1895–1898.* Chapel Hill: University of North Carolina Press, 2006.

Topik, Steven, Carlos Marichal, and Zephyr Frank, eds. *From Silver to Cocaine: Latin American Commodity Chains and the Building of the World Economy, 1500–2000.* Durham, N.C.: Duke University Press, 2006.

Topik, Steven, and Allen Wells. *The Second Conquest of Latin America, 1850–1930: Coffee, Henequen, and Oil during the Export Boom.* Austin: University of Texas Press, 1997.

Trelease, Allen W. *White Terror: The Ku Klux Klan Conspiracy and Southern Reconstruction.* Baton Rouge: Louisiana State University Press, 1971.

Trouillot, Michel-Rolph. *Silencing the Past: Power and the Production of History.* Boston: Beacon Press, 1995.

Turits, Richard Lee. "A World Destroyed, a Nation Imposed: The 1937 Haitian Massacre in the Dominican Republic." *Hispanic American Historical Review* 82, no. 3 (August 2002): 589–635.

Veeser, Cyrus. "Inventing Dollar Diplomacy: The Gilded-Age Origins of the Roosevelt Corollary to the Monroe Doctrine." *Diplomatic History* 27, no. 3 (June 2003): 301–326.

——. *A World Safe for Capitalism: Dollar Diplomacy and America's Rise to Global Power.* New York: Columbia University Press, 2002.

Viales Hurtado, Ronny José. *Después del enclave, 1927–1950: Un estudio de la Región Atlántica Costarricense.* San José: Editorial de la Universidad de Costa Rica, 1998.

Vitalis, Robert. *America's Kingdom: Mythmaking on the Saudi Oil Frontier.* Stanford: Stanford University Press, 2007.

——. "Black Gold, White Crude: An Essay on American Exceptionalism, Hierarchy, and Hegemony in the Gulf." *Diplomatic History* 26, no. 2 (Spring 2002): 185–213.

Von Eschen, Penny M. *Race against Empire: Black Americans and Anticolonialism, 1937–1957.* Ithaca: Cornell University Press, 1997.

Von Hagen, Victor. *Maya Explorer: John Lloyd Stephens and the Lost Cities of Central America and Yucatán.* 1947. San Francisco: Chronicle Books, 1990.

Wade, Peter. *Race and Ethnicity in Latin America.* London: Pluto Press, 1997.

Ward, Geoffrey C. *Unforgivable Blackness: The Rise and Fall of Jack Johnson.* New York: Alfred A. Knopf, 2004.

Watt, Ian. *Joseph Conrad, Nostromo.* Cambridge: Cambridge University Press, 1988.

Weaver, Blanche Henry Clark. "Confederate Emigration to Brazil." *Journal of Southern History* 27, no. 1 (February 1961): 33–53.

Weber, David J. *The Spanish Frontier in North America.* New Haven: Yale University Press, 1992.

Wesley, Charles H. "Lincoln's Plan for Colonizing the Emancipated Negroes." *Journal of Negro History* 4, no. 1 (January 1919): 7–21.

Whitfield, Stephen J. "Strange Fruit: The Career of Samuel Zemurray." *American Jewish History* 82, no. 3 (March 1984): 307–323.

Wiebe, Robert H. *The Search for Order, 1877–1920.* New York: Hill and Wang, 1967.

Wilder, Craig Steven. *A Covenant with Color: Race and Social Power in Brooklyn.* New York: Columbia University Press, 2000.

Wiley, James. *The Banana: Empires, Trade Wars, and Globalization.* Lincoln: University of Nebraska Press, 2008.

Wilkins, Mira. *The Emergence of Multinational Enterprise: American Business Abroad from the Colonial Era to 1914.* Cambridge, Mass.: Harvard University Press, 1970.

——. *The Maturing of Multinational Enterprise: American Business Abroad from 1914 to 1970.* Cambridge, Mass.: Harvard University Press, 1974.

Williams, Derek. "Popular Liberalism and Indian Servitude: The Making and Unmaking of Ecuador's Antilandlord State, 1845–1868." *Hispanic American Historical Review* 83, no. 4 (November 2003): 697–733.

Williams, Robert G. *States and Social Evolution: Coffee and the Rise of National Governments in Central America.* Chapel Hill: University of North Carolina Press, 1994.

Williams, Walter L. "United States Indian Policy and the Debate over Philippine Annexation: Implications for the Origins of American Imperialism." *Journal of American History* 66, no. 4 (March 1980): 810–831.

Williams, William Appleman. *The Contours of American History.* Chicago: Quadrangle, 1961.

——. *Empire as a Way of Life.* New York: Oxford University Press, 1980.

——, ed. *From Colony to Empire: Essays in the History of American Foreign Relations.* New York: John Wiley and Sons, 1972.

——. *The Tragedy of American Diplomacy.* New York: W. W. Norton, 1959.

Wood, Peter H. *Black Majority: Negroes in Colonial South Carolina, from 1670 through the Stono Rebellion.* New York: W. W. Norton, 1974.
——. *Weathering the Storm: Inside Winslow Homer's Gulf Stream.* Athens: University of Georgia Press, 2004.
Woodward, C. Vann. *Origins of the New South, 1877–1913.* Baton Rouge: Louisiana State University Press, 1971.
——. *The Strange Career of Jim Crow.* New York: Oxford University Press, 1966.
Woodward, Ralph Lee. *Central America: A Nation Divided.* New York: Oxford University Press, 1999.
——. *Rafael Carrera and the Emergence of the Republic of Guatemala, 1821–1871.* Athens: University of Georgia Press, 1993.
——. "Unity and Diversity in Central American History." *Latin American Research Review* 27, no. 3 (1992): 254–266.
Wrobel, David M. *The End of American Exceptionalism: Frontier Anxiety from the Old West to the New Deal.* Lawrence: University Press of Kansas, 1993.
Yashar, Deborah J. *Demanding Democracy: Reform and Reaction in Costa Rica and Guatemala, 1870s–1950s.* Stanford: Stanford University Press, 1997.
Young, Robert J. C. *Postcolonialism: An Historical Introduction.* Oxford: Blackwell, 2001.

Unpublished Secondary Sources

Anderson, Wayne F. "The Development of Export Transportation in Liberal Guatemala, 1871–1920." Ph.D. diss., Tulane University, 1985.
Gillick, Steven S. "Life and Labor in a Banana Enclave: Bananeros, the United Fruit Company, and the Limits of Trade Unionism in Guatemala, 1906 to 1931." Ph.D. diss., Tulane University, 1994.
Kraft, Douglas W. "Making West Indians Unwelcome: Bananas, Race, and the Immigrant Question in Izabal, Guatemala, 1900–1929." Ph.D. diss., University of Miami, 2006.
Palmer, Steven. "A Liberal Discipline: Inventing Nations in Guatemala and Costa Rica, 1870–1900." Ph.D. diss., Columbia University, 1990.
Williams, John L. "The Rise of the Banana Industry and Its Influence on Caribbean Countries." M.A. thesis, Clark University, 1925.

Index

labor segmentation (*continued*)
  Northern industry and, 5–6, 92–93
  United Fruit's transition to, 82–83,
    103–105, 114–115, 118–120
  West Indian resistance and, 1–3, 38,
    82–83, 87, 112, 119–120, 128, 143–144,
    188–191
ladinos, 10, 40, 43, 45, 70–73, 107, 110, 115,
    135–141, 143–144, 171, 175, 196
Lansing, Robert, 123
layoffs, 129–130, 139, 145, 149, 155, 184
Leopold II, King, 47, 67
Lesseps, Ferdinand de, 51
Liberal Party (Guatemala), 42–46, 70
Liberal Party (Nicaragua), 27–28, 153
Limón province (Costa Rica), 37–39, 66–68,
    91–93, 127–128, 130–134, 160–164,
    184–191, 202–203
Lincoln, Abraham, 29–30, 36, 84
Lira, Trinidad, 155
Livingston (Guatemala), 40, 43–45, 107, 113,
    142
Logan, Thomas, 31
Lôme, Enrique Dupuy de, 56
Louisiana, 53, 55, 61, 107
Lugg, Lucas Samuel, 154
Luther, Martin, 191
lynching, 3, 52, 60, 72, 150

Maceo, Antonio, 55–56
Machado, Gerardo, 154
Macphail, Neil, 109
malaria, 37–38, 45, 59, 89, 99
Mallet, Claude, 90–91
Managua (Nicaragua), 24
mandamiento labor (Guatemala), 40, 42, 70,
    106
Manifest Destiny, 24, 27, 46
Marsh, M. M., 186
Martínez, Maximiliano Hernández, 193
Massachusetts, 92–93, 115
Mayan Indians, 10, 40, 43, 70–71, 171, 194,
    196
McEnery, Samuel, 61–62
McGrigor, C. G., 104
McKinley, William, 56–57
Mee, George, 124–125
Meiggs, Henry, 37
Meily, John J., 160
menial work, 5–6, 72, 82–83, 111

mestizos, 33, 64–65, 153, 163
Mexican Revolution, 123, 152–153
Mexico, 7, 13, 20, 22, 27, 32, 46, 120, 123,
    152–153, 158, 166–167, 182
mining, 32, 49–50, 74, 152–153
Miskito Indians, 21–22, 29, 54
monopolies, 38, 44, 54, 69, 72, 74, 90,
    99–100, 126–129, 137, 160, 167, 205
Monroe Doctrine, 22, 61, 84, 158
Monzón, Luis, 141–142
Mora, Juan Rafael, 35
Morant Bay Rebellion, 7–8
Morgan, John Tyler, 61, 88
Morris, T. J., 154
mosquitoes, 88, 191
Mullins, W. E., 97, 127, 130
Munro, Dana G., 64, 71

NAACP, 199–200
Nanne, William, 37–38, 44
Nazis, 179, 202
Negro World, The, 123, 133
Ness, Barney, 150
New Orleans, 2, 28, 37, 53, 69, 124, 183
newspaper coverage, 19, 22, 29–30, 56, 60,
    105, 129–130, 135, 138, 154–155, 165,
    169–170, 185, 192
New York, 19, 24, 101–102, 199
Nicaragua
  banana industry in, 53–54, 69
  British protectorate, 21–22, 29
  canal, 22, 35, 51, 61–62, 85
  Conservative Party, 27–28
  filibuster invasion of, 19–20, 27–29, 35
  Liberal Party, 27–28, 153
  mestizos, 33, 64–65, 153, 163
  national origins, 9
  race relations, 24, 29, 85–86
  U.S. government relations with, 22–25, 51,
    54, 85–86, 131, 153, 165, 173, 193
Nicaraguan Canal Syndicate, 61
Noah, Abraham, 66
North Coast National Labor Party
    (Honduras), 150
Northern Railway (Guatemala), 12, 45, 70,
    72–74, 100, 106, 110, 134, 160, 190
Nostromo, 48–49

O. Henry, 53, 79
oil industry, 152–153, 182, 207